Sound Targets

Sound Targets

American Soldiers and Music in the Iraq War

Jonathan Pieslak

INDIANA UNIVERSITY PRESS

BLOOMINGTON AND INDIANAPOLIS

This book is a publication of

Indiana University Press

601 North Morton Street
Bloomington, IN 47404-3797 USA

http://iupress.indiana.edu

Telephone orders	800-842-6796
Fax orders	812-855-7931
Orders by e-mail	iuporder@indiana.edu

MANUFACTURED IN THE UNITED STATES OF AMERICA

Library of Congress Cataloging-in-Publication Data

Pieslak, Jonathan R.
    Sound targets : American soldiers and music in the Iraq war / Jonathan Pieslak.
        p. cm.
    Includes bibliographical references and index.
    ISBN 978-0-253-35323-8 (cloth : alk. paper) — ISBN 978-0-253-22087-5 (pbk. : alk. paper) 1. Iraq War, 2003—-Music and the war. 2. Popular music—Social aspects. 3. United States.—Armed Forces—Iraq. 4. Soldiers—United States—Social conditions. I. Title.
    ML3477.P54 2009
    956.7044'38—dc22

                                        2008046562

1 2 3 4 5 14 13 12 11 10 09

To the power of music: may it also help us reconcile with one another.

CONTENTS

Map of Iraq   XII

Introduction   1

1 Music and Contemporary Military Recruiting   16

2 Music as an Inspiration for Combat   46

3 Looking at the Opposing Forces   58

4 Music as a Psychological Tactic   78

5 Music as a Form of Soldier Expression   100

6 Metal and Rap Ideologies in the Iraq War   135

Postscript   185

Appendix 1: Soldier E-mail and Sample Questions
from Soldier Interviews   189

Glossary of Military Ranks   191

Notes   192

Bibliography   209

Index   216

ACKNOWLEDGMENTS

First and foremost, I would like to thank the soldiers who contributed to this book. Many were apprehensive about speaking to me because of the discrepancy they feel exists between their experiences and media reporting about the Iraq War. I am grateful that they gave me the opportunity to ask them questions and greatly appreciate their openness, honesty, and strength to speak about very difficult topics, like the loss of a fellow soldier. While my focus was on music, they willingly shared much more than I could have ever expected, and many times they referred me to a friend or resource that proved invaluable. I am happy and proud to consider many of you new friends, and I wish you all the best in the future. Thank you; I am personally richer for having met and spoken with you.

The research process for this book was often based on networking and contacts. As such, I am grateful to the following people who assisted in this capacity: Gabrielle Dalton, Amber Ferenz, George Gittoes, David Little, Christopher Sabis, David Schober, and Ann Marie Sorrow. At the City College of New York, institutional support was generously made possible by the Dean of the Humanities Fred Reynolds; Deputy Dean Geraldine Murphy; Provost Ze'ev Dagan; President Gregory Williams; and a PSC-CUNY Research Foundation Grant. My colleagues Shaugn O'Donnell and Joe Popp at CCNY were especially supportive. Special thanks are also due the many scholars and experts, too numerous to be individually listed here, outside the field of music who answered my e-mails and questions. I appreciate your willingness to respond to my inquiries. I would also like to thank those scholars who have responded to my work. Their comments, and particularly their passionate disagreements, were important parts of my thinking and rethinking aspects of this book. While they may no doubt maintain some of their objections, the book has improved from their insights and I appreciate their time and engagement with my research.

I am especially grateful to Jane Behnken and the staff at Indiana University Press for their support of this project. Taylor and Francis generously granted me permission to reprint sections of my article "Sound Targets: Music and the War in Iraq," which originally appeared in the

Journal of Musicological Research 26, nos. 2–3 (2007): 123–50. That article laid the foundation for much of the work I pursue in this book, and sections of it are interspersed throughout the text.

Other people helped in less tangible ways and motivated me through the example of their character: Jim Holtom and the Holtom family, Holly McGeogh, Wade Oglesby and his family, Mike and Katrina Rojas and their families, Melissa Sewell, Sue Tottle, and Paula and Michael Zasadny.

My family and friends have been exceedingly supportive of this book and I wish them many thanks and love: the Gignilliat family; Kimberly, Gavin, and Gabriel Hindman; Annette, Joe, and the entire Kane family; Brian, Suzanna, and Ben Pieslak; my mother, Judith Pieslak, and my late father, Robert Pieslak; Karen, William, Hannah, and Gwendolyn Pohlmann; Joel Puckett; D. J. Sparr; George and Janet Staples; and Mary and Fred Van Geuder. And to anyone I may have overlooked, please know that I send you the warmest appreciation.

Finally, I wish to thank my wife, Sabina. She carefully read the drafts of this book and offered insightful comments. In many ways, Sabina bore the brunt of the sacrifices made in writing this work. Living with the Iraq War is not easy, and she was forced to deal with the conflict almost daily. I have experienced joy, anger, laughter, confusion, tears, and almost every possible emotion from working on this book, and she was tirelessly by my side. Thank you, my love.

Sound Targets

Iraq. Central Intelligence Agency map

Introduction

When the Iraq War began in March 2003, I was involved, like many Americans, with sending care packages to troops. My sister-in-law's brothers had been deployed, and our families took turns sending them monthly boxes filled with socks, deodorant, toothpaste, and other basic necessities. I contacted the United Service Organizations (USO) and asked if it was possible to send packages to additional soldiers.[1] From my sister-in-law's brothers we had learned that many men and women serving in Iraq were in need of such assistance; in fact, much of what we were sending was being shared among members of their unit. The USO subsequently provided me with the contact information of an Air National Guard unit from Nashville, Tennessee. In looking over soldiers' requests, I noticed that, in addition to the usual toiletries and clothing, the soldiers requested music, which seemed like a coincidence given that the unit was from Nashville, "The Music City." I sent a package with about a dozen CDs, among other things. Six weeks later, I received a letter from Major Rob Crawford thanking me for the music and letting me know that the CDs had become part of a "library that all of our troops share" (see figure I.1). I soon sent over additional boxes with CDs to contribute to this growing library of shared music.

In January 2004, my scholarly interest in the relationship between American soldiers and music developed almost by accident. I was working on an article about rhythm and meter in metal music when I came across an interesting statistic on a fan web site of the thrash/death metal band Slayer. The posting stated that during the Persian Gulf War, Operation Desert Storm (1991), over 40 percent of Slayer's fan mail came from American sol-

Dear Friend, JONATHAN   5 June 2003

    I just wanted to personally thank you for the music you sent the troops recently. I have added your music to the library that all of our troops share. We greatly appreciate the support of you and Americans like you. We have received music from all around the world and all types of music.

    We are an Air National Guard unit from Nashville, TN (The Music City) called to Active Duty in March for Operation Iraqi Freedom. We fly the C-130 cargo aircraft all over the theater in to provide airlift to all members of the Armed Forces in and around Iraq. Thank you again for your support. God Bless you and God Bless America!

Sincerely,

Rob Crawford
MAJ, TN Air National Guard

FIGURE I.1. Letter from Maj. Rob Crawford

diers based in the Middle East.[2] This struck me as a fascinating claim. Slayer is an extremely popular metal band, and it was remarkable that 40 percent of their fan mail would have come from deployed soldiers during the war. While Slayer singer Tom Araya suggested in a 1992 interview with *Esquire* magazine that this percentage was actually closer to 20 percent, some obvious questions arose nevertheless.[3] Why did fan mail from American soldiers increase during the war? What were soldiers experiencing in this music that caused a surge of fan mail? How do the music and lyrics operate in their lives as soldiers in combat zones? These and many other questions motivated my initial interest and led me to investigate this topic in relation to the Iraq War.

My subsequent research revealed that many enlisted-rank soldiers use metal and rap music as an inspiration for combat. Some soldiers, alone or in a group, listen to metal or rap before missions, patrols, and raids as a way to prepare themselves for the possibility of combat. Furthermore, I learned that new technology allows for music on and off the battlefield in unprecedented ways. Tanks, Strykers, and Humvees are equipped with audio and communication technology that enables soldiers to construct improvised sound systems with which to listen to music while on patrol. And as digital technology has advanced over the last decade, the ways in which American soldiers interact with music has continued to evolve. In the Iraq War, music appears to play a more direct and significant role in the lives of soldiers than in previous American military conflicts. One soldier I interviewed, who adopted the pseudonym "American Soldier," emphasized, "Music was a huge thing for me while in the war, [and] music played a great deal in deployment. I listened to it as much as I could. I really don't know what I would have done without my iPod over there. The military ought to issue an mp3 player to every Soldier!"[4]

During deployment, soldiers experience music in a wide variety of ways. Most American soldiers bring portable audio devices with them, such as laptop computers, CD players, iPods, or mp3 players, to make their personal music preferences available in daily life. In my interviews, I asked soldiers about the general musical environment and how music fit into a typical day in Iraq (see appendix 1 for a list of sample interview questions). Their responses suggest that soldiers' listening practices involve almost every musical genre in a wide range of contexts. Regarding the musical environment during his deployment, Sergeant First Class C. J. Grisham, a noncommissioned officer who served during the initial invasion of Iraq in March 2003, explained, "Almost everyone had a CD player. You walk into any tent and if anybody is there, they've got headphones on. And if there isn't anybody there, then they're playing music without headphones. It almost seemed like if we weren't watching a movie, we were listening to music. As for me personally, from the moment I woke, I had music wake me kind of up and get

FIGURE I.2. *Doonesbury,* 26 November 2007. Reprinted with permission of Universal Press Syndicate.

me going."[5] All the soldiers I interviewed said that they frequently listened to music and for a variety of reasons: personal enjoyment, remembrance of loved ones, relaxation, religious purposes, to stave off boredom, or to heighten their aggressiveness. The circumstances varied as well: before and after missions, or while traveling, working, relaxing at a camp or base, hanging out with fellow soldiers, and so on.

Soldiers' interactions with music also vary considerably depending on factors such as personal preference, ethnicity, geographic background, Military Occupational Specialty (MOS, i.e., their job), rank, age, gender, and social class, among others. For instance, the typical age difference between enlisted-rank soldiers and their officers tends to correspond to a wide disparity in listening choices and habits. Garry Trudeau's Doonesbury comic strip from 26 November 2007 (figure I.2) satirizes how musical preferences can vary according to the age differences within the ranks.

Specialist Colby Buzzell, a M240 Bravo machine gunner in the army infantry who served a year-long tour in Iraq beginning in November 2003, observed that enlisted-rank soldiers in the army come from diverse backgrounds and regions and they have widely varied musical preferences: "You'd get people from all sorts of walk[s] of life. You'd get these southern boys who were all into country music, and you'd get the hip-hop gangsters who are into gangster rap, and they'd all listen to that. You'd get the punk kid who was into punk music. I had no idea people listened to country music until I joined the Army. I, seriously, had no idea country music was that big until I joined the Army."[6] Buzzell's comment highlights how musical tastes invariably mix during deployment, since space is limited and most enlisted soldiers share living quarters.

Most soldiers do not have direct access to new record releases or online music retailers, so they tend to acquire new music by sharing and transferring songs from each other's collections. Staff Sergeant Erik Holtan, who primarily served in Baghdad as part of a medical readiness team from 2004 to 2005, explains, "The biggest thing over there is that we share music—don't tell the record companies that—but we didn't have access to buy music online just because the firewalls prevented that. So, I figured out that we all have thumb drives, we all bought external hard drives for our pictures and things, so why don't we just transfer all our music. You get to know people and a lot of people have laptops, so you just transfer all your music. I remember this one guy gave me 30,000 songs."[7] Likewise, Buzzell said that he asked members of his platoon for their CDs, and before he left Iraq he had amassed 932 hours of music.[8]

Another important factor that influences soldiers' relationship to music is their MOS. Depending on the nature of their duty, soldiers may leave the military camps in Iraq only on occasion, and in some instances this has musical consequences. Specialist Joshua Revak, for example, served in an M-1 Abrams tank in 2005 and 2006 and frequently listened to gangsta rap with his tank mates as a way to inspire themselves for the possibility of combat and to maintain a sense of heightened awareness during missions. On the other hand, Sergeant Stephen Johnson, who served for over a year in Iraq in 2006 and 2007, was assigned to unmanned aerial surveillance and did not leave the military bases regularly. His engagement with gangsta rap music was decidedly different from Revak's: he did not go on missions that typically encountered combat and did not use this music to facilitate an aggressive mindset. In another example, Sergeant First Class Ronald Botelho, who was deployed to Iraq three times, listened to indigenous Iraqi music before leaving the military camps.[9] This was based on his specific duties; Botelho collected information from Iraqis and listened to indigenous music to learn about local culture.[10]

This book documents and interprets some of the roles that music plays in American soldier life in Iraq. Given the size and diversity of the American military there, my ethnography focuses primarily on soldiers of the enlisted rank, many with combat experience. I address music in military recruiting and Basic Combat Training, the uses of music as a preparation for combat and as an operational tactic on the battlefield, and how soldiers express their wartime experiences in the form of music. In this way, the book guides the reader through a sequence of stages characterizing an enlisted soldier's service in the military. Metal and rap emerge as a common thread among these areas of study. I investigate how these musical styles are employed within these military contexts and their profound effects on soldiers in the Iraq War. However, these are not the only genres or circumstances in which music plays a significant role for soldiers in Iraq; in fact, almost every genre of music can be said to influence the musical lives of soldiers.

The research for this study has presented some unusual challenges. Although the nature of my interest relates directly to how music is used in combat zones, onsite fieldwork has not been possible due to political instability, which in turn made travel and accommodation to the Green Zone in Baghdad prohibitively expensive. As such, I make no claims that this is an exhaustive study; rather, it presents my documentation and analysis based on the information provided by a cross-section of soldiers who have now returned from Iraq. In addition to the obvious safety risks, onsite fieldwork would have been problematic as active-duty soldiers in Iraq have become less inclined to speak to the media or to people outside the military. Some are under direct orders from their commanding officers not to speak to news reporters. Soldiers frequently have different views about the war from what circulates in popular American television and newspapers, and many feel there is an inconsistency between their experiences and what is projected by the media. Interviewing soldiers on leave or based in the United States as well as those no longer in the military seemed more fruitful because these individuals tend to speak more freely than those on active duty in Iraq.

I contacted soldiers through a number of different resources: friends, family, the internet, and sometimes dumb luck—as when I discovered that an Iraq War veteran lived in my building. Casual conversations would occasionally transform into frantic searches for pens, pencils, and paper to scribble down an e-mail or phone number for a potential interview. Over the last few years, the internet has become the norm through which soldiers voice their experiences, and I contacted some soldiers through their blogs. Many soldiers have established web sites and blogs expressing their attitudes about the war and experiences in the combat field, and these blogs sometimes form the primary material for books about soldier life in Iraq.[11] In May 2008, www.milblogging.com had 1,987 military blogs, with 432 blogs specific to soldiers deployed to Iraq; these represent both sexes and almost all races, ages, ranks, and sites of service in Iraq.

Since I had to primarily rely on phone and e-mail interviews, the interpersonal connection that comes from being in the same room with another person was lost. I felt that the interview process would be dehumanized to a certain degree, so I tried to inform myself as much as possible about each soldier before talking about his or her music. I began each interview with questions about the soldier's background: Where were you born? What was it like growing up? Did music factor into your life as a child? How did you become involved with the military? Did your background influence your musical life in Iraq? This was useful in reaching my goal to know the soldiers on a personal level. Erik Holtan, for instance, was a little embarrassed but revealed that he is a big Mötley Crüe fan, and we shared a laugh about having a mutual fondness for the band.

My conversations with soldiers would then move to general questions about music in Iraq: While deployed, did you listen to music? If so, what kinds of music? Did your musical preferences change while in Iraq? How did music fit into a typical day, if at all? The soldiers' responses clarified some aspects of the musical cultures of American soldiers in Iraq and, perhaps more important, highlighted how their musical interactions varied due to the specific circumstances of their deployment. Sergeant William Thompson, an Army counter-intelligence soldier who served in 2004, was relatively stationary in Baghdad and able to keep a laptop computer and keyboard with him. He recorded an album of jazz-inspired music during his deployment. On the other hand, Marine Corps sergeant Jason Sagebiel, who served in Iraq from March to September 2003, moved around considerably, and his duties as a scout-sniper required him to carry significant amounts of equipment. He had little or no interaction with recorded music. I also asked soldiers about specific listening contexts and how they may have used music to assist them, like listening before or during missions or in psychological operations (PSYOPS), and if they were involved in making music themselves.

I interviewed eighteen soldiers in person, over the phone, and via e-mail. Our communications ranged from a single e-mail message to a three-hour phone interview and daily correspondence. Compiling exact demographic and background statistics was difficult because, in some cases, the soldier preferred not to reveal his or her name, ethnic background, age, socioeconomic status, or other personal information. I can only be sure of the following profiles for the soldiers with whom I spoke: two women and sixteen men; two African Americans, two Hispanics, and twelve whites. The soldiers ranged in age from their early twenties to their early fifties, and the nature of their service spanned from the National Guard to over thirty years of experience in the active military. The soldiers now live throughout the United States, including in New York, Los Angeles, Arkansas, Louisiana, and Minnesota. At least half come from lower-middle-class and middle-class backgrounds.

From what I could assess, my pool of soldiers was relatively proportional to the demographic makeup of the military. The Department of Defense provides the following statistics: 89 percent male, 11 percent female; 16.25 percent African American, 1.23 percent Asian, 78.5 percent white, and 4.02 percent other. Hispanic ethnicity is listed as a separate question in military ethnicity polls, which makes the military/population ratio a better way to assess the percentage of a racial group in the U.S. population relative to its percentage in the military. A mark of 1.00 means that a race in the military is represented exactly by its percentage within the overall population, while higher ratios indicate that a group is overrepresented in the military: African American 1.44, Asian .31, White 1.01, Hispanic .89. These ratios also approximately represent the racial demographics of troops deployed to Iraq. Casualty statistics through March 2008 show the following percentages by ethnicity: 9.5 percent African American, 1.9 percent Asian, 10.7 percent Hispanic, 74.8 percent white, 3.1 percent other.

In the first chapter, I discuss music in military recruiting. Since its return to an all-volunteer force in 1973, the U.S. military has engaged in active recruiting campaigns, including television commercials and propaganda videos. Music in these advertisements typically portrays military service as an honorable duty, or a source of action, adventure, and excitement. Around 2003, the navy launched its "Accelerate Your Life" campaign, employing metal music and songs by the popular hard rock/metal band Godsmack in commercial sound tracks. This campaign demonstrated a dramatic change in style from the music of prior recruitment efforts. Since then, other military branches, including the army and Marine Corps, have used hard rock and metal in their advertisements as well. I analyze this change in depictions of action, adventure, and violence within television, film, and MTV through the 1980s and 1990s to explain this shift in music in recruiting ads. Additionally, I discuss music, or the lack thereof, in basic training. Personal music devices, like stereos and mp3 players, are not allowed in basic training. Music exists almost exclusively in the form of running and marching cadences sung by drill sergeants and recruits, with the purpose of building morale and camaraderie, or to assist in physical training exercises.

Chapter 2 examines music as an inspiration for combat. While carrying out patrols and missions, soldiers can listen to music in tanks and Humvees through self-made sound systems, portable CD players, and mp3 players. Although soldiers may engage in a variety of activities before combat, like playing video games, sleeping, or praying when time permits, almost every soldier I interviewed recalled listening to music at some point before going on patrol or within a military vehicle. Many soldiers believe that listening to music, primarily metal and rap, before or during missions, psychologically prepares them for combat. I provide excerpts from my interviews with soldiers in which they describe these experiences. Aspects of ritualization and community building emerge from these interviews as soldiers discuss planned, pre-mission gatherings involving music and chanting or yelling.

Chapter 3 offers an introduction to the music of anti-American and anti-Israel movements among opposing forces in Iraq and focuses on how these forces utilize music in recruiting efforts and as inspiration for combat. The comparison reveals some interesting similarities to the music of American military forces: both groups use culturally conditioned signifiers of meaning to project the idea that military/militia service is an honorable duty.

In chapter 4, I introduce the two principal ways music has been employed as a psychological tactic in battlefield operations: music played from loudspeakers and in detainee interrogation. Since the success of Operation Just Cause in Panama 1989, the military has projected music, particularly hard rock/metal, from special PSYOPS speaker trucks in order to induce a sense of frustration and irritation among opposing forces during specific combat missions. I investigate how music has been employed in this way within battlefield tactics in Iraq. My interviews with army interrogators also reveal how hard rock/metal music has operated as a tool to break the will of detainees if they refuse to answer questions during interrogation. This new technique has provoked widespread debate as an ethical as well as a legal issue. I address the complex issue of music as torture in interrogation in light of soldiers' training and practices, which are determined primarily by international law and U.S. military policy.

The fifth chapter explores how music has become a voice through which soldiers express their feelings about wartime experiences. In the past, soldiers mostly practiced text adaptation as the primary form of musical expression. Even with the availability of musical instruments, particularly acoustic guitars, soldiers more often played and sang existing songs or wrote parody lyrics. The Iraq War, however, has seen a proliferation of original music composed by soldiers. Soldiers express a wide variety of textual themes in their compositions, such as patriotism, grief over the loss of a friend, and the realities of daily soldier existence. Additionally, new recording, mixing, and editing programs for laptop computers now allow soldiers to record music in the setting of combat theaters. In one instance, 4th25 (pronounced "Fourth Quarter"), a group of American soldiers led by Sergeant Neal Saunders, released the first rap album written and recorded entirely in Baghdad, *Live from Iraq*. I examine the diversity of lyrical themes and styles that emerge from this music and focus on how original music serves as a vehicle for soldier expression.

In the final chapter, I analyze my previous findings within the framework of metal and rap ideologies. Like all popular music genres, metal and rap are part of a larger system of sociopolitical beliefs. I examine how themes of power, chaos, violence, and survival operate within these contexts, and how race, gender, and social class, which are important components of both metal and rap, are involved as well. My discussion explores, first, why metal may have been chosen over other popular music genres in military recruiting. The use of metal is not only a projection of the power of military institutions, but can be seen as a sonic appeal to feelings of individual empowerment. Second, I analyze the influences of metal and rap as an inspiration for combat. Some soldiers experience an intense emotional interaction with the music and its lyrical themes, and I consider ways in which metal and rap may function, to varying degrees, as catalysts for psychological transformation.

With regard to psychological tactics, I suggest that the primary source of antagonism for music in battlefield operations is timbre. More than volume or cultural resonance, timbre operates in highly impacting ways as a form of aural harassment during detainee interrogation. Next, I explore the relationship between the music of 4th25 and gangsta rap. While *Live from Iraq* adopts much of the rhetorical framework of gangsta rap, the attitudes expressed within the album, and particularly Saunders's personal views, stand ideologically opposed to many of the fundamental components of gangsta rap. In closing, I discuss areas of study, like the role of music as nostalgia and post-deployment soldier therapy, which seem promising avenues for future research.

Given that there is little scholarship now on the subject of American soldiers and music in Iraq, I wanted my theoretical and methodological frameworks to materialize from soldiers' experiences. Ethnomusicologist Bruno Nettl proposes that "each culture is likely—perhaps certain—to have its own musicology," and my goal was to let the musicology emerge from a culture of musical practices that music scholars know very little about.[12] Because of this approach and my reliance on soldiers who have returned from Iraq, however, it is important to present soldiers' accounts as an ethnography of memory. Psychologist Daniel L. Schachter suggests that "we do not store judgment-free snapshots of our past experiences but rather hold on to the meaning, sense, and emotions these experiences provided us. . . . Memories are records of how we have experienced events, not replicas of the events themselves."[13] I had to rely on soldiers' stories without observing their musical habits during the war or having the ability to notice anything that they might not have relayed in their interviews.

Many researchers find onsite fieldwork invaluable for gaining insights into musical cultures and that participation in musical events greatly enhances their understanding of the music's sociocultural contexts, listeners' memories, and variable meanings. In her examination of music and memory among Syrian Jews, for example, Kay Kaufman Shelemay points out that "observation of musical performance provides an additional unique perspective, one where the ethnomusicologist stands to make a contribution to understanding the moment in which a memory is constituted. . . . Ethnographic observance of performance can provide insights into social and cultural factors that help shape the psychology of remembering."[14] In my case, I was limited to a great degree. I was not able to travel to Iraq and I am not a soldier; thus, my research and conclusions are limited by what I was told and not what I personally experienced or observed. On the other hand, soldiers were interviewed individually and deployed to Iraq at different times to various locations. Many of their accounts are corroborated by other soldiers. By using interviews as my primary research source in conjunction with books, articles, and documentaries, it has been possible to gain a fairly clear idea of how music operates in the Iraq War as it relates to my areas of focus.

Another difficulty arises with regard to my position as a researcher. For the last few decades and at least since George Devereux's *From Anxiety to Method* (1967), scholars have been proposing that it is impossible to thoroughly separate oneself from one's own embeddedness in social and political contexts when conducting research.[15] As Michael H. Agar, Charles L. Briggs, Clifford Geertz, and many others have discussed, claiming simple neutrality or objectivity on a subject ignores the researcher's own position as subject in a complex web of social and political influences.[16] As Philip V. Bohlman summarizes, "Musicology is a political act."[17] Even in the laboratory sciences, Bruno Latour and Steve Woolgar have shown how the collection and interpretation of observations is often influenced by factors outside the realm of scientific knowledge.[18] Moreover, any study involving the Iraq War may introduce further questions concerning the position of a researcher given the highly charged political feelings some readers might have about the war.

There are no easy solutions to these problems. Scholars have negotiated the varying difficulties involved in the reflexive subjectivity of the ethnographer in a number of ways—Ruth Behar's concept of "vulnerability," Harris

Berger's "critical phenomenology" and dialogue, and others.[19] Underlying these concepts, however, is the idea that one should present, examine, and ultimately embrace the many influences surrounding research. I outline, to the best of my reflexive ability, my approach and position relative to these issues. In trying to negotiate the difficulties of "musicology as a political act" on a topic with political resonance, I want to present my work as transparently as possible.

When I began research in 2004, I believed—and still do—that I should try to maintain an open mind to all the perspectives on the issues surrounding music and the Iraq War. Any scholarship involving the Iraq War risks becoming a forum for expressing the political views of the author, and my aim is to document certain musical practices of American soldiers in Iraq, not to engage or critique the politics of war or larger issues of American policy in Iraq and the Middle East. As I was pursuing research on this topic, it quickly became clear that my presentation could be easily manipulated to enhance a position either for or against the war. While I admit that a true neutrality in my approach is impossible, it has, nonetheless, been the goal: acknowledging the limitations of impartiality does not necessitate a partisan position.

Knowing these problems, I want to share with the reader as much as possible my research process. To that end, I have created a web site in conjunction with this book, http://soundtargets.com, which provides recordings of some of my interviews and links to the video examples I discuss. "A picture is worth a thousand words" certainly applies here, and I recommend listening to these interviews because they allow the soldiers to speak in their own voices. Throughout the text, I quote them often and at length in order to provide a more comprehensive context for their words. However, inflection, tone, and emphasis are not easily transferable to the written page, and the audio allows for a more personal experience of what is being said. I want the reader to be able to examine my ability to conduct interviews with or without predisposition.

Some may argue that it is only natural for my opinions about the war to influence my research, and that I should have taken a firm stand from the beginning, either against or in support of the war, and conducted my work from one of these positions. But this strategy would have produced a number of problems in the ethnographic process. Soldiers were decidedly more willing to talk to me because I did not set out to argue political issues, and many trusted that I was not going to decontextualize their words for the purposes of defending or criticizing the war. In fact, one soldier told me over the phone that it was exactly because I did not want to talk about politics that he agreed to share his experiences. He mentioned that had my study been politically slanted, he would have refused to participate. To be sure, soldiers have political opinions, but many were enthusiastic to talk just about music.

The e-mail inquiries I sent to soldiers made clear that political propaganda—for or against the war—was not the purpose of my work (see appendix 1 for a sample e-mail sent to soldiers). Some soldiers are reluctant to speak about their experiences in the war for fear of being misinterpreted, and I believe that the intentional limitation of political discussions in my study was an important factor in many soldiers agreeing to answer my questions and in my developing rapport with them during the interviews. The restricted focus on musical issues was also helpful in this regard. Certainly, it could be argued that, even though the contexts in which I am examining soldiers' listening practices are not directly involved in the politics of the war, the reasons for their deployment are; and as such, the larger context of their musical practices is the product of global politics and U.S. government policy in the Middle East. I agree. But a scholar can discuss how college football players listen to music before a game as a way to inspire their performance without having to unpack the larger issues of their academic curriculum, athletic department budgets, and how football can strain a college's resources by diverting money from underfunded disciplines. The issue of how far up the contextual ladder any study should climb is debatable. In *Sound Targets*, I focus on the local consideration of soldiers' musical habits. This is not to deny the value of examining larger contextual issues, but I found a "boots on the ground" consideration to be the least problematic from a research and scholarship perspective. For some soldiers, the larger political issues do not significantly factor into their lives during deployment; as Neal Saunders noted, "We don't deal with whether Bush is an idiot or a liar. He ain't over there with us. I'm worried about whether this other dude is an idiot or a liar—the soldiers that are fighting beside me."[20]

My biographical relationship to this work is worth mentioning as well. I am a thirty-four-year-old white, heterosexual male from an upper-middle-class background. While my father served in the Army Reserves, I was not born until he was honorably discharged, and his service was rarely a topic of family discussion. My great-uncles served in World War II, but this too was not a significant component of my interaction with them. Am I predisposed to a sympathetic viewpoint of military personnel? Possibly, but I do not know to what extent and in what ways. And I doubt I could convincingly self-analyze my position in this regard. Conversely, one could argue that because I come from an educated, academic background, I am more inclined to liberal ways of thinking. Again, there are no easy solutions to these problems. However, one of the ways to confront the issues involved in the politics of musicology on a political topic is through transparency, thereby allowing the reader to draw their own conclusions, and this is one of my goals in including the web site as part of the book project. I accept the criticisms that may be lodged against me and my position as a researcher, and, after thinking about this situation from a different perspective, I welcome them. This study represents the first ethnography-based book on music and American soldiers in Iraq; it is only natural that these issues will arise and be debated. I hope that further discussions will advance the theoretical frameworks involved in music and war.

My research also presented practical and ethical challenges. In my attempts to contact interrogators, for example, I was once rejected for security reasons. A former army interrogator in Iraq, who wished to remain anonymous, wrote me an e-mail explaining, "I was told that I can not answer any [questions] that involve interrogation techniques. Our enemy uses the media to disseminate and collect information."[21] This response led me to consider how my writing could possibly be involved in the war itself. The interrogator's reason for refusing to answer my questions implied that, hypothetically, if I were able to obtain information about interrogation that was classified, or in some way not intended for public knowledge, publishing this information might violate security restrictions. Clearly, the military felt it was important not to risk the possibility that certain information could become known among its adversaries. This made me consider how conducting research on a topic related to a war that is still being fought could potentially influence the tactics of either side. Fortunately, I did not, to my knowledge, gather any such information, and I have tried to maintain an awareness as to what might compromise secure information.

Additionally, the interview process presented numerous difficulties. Although I mainly focused on music, my discussions with soldiers often involved stories about life and death situations in combat, where fellow soldiers were killed or wounded. In some cases, these casualties were close friends of the soldiers. I wanted to maintain a sensitivity to the fact that many of these experiences may have been traumatic, and by asking soldiers to speak about those events I could have been opening deep wounds. The experience of being a soldier in Iraq is something that I can never fully comprehend. As such, I recognize a level of discord between my awareness of this war and the experiences and perspectives of soldiers.

The many difficulties addressed above are only some of the challenging issues that arose in my work on this topic, but I believe the insights offered in the following pages outweigh the problematic aspects. It is likely that this book raises more questions than it answers: Are these practices distinctly American? What, if any, are the differences between soldiers in Iraq as opposed to Afghanistan? What are the differences in listening practices between soldiers who regularly encounter combat and those who do not? How are soldiers' combat-zone musical interactions different from those at military bases not located in Iraq? These and many other questions will surely emerge from my research, and I hope the reader will not find this to be a shortcoming but rather a function of the nature of introductory work where new ideas seem to unfold at every turn. My hope is that this book will provide a platform for others to pursue topics related to music and the Iraq War.

The relationship between music and war has a long and distinct history. For as long as war has been waged, music has played important roles: God instructed the Israelites to blow silver trumpets when they were attacked (Numbers 10:9), fife and drum corps rallied the soldiers of the American Revolution, the boogie woogie bugle boys encouraged the troops of World War II, and pop musicians like Jimi Hendrix and Jim Morrison provided the musical backdrop for the so-called "first rock 'n' roll war" in Vietnam. The present war in Iraq is no exception. My research has taught me that soldiers' musical practices are dynamic, always changing and taking new forms throughout history. This book offers a glimpse into the lives of soldiers in the present conflict in Iraq, and I hope it will provide a valuable contribution to the literature on music and war.

1 | Music and Contemporary Military Recruiting

The Continental Army began recruiting soldiers in 1775 to fight in the American Revolution. Since then, American military forces have been mostly comprised of volunteer soldiers, though with periods of conscription (known in more recent times as the draft) during wartime, as in the Civil War and World War I. A dramatic shift in military recruiting came about with the Selective Service Act of 1948, the first establishment of peacetime conscription.[1] Previously during peacetime, the military had developed a variety of advertising campaigns to attract servicemen, including advertisements and posters like James Montgomery Flagg's famous "I want *you* for the US Army!" which was used from World War I to World War II. The Marines' slogan, "We're Looking for a Few Good Men," still in use, can be traced back to a 1799 advertisement in a Boston newspaper.[2] After 1948, however, peacetime conscription made it possible for the military to relax recruiting campaigns, and by the mid-1960s, branches like the army acquired soldiers primarily through this route.[3]

It was during the Korean War (1950–53) that the draft came to be viewed by many as unfair; similarly, the Vietnam War (1959–75) was accompanied by a strong public outcry against conscription. In both wars, it was not uncommon for those of higher socioeconomic brackets, including college and university students, to be able to avoid military service via deferments. Although the process of conscription shifted to a lottery system in 1970, historian Thomas W. Evans notes that this "did not erase the sense of unfairness, merely changing the focus from victimization of the underprivileged to victimization of the unlucky."[4] This was the background for the U.S. military's return to an all-volunteer force in 1973, after which the modern age of military recruiting began.

Following peacetime conscription, the military has tried to sell itself to a target audience of 17- to 25-year-old men (and more recently women) by portraying military service as an attractive career option. It does this in two principal ways: recruiters and advertising. Much of a recruiter's work takes place in high schools and colleges, where the target audience is centrally located. As a provision of the No Child Left Behind Act (2001), high schools must provide contact information for all students to military recruiters or possibly lose funding. Students are automatically included unless they request that their information be withheld or they "opt out." Military recruiters often attend "career day" and "college day" activities at high schools, setting up booths alongside those of colleges and universities.[5] Recruiters are an essential means of enlisting soldiers. In 2005, for example, the U.S. Army spent $346.5 million on recruiter support among the Active Army, Army National Guard, and the Army Reserve.[6] The army considers advertising at least as important as recruiters, and spends over $100 million more on advertising than on recruiter support; the Active Army, Army National Guard, and the Army Reserve spent $459 million on advertising in 2005.[7] Television advertisements and propaganda videos consume a considerable amount of the advertising budget, and music figures prominently in these recruiting efforts.[8]

The music of military advertising should be understood against the backdrop of the advertising industry, in which music has always been a vital component. Jingles—short melodies aimed at memorability and product recollection—were some of the first music composed for advertising and have persisted to the present day both on television and radio. The documented history of music and advertising dates back to the nineteenth century. Carrie McLaren observes that "pretty much as soon as there was such thing as a music industry (and such thing as an advertising industry), music was employed to sell. The music and advertising industries took shape in the late 1800s and cemented their relationship with commercial radio broadcasting in the '20s."[9] One of the important developments in the history of music and advertising occurred in 1908 when the Oldsmobile Motor Company promoted its automobiles with the popular Johnny Marks song "In My Merry Oldsmobile."[10] Since then, companies have constantly sought licensing agreements from popular music artists to broadcast their songs in commercials or to sing their advertisement jingles. This relationship has also worked in reverse. In 1964, for example, John Delorean commissioned a song, "Little GTO," for the advertising campaign of the new Pontiac car, and the song then became a top 40 hit. "I'd Like to Teach the World to Sing (in Perfect Harmony)" was originally composed by the New Seekers in 1971 for a Coca-Cola commercial, and later reached #7 on the U.S. popular music charts as a single and #1 in the United Kingdom and Japan.

In 1981, the relationship between music and advertising significantly changed with the founding of Music Television, MTV. Promoted as "the Biggest Advertising Merger in History," merging television and music, the network aired music videos, short films accompanying popular music songs. MTV's enormous success further commodified music by making it the advertised product, thereby switching the traditional relationship between music and television advertising.[11] In the past, music was composed to help sell a product; with MTV, music itself was the product and, at least at the beginning of the network, the visual imagery of the music video usually accompanied a song that had already achieved popular success on the radio. As popular music genres became more deeply associated with specific visual imagery, the military began to draw upon such sound/image associations for its advertisements and propaganda videos. The musical styles used in military recruiting efforts were the result of a variety of influences, many of which are cultural and originate within the mass media. In this chapter, I trace developments in the music of military advertisements and illustrate how, through the 1980s, 1990s, and into the twenty-first century, depictions of action, adventure, and violence in television, film, and music videos shaped this music.

SOUND, IMAGE, AND MEANING:
A THEORETICAL INTRODUCTION

With the end of conscription, the military reengaged in aggressive advertising campaigns. Music played an important role in these efforts to attract soldiers and was utilized most prominently in television advertisements and propaganda videos. The music in these recruiting resources works synergetically with the visual imagery, resulting in combinations of sound and image. The theoretical literature on the relationship between sound and image is somewhat limited because, as anthropologist Kelly Askew notes, the anthropology of media has traditionally prioritized the study of images over sound: "But for reasons yet to be explored, they (aural forms of media) have attracted less attention than they deserve."[12] Film scholar Roger Hillman echoes Askew's position: "The visual aspect of film still holds most critics in thrall, and the dimension of sound, including music, frequently receives token mention, if any."[13] The seminal work of cultural theorist Michel Chion, however, helps to address this gap and provides an insightful framework for understanding the relationship between sound and image. In his research on music and cinema, Chion proposes that music and sound have no intrinsic bond, but when combined, they generate a distinct mode of perception, "audio-vision."[14] Sound creates "added value" to the experience of visual perception:

> By *added value* I mean the expressive and informative value with which a sound enriches a given image so as to create the definite impression, in the immediate or remembered experience one has of it, that this information or expression "naturally" comes from what is seen, and is already contained in the image itself. Added value is what gives the (eminently incorrect) impression that sound is unnecessary, that sound merely duplicates a meaning which in reality it brings about, either all on its own or by discrepancies between it and the image.[15]

Chion understands the role of music in film as more than association; music exists in a "symbolic contract" with image, forming a single perceptual entity.[16] Sound does more than simply reinforce a meaning inherent in an image: it is an equal partner in constructing meaning. Greater than the sum of the individual parts, sound and image mutually interact and inform one another, such that the role of sound is not subservient to that of the image: "We never see the same thing when we also hear; we don't hear the same thing when we see as well. We must therefore go beyond preoccupations such as identifying so-called redundancy between the two domains and debating inter-relations between forces (the famous question asked in the seventies, 'which is more important, sound or image?')."[17]

While my discussion is primarily devoted to music, I consider, like Chion, sound and image to exist in a "symbolic contract." Any discussion of sounds and images is somewhat limited by what one can accomplish through description on the written page. Therefore, the reader may wish to reference the accompanying web site (http://soundtargets.com), which provides links to the videos I discuss.[18] Chion's concept of "audio-vision" is useful to my analysis of music in military recruiting because it identifies music as an indispensable component of film, television, video, or any media that pairs images and sound. Adopting Chion's perspective allows sound to be discussed as a distinct signifier of emotion, and the music employed in military television advertisements and propaganda videos is an important communicator of meaning.

Naturally, this brings us to the issue of musical meaning, and here the literature is vast. The questions of what music means (if anything), how musical meaning is created, how we interpret meaning, and how we talk about meaning have been contemplated and answered very differently by philosophers and semioticians of music. Much of the early influential work on meaning and music was written by Leonard Meyer, Jean Molino, and Jean-Jacques Nattiez.[19] Meyer, for instance, employs gestalt perception principles to explain meaning as the fulfillment or denial of anticipated musical events or structures.[20] Molino and Nattiez examine how music can be structurally referential and propose a tripartite model for understanding musical interpretations; they primarily argue for the position of one component of the model, *niveau neutre*—the idea that music is an autonomous text, existing on a "neutral level." Others scholars have found the *niveau neutre* idea problematic, among them David Lidov, Mark Johnson, and Robert Walser. Walser suggests, "While Nattiez recognizes the conventional basis of semiological meanings, he seems to want to retain some sort of absolute notion of truth, against which interpretations can be measured. . . . Underpinning all semiotic analysis is, recognized or not, a set of assumptions about cultural practice, for ultimately music doesn't have meanings: people do."[21] Many scholars have since built upon the work of Meyer, Molino, and Nattiez, but understand meaning to result from individual listener responses within wider sociocultural interpretative contexts.[22]

Another influential perspective on music, emotion, and meaning is proposed by Thomas Turino, whose theory of meaning is derived from the semiotics of American philosopher and scientist Charles Peirce (1839–1914).[23] Adopting Peirce's term "index" ("a sign that is related to its object [what it signifies] because of co-occurrence between the sign and object in the actual experience of a perceiver"), Turino suggests that indexical signs, like music, "are associational and particularly context dependent . . . are dependent on personal as well as shared experiential associations over time, and these facets give them a more affective, personal, or group-specific quality ('our song'), as well as variable semantic character, because people's experiences and associations differ."[24] Indices may also hold multiple meanings simultaneously. In other words, musical meaning is not traceable back to a neutral text, as it was for Nattiez, but is constructed differently by listeners who interpret a multiplicity of meanings based on personal, social, and cultural experiences and associations. Charles Keil and Steven Feld's work effectively demonstrates that musical meaning can also be highly variable and shifting even for an individual.[25]

This brief survey of musical semiotics is intended to inform our conception of how music operates within the context of advertisements, film, television, and media texts. Nicholas Cook makes a useful application of contemporary semiotic ideas in his discussion of musical meaning in television commercials, which directly relates to my forthcoming arguments. He observes that music in media texts is vital to the creation of meaning and possibly more important than any text, slogan, or narration: "Music, then, does not just project meaning in the commercials; it is a source of meaning. . . . It generates meaning beyond anything that is said (and sometimes anything that *can* be said) in words."[26] Music in media, like commercials, can draw upon culturally conditioned signifiers of meaning and lend meaning to the images. As we have seen, individuals will interpret music in multiple ways, but music can be also intended to generate meanings that reach across individual boundaries and create common meaning for groups of people. Particularly in commercials where a product is being sold, it makes sense that advertisers would attempt to draw upon more general cultural codes of musical meaning to affiliate their product with an emotion or affect that is readily recognizable.

Claudia Gorbman is another important figure, besides Chion, in the literature on the relationship between sound and image. In her book *Unheard Melodies,* she observes that, apart from the text and images, the music itself can be considered its own cultural "language" of meaning: "Any music bears cultural associations, and most of these associations have been further codified and exploited by the music industry. Properties of instrumentation, rhythm, melody, and harmony form a veritable language."[27] It is in this way that I would like to engage the music of military recruiting. The music used in military propaganda and advertisements can be understood as signifiers of musical meaning within American culture that are used to project qualities of military service. The soundtracks utilize specific musical codes to create meaning within the commercials and affiliate military service with different meanings as transmitted through music.

THE MUSIC OF MILITARY ADVERTISING AND ITS INFLUENCES

The music of contemporary military recruiting tends to be "structure/continuity" music, a term suggested by David Huron referring to music that creates continuity and dramatic emphasis to a series of images.[28] This music lends meaning to the images in military advertising, which are accompanied by text and, almost always, a slogan. The slogan is typically presented in the final scene of the commercial and, along with the text, may or may not be narrated. The list below presents recent slogans of the four main U.S. military branches.[29]

Air Force
Aim High (1980–2001)
No One Comes Close (1990s)
Cross Into the Blue (2001–06)
Do Something Amazing (2006–present)

Army
Be All That You Can Be (1981–2001)
An Army of One (2001–06)
Army Strong (2006–present)

Marines
The Few. The Proud. The Marines.
We're Looking for a Few Good Men (both appear in various forms since the nineteenth century)

Navy
It's Not Just a Job, It's an Adventure (ca. 1981–90)
You and the Navy: Full Speed Ahead (1990–2001)
Accelerate Your Life (2001–present)

In its interaction with texts, images, and slogans, the music of military recruiting conveys two principal messages: military service is a heroic, patriotic, and honorable duty; and military service is a source of action, adventure, and excitement. While each branch of the military attempts to distinguish itself to a certain degree within these two categories, the majority of music in commercials and videos generally supports these messages. The following examples illustrate how music is used to convey these two ideas.

Video example 1, a Marine Corps advertisement, shows Marines in a variety of training exercises, such as presenting arms, running across fields, jumping from airplanes, and related activities. Although each scene lasts only a second or two, much of the action within these scenes appears in slow motion, coordinating with the mood of the music. The music begins with brass playing a slow, chorale-like theme in major mode, doubled by a synthesizer (synth) choir sound. The tonal harmony outlines a I-V⁶-I progression under scale degrees 3-(4)-5-3; strings enter on the next phrase (example 1.1). The theme then repeats with a contrapuntal line added by the strings, and the words "for Honor" appear against a black background approximately twenty-three seconds into the minute-long commercial. There is no narration or text until this point and no sound in the entire commercial other than the music. The scenes continue for another seven seconds and the music of the first phrase repeats in a slight variant. We see the faces of Marines looking attentively at the camera and their commanding officers. A fighter jet is raised to the launch platform of a ship, and the image focuses closely on the face of a Marine; the words "for Courage" emerge. After seven seconds of Marines pointing rifles, swinging on ropes across training obstacles, and jumping from airplanes, "for Country" appears on the screen. The remainder of the video shows helicopters and tanks moving across the landscape, and a close-up of a Marine's face. The famous slogan finally unfolds: "The Few. The Proud. The Marines." The brass, strings, and synth choir play the slow opening theme once more, but with full melodic closure, I-V^6-I supporting scale degrees 3-(4)-2-1, as the advertisement ends.

EXAMPLE 1.1. Reduction of the Marine Corps video theme and first phrase

Video example 1 conveys the message that service in the Marine Corps is an honorable, courageous, patriotic act. In fact, the commercial states this explicitly with "for Honor, for Courage, for Country," but the first phrase, "for Honor," does not appear until almost halfway through the advertisement. Before the video shows us how we should be interpreting the images, the music is the principal communicator of meaning. The slow chorale theme in major mode along with the synth choir sound may invoke, for those from a religious, particularly Christian, background, the solemn nature of religious service. The brass texture that begins the theme introduces a timbral connection with the military, as brass instruments are commonly associated with military music and fanfare. The music suggests a solemn, brave, and patriotic character to the Marines and their duties. This interpretation is reinforced when the text is presented.

Similar strategies are employed in an "Army Strong" video (video example 2). In the beginning of this example, the following text appears across six different scenes set against a black background: "Webster defines strong as having great physical power, as having moral or intellectual power, as striking or superior of its kind. But with all due respect to Webster, there's strong, and there's Army strong." The music accompanying these images consists of strings and brass in a static texture, moving slowly over a melody, E-D-F♯-D-E. Once the text is presented, after approximately twenty seconds, an image of U.S. Army soldiers standing together in a desert landscape appears. The music immediately increases in tempo and begins a theme that recurs in variations throughout the advertisement (example 1.2). Then, we see camouflaged soldiers running across a field, surveying electronic maps, and jumping out of airplanes. The text, "It is a strength like none other," is shown. The interplay between scenes of text and soldier activities consumes the remainder of the advertisement. Every few seconds images of soldiers in training activities, close-ups of soldiers' faces, or related scenes are presented. Some scenes unfold in slow motion and alternate with the following text:

> It is a physical strength, it is an emotional strength. It is a strength of character, and strength of purpose. The strength to do good today and the strength to do good tomorrow. The strength to obey, and strength to command. The strength to build and strength to tear down. The strength to get yourself over, and the strength to get over yourself. There is nothing on this green earth that is stronger than the U.S. Army because there is nothing on this green earth that is stronger than a U.S. Army soldier. Army strong.

EXAMPLE 1.2. "Army Strong" theme

The message conveyed in the "Army Strong" advertisement is clear: army service makes you strong, and it is noble and heroic. Like the Marine Corps video, the music of "Army Strong" contributes "added value" to this message. Even though both examples contain texts that directly communicate how we should interpret the music, these soundtracks draw upon culturally conditioned signifiers of meaning to project their respective messages. As an example, let us consider the "Army Strong" theme and my description of this music as strong, noble, and heroic. Following Gorbman, one possible way of interpreting the meaning conveyed by the "Army Strong" theme is through its similarities to music associated with these characteristics in American culture.

The theme music composed by John Williams for the 1978 movie *Superman* provides a good basis for comparison. *Superman* is an icon of American strength, nobility, and heroism, and this theme music is well known in popular culture (an excerpt is presented in example 1.3). While the *Superman* theme is played at a much faster tempo, among other differences, there are some interesting connections that emerge between this theme and "Army Strong." Both are similarly orchestrated as a predominantly brass instrumentation plays the principal melodies with string/wind accompaniment, and the themes undergo a series of repetitions and variations throughout each example. They are closely related in scale structure and melodic organization as well. The *Superman* example repeats the melodic fragment of m. 1 in m. 3. A distinguishing feature of this measure—present in almost every bar of the excerpt—is the motive of a perfect fifth, C-G, which creates a rhythmic emphasis on the second beat. Turning to the "Army Strong" example, we find a great deal of parallelism. The melodic fragment of m. 1 is reiterated in m. 3, and in mm. 5 and 7. The motive of a perfect fifth in m. 2, a descending G-C, emerges as the first melodic leap and repeats in m. 6. The perfect fifth interval then appears in mm. 9 and 11 as F-B♭. These motivic leaps also create a rhythmic emphasis on beat 2 in mm. 2, 6, 9, and 11. Moreover, both themes demonstrate an x, x, y subphrase structure. In "Army Strong," the first four bars are repeated (x), followed by a different subphrase (y) that completes the melody, mm. 9–12. Likewise, the *Superman* theme repeats a passage (x), mm. 1–2, which is followed by a different subphrase (y), mm. 5–8, that concludes the excerpt. In these ways, the "Army Strong" theme might be described as strong, noble, and heroic in light of its similarities to music within American culture that is codified with these characteristics, like the *Superman* theme. While the texts and images of military advertisements communicate meaning, the music, in its own

EXAMPLE 1.3. *Superman* theme

right, projects meaning based on associative, cultural "codes" that provide a framework for interpretation. This is not to suggest that all listeners will hear the music as signifying these qualities, but these types of associations seem to be implied by the music and represent one possible interpretation of meaning, which could be recognized by a significant number of listeners.

The "Army Strong" and Marine Corps advertisements demonstrate numerous resemblances. In both examples, music is the only sound element and the timbres of the music have much in common: the instrumental texture of "Army Strong" is dominated by brass and accompanied by strings, synth choir, and some woodwinds. Meanwhile, the Marine Corps video prominently displays a brass instrumentation along with strings and synth choir. Both videos show soldiers engaging in military training activities that are often exactly the same: jumping from airplanes, running across fields, riding in boats, and aiming rifles. Close-ups on the faces of the soldiers serve as an important component of each advertisement as well, and much of the action in each video takes place in slow motion. Structurally, they are almost identical in that action scenes alternate with text appearing against a black background. If the text and slogan did not serve as a guide, one might not be able to distinguish the two videos. They also generally convey the same message: military service is a patriotic, noble, courageous, heroic, honorable duty. For the sake of brevity, I call this type of soundtrack "honorable duty" music, where "honorable" implies any of these or related values.

Indeed, most of the armed forces depict service in their respective branches in similar ways; video and television advertisements show soldiers engaging in activities, text or narration describes the qualities inherent in service, a slogan concludes the commercial, and honorable duty music contributes as a signifier of this message.

While honorable duty music is prevalent in military videos, the army's "Be All That You Can Be" campaign (1981–2001) demonstrates an exception to the use of structure/continuity music in television commercials. This campaign represents the longest-running slogan since the army became an all-volunteer force. In these advertisements, the slogan is not narrated or projected on the screen as text, but sung as a jingle. Video example 3 presents an Army Reserve version of the "Be All That You Can Be" television commercial. The images are remarkably similar to the previous two examples. We see helicopters flying over the shoreline, soldiers running down a hillside, and camouflaged jeeps moving along a dirt road. In place of text, a narrator describes these scenes: "One weekend a month you can take off for the beach, the mountains, or a drive in the country, in the Army Reserve." The famous jingle is then sung by male voices. The narration continues, "It's no picnic, but it's the kind of excitement no other weekend offers. And you'll still have three weekends a month to take off on your own." The commercial concludes with the sung melody, "find your future, in the Army Reserve," and a man and woman dressed in street clothes drive away on a motorcycle. Although the scenes are consistent with those of the other videos, the music and message of this advertisement are expressed differently. Unlike the structure/continuity type of honorable duty music, a jingle conveys the idea that service in the Army Reserve provides action and adventure. The narrator emphasizes the diversity of locations one would encounter in the Army Reserve ("beach," "mountains," and "the country") and stresses the uniqueness of the experience: "It is the kind of excitement no other weekend offers." This example illustrates the second principal advertising strategy of military recruiting: the military is a source of action, adventure, and "excitement."

For the most part, branches of the military portray themselves in television advertisements and propaganda videos in these two ways (honorable duty and opportunities for action/excitement), and music plays a vital role in projecting these messages. In approximately 2003, however, the U.S. Navy took a new approach to the action/excitement strategy in its "Accelerate Your Life" recruiting campaign. The music that accompanied the familiar scenes of sailors in action was not a lively jingle or honorable duty music, but metal.[30] Included in these commercials were excerpts from the songs

"Awake" and "Sick of Life," by the nü metal band Godsmack from their 2000 album *Awake*.[31]

Before these navy commercials, no military branch had employed music remotely similar to metal in military recruiting. Although references to popular music genres had appeared, none of this music even slightly resembled metal. For instance, the U.S. Air Force "No One Comes Close" video (video example 4) opens with images of a fighter jet moving quickly across the sky, followed by a sequence of scenes that alternate between images of the flying jet and men operating radar and computer equipment. A male voice states, "America's Air Force has a plane so advanced it dominates everything in the air." The atmosphere of the music up to this point might be described as mysterious. A piano accompanies a solo female voice ascending in a slow, step-wise, vocalise melody, D-E-F-G. The music stops as the narrator states, "Yet on radar, it's small as a bird." At this point, the music changes dramatically to an up-tempo, quasi-techno groove, influenced by the techno/electronica popular music style and bearing a striking similarity to The Chemical Brothers' "Block Rockin' Beats"—the tonal center, tempo, modality, timbres, and syncopated rhythms are all alike. The remaining images present the fighter moving quickly across the sky and the narrator continues: "The meanest, baddest bird on the planet. Join the team that keeps us flying. America's Air Force. No One Comes Close." The techno groove persists as the U.S. Air Force logo and slogan, "No One Comes Close," conclude the advertisement. The recruiting strategy in this video falls into the action, adventure, excitement category, but with a slight twist. The advertisement focuses on the technological advances of the U.S. Air Force and suggests that by joining, one would be involved with this cutting-edge aviation technology. The techno/electronica-inspired music from the second half of the commercial reinforces this message. By referencing the popular music genres of techno and electronica, the music creates associations (cultural "codes") between being "hip" and "cool" and the technology one would encounter in the air force.

Video example 4 demonstrates how music in military recruiting references popular music styles and constitutes the closest music I could find to metal. Of course, techno/electronica sounds nothing like metal, and this is the point. When the navy began employing metal music and Godsmack songs in their videos, this change entailed a significant break from other popular music genres that had been referenced in military advertisements. Popular music songs have appeared in advertising since 1908, and the military has licensed popular music songs for its commercials; "Won't Back

Down" by Johnny Cash, for example, appears in an "Army of One" advertisement. However, before the "Accelerate Your Life" advertisements, like the one in video example 5, a distorted, power chord guitar sound had rarely been heard in military videos, and now it suddenly became a primary timbre.

Although the music changed significantly, the structure and images of video example 5 closely resemble the other advertisements I have discussed. There is no sound element other than music, and sailors engage in training maneuvers, like leaping from helicopters, swimming underwater in scuba gear with rifles, and rappelling down ropes off helicopters. The only noticeable difference is that the close-ups of the sailors show slightly more serious and intimidating facial expressions. While the video demonstrates the recruiting strategy of action, adventure, and excitement, the metal soundtrack contrasts greatly with the music of previously discussed video examples. But just as the techno/electronica music signaled the technological advances of the air force, the metal music seems to be musically representing aspects of naval service. It appears to suggest that service in the navy is analogous to the experience of metal. The U.S. Navy rocks.

Over the last four years, other branches of the military have begun to use metal-influenced music in their recruiting efforts, such as the Marine Corps video in video example 6. After a seventeen-second introduction outlining the history and values of Marine Corps service, the music builds ominously to a bass, synth, drums, and distorted guitar climax playing a power chord, nü metal-style riff. As might be expected, the images of this section show marines in training exercises: presenting arms, running out of an airplane with rifles, and moving across terrain in tanks and armored vehicles. This particular video, though, is distinct among the advertisements surveyed here in that it presents images of shots being fired. In the majority of videos, guns may be shown or pointed, but they are rarely fired. It is therefore significant that most of the images showing bombs dropping, artillery shells being fired, or guns shooting are set to metal music. The most overtly violent scenes in video example 6 are coordinated with the distorted guitar riff.

The image of a tank firing its main battle gun, approximately eighty-seven seconds into the video, begins a quick and somewhat curious musical transition. A cymbal crash ends the nü metal riff and almost immediately we hear honorable duty music. Brass instruments play a slow, major mode melody with string and synth choir accompaniment. In a matter of seconds, the music moves from a bass, drums, and distorted guitar metal riff to slow brass music. With this dramatic change, the video synthesizes the two principal advertising strategies, honorable duty and action/excitement, in the context of a single video.

The influence of metal music in recent military recruiting advertisements is perhaps best demonstrated by the 2006 video "The Creed" (video example 7). Section 8 Studios produced the video and original music for the New Jersey National Guard, making it one of the first complete songs in a popular music style specifically commissioned for the purposes of military recruiting.[32] "The Creed" features detuned, heavily distorted guitar timbres, syncopated riffs in $\frac{4}{4}$ time, and pitched sung vocals, all of which reference the nü metal subgenre. The lyrics are primarily derived from army slogans. The chorus, for example, "I will never quit, I won't accept defeat, placing the mission first," is taken from the U.S. Army's "Warrior Ethos":

> I will always place the mission first.
> I will never accept defeat.
> I will never quit.
> I will never leave a fallen comrade.

The remaining phrase, "I will never leave a fallen comrade," is introduced in the bridge section of the song where the male vocals repeat four times, "Know in your heart, I will never leave you behind." Furthermore, the text that begins the video presents the seven army core values: leadership, duty, respect, selfless service, honor, integrity, and personal courage. The images of "The Creed" are familiar to military recruiting videos. Soldiers and recruits engage in training exercises, like pointing rifles, running across obstacles, doing push-ups and sit-ups, and performing search and recovery exercises, among others.

Structurally, "The Creed" is organized as a music video, more closely related to what one sees on MTV than any of the videos analyzed thus far. It is over four and a half minutes long—around the average length of a metal song, but about a minute longer than the other videos—and this duration appears to be determined by the music. In the previous videos, the music was largely structured around the intended length of the video. The metal music of the navy's "Accelerate Your Life" advertisement, video example 5, was edited to fit the format of a thirty-second television commercial. The excerpts from the Godsmack songs, "Awake" and "Sick of Life," appearing in other navy advertisements, are likewise edited to fit within the format of short television commercials. In music videos, however, the preexisting song governs the duration of the video and the images are set within the structure of the music. The images of "The Creed" are constructed around the song in the manner of MTV videos, where the music becomes the primary creative element.[33] By referencing the format and structure of music videos, "The Creed" places even more emphasis on the role of music in communicating meaning. Here as well, the metal music conveys the idea that military service is an opportunity for action, adventure, and excitement.

Given the emergence of metal as a sound track in military recruiting advertisements and videos, it seems logical to ask: Why did metal music become an important part of military recruiting? What motivated this major stylistic shift in the music the military employed to attract soldiers? One explanation is that metal music contributes to the long-standing recruiting strategy of depicting military service as a form of action, adventure, and excitement. This strategic message persists from early videos, like the Army Reserve's "Be All That You Can Be" (video example 3), to more recent advertisements like "The Creed." The notable difference, however, lies in the musical representation of the military as a source of action and "excitement."

The use of metal music in military recruiting can be understood by considering the genre in mainstream media, like television and film. Throughout the 1980s, 1990s, and into the twenty-first century, mainstream television and film gradually incorporated aspects of metal music in soundtracks to scenes of action and violence. As I show, metal, or what might be better described as metal- or rock-influenced timbres, slowly became associated with portrayals of action and violence in film and television, and these associations greatly contributed and in some cases led directly to the military's use of metal music in its recruiting videos.

The Influence of Television

One of the most popular action/adventure television series in the 1980s was *The A-Team*, which aired from 1983 to 1987. A narrated storyline introduced the show: "In 1972, a crack commando unit was sent to prison by a military court for a crime they didn't commit. These men promptly escaped from a maximum-security stockade into the Los Angeles underground. Today, still wanted by the government, they survive as soldiers of fortune. If you have a problem, if no one else can help, and if you can find them, maybe you can hire—The A-Team" (video example 8). After this narration, which is accompanied by snare drum rhythms and timpani accents, gunshots riddle the screen, spelling out "The A-Team," and the theme music begins. The music employs three principal timbres: strings, brass, and snare drum. The strings and upper brass play the main melody in unison, while the lower brass provide a contrapuntal bass line. The snare drum continues the military-style rhythmic patterns of the narrated section. Approximately forty-seven seconds into the introduction, the music makes a timbral and stylistic shift. The strings and brass drop out, giving way to a distorted electric guitar, bass, and drum set. The guitar and bass repeat a power-chord riff in $\frac{4}{4}$ time while the drums place snare accents on beats two and four. After this section, the music returns to the texture dominated by strings, brass, and snare drum.

This passage of *The A-Team* theme clearly reveals the influence of metal and hard rock timbres. The classic hard rock backbeat with the power chord riff in $\frac{4}{4}$ time played by distorted electric guitar is one of the primary timbral signifiers of hard rock and metal music.[34] The pitch structure also references metal and hard rock, genres that tend to be modal with an emphasis on Aeolian/Dorian or Phrygian/Locrian scales.[35] In this excerpt from "The A-Team" theme, the pitch collection outlines a D Aeolian mode (D, E, F, G, A, B♭, and C). While the metal-influenced sounds and pitches do not dominate the instrumental texture of the entire theme music, they provide a significant reference to the popular music genre in this section.

The military overtones of the introduction and the depictions of violence are also worthy of notice. The beginning images show a military helicopter landing and armed men running into a heavily forested area. Many of the vehicles seen in the first thirty seconds of the introduction appear to belong to the military. Additionally, three scenes in the theme are more overtly violent than the others, in which the main characters shoot rifles. In fact, two of the three scenes where gunshots are fired occur during the segment of metal-influenced music, which accounts for only twenty seconds of the ninety-five-second introduction. Like the Marine Corps advertisement (video example 6), the scenes of gunfire in *The A-Team* introduction correspond with metal music.

To emphasize the important pairing of metal-influenced music with action and violence, I make a brief comparison with another television program of the same era. *The Greatest American Hero* (1981–86) was an action/comedy series about a teacher who reluctantly becomes a superhero after finding an alien super-suit. Both series were produced by Stephen J. Cannell. The theme music for *The Greatest American Hero* was composed by Mike Post, who co-wrote the theme music to *The A-Team* with Pete Carpenter. The short pop song that serves as the theme music for *The Greatest American Hero* includes synthesizer/piano, bass, drums, strings, and a tenor male voice (video example 9). There are no distorted guitars or power chords, but there are also no images of violence. The main character is not seen shooting a gun, and only one scene in the introduction pictures a gun; the gun is held by the character, Bill Maxwell, an FBI agent in the series. *The A-Team* introduction is more graphically violent than that of *The Greatest American Hero* due to the former's images of guns and gunfire. While *The A-Team* includes metal-influenced timbres in scenes of violence, *The Greatest American Hero* does not reference metal. As it relates to scenes of violence, including guns and gunfire, the presence of metal in *The A-Team* is a distinguishing musical feature that separates such scenes from content that is less graphically violent.

Two further examples support the idea that, through the 1980s and into the 1990s, television began portraying action, adventure, and violence with music that referenced metal. In *Magnum PI* (1980–88), a former Navy SEAL becomes a private investigator. The beginning of the theme music for this series presents a distinctive guitar part (video example 10). The guitar repeats a fast sixteenth-note riff between F and E♭. The timbre of the guitar has a partial distortion effect, and while this reference is subtle, it demonstrates one of the first examples of a hard rock or metal music allusion in a mainstream television action series. Additionally, a distorted solo guitar melody is heard approximately halfway through the introduction in the call and response section of the theme music. During the music of the opening fifteen seconds, which includes the partial distortion effect on the guitar, the scenes are the most violently suggestive in the entire theme. The main character, bare-chested, slams a cartridge into his handgun and runs through a forest with his gun raised. At no other time in the introduction do we see a gun.

The theme music composed by Jan Hammer for *Miami Vice* (1984–89), a series about two vice detectives, provides another useful example. According to the storyline, one of the two detectives, James "Sonny" Crockett, served two tours in Southeast Asia after being drafted by the army; just as in *The A-Team*, *Magnum PI*, and *Miami Vice*, many characters in action/adventure television series are portrayed as having military backgrounds. The images displayed during the *Miami Vice* theme (video example 11), however, differ from those in the other examples. Instead of the main characters in action, we see scenes suggesting the city of Miami: palm trees, flamingos, the ocean, Jai-Lai, and finally the Miami skyline. While guns are not depicted, the series is well known for its violent content; a shot is fired in almost every episode and a wide assortment of firearms was shown over its six-year history. The theme music begins with a short percussion introduction before a distorted guitar enters, mostly repeating a C power chord. The main melody also appears as a distorted guitar timbre, approximately nineteen seconds into the theme. This is a more conventional hard rock or metal instrumentation and texture, with a solo distorted electric guitar playing the melody and a rhythm distorted electric guitar playing a power chord riff. The percussion places clear snare drum emphases on beats two and four, suggesting a hard rock or metal backbeat.

As all these examples begin to suggest, throughout the 1980s, hard rock and metal had an evolving association with scenes of action and violence.[36] Other television series, such as *Hardcastle and McCormick* (1983–86) and *Hunter* (1984–91), further demonstrate the increasing references of metal timbres in theme music. Conversely, action/adventure shows from previous decades did not make these musical allusions. The theme music to *Hawaii Five-O* (1968–80), *The Six Million Dollar Man* (1974–78), and *Charlie's Angels* (1976–81) do not exhibit the timbral signifiers of a distorted electric guitar and power chords, even though the overall plots of these shows have much in common with those discussed above. For example, the images of *Hawaii Five-O* are similar to *Magnum PI*. Both introductions present two successive scenes where guns are shown, but in *Hawaii Five-O* the instrumentation of the music involves brass and woodwinds rather than distorted electric guitar. *Charlie's Angels* offers another good point of comparison; the introduction to the show is dominated by guns (video example 12). If one considers the animated profiles of the characters, five scenes depict guns or gun images and four shots are fired. The instrumentation, however, mostly comprises brass, strings, electric bass, drums, and a background clean-tone, wah-wah guitar.

Before the 1980s, the timbral signifiers of metal were rarely associated with television depictions of action/violence. Certainly, the producers of a show like *Charlie's Angels* could have chosen the contemporary metal music of that time, like Black Sabbath, Led Zeppelin, or music that was influenced by these bands, to accompany such scenes. These musical references, however, are absent from the soundtrack. The case of *Charlie's Angels* illustrates how the developing association between metal and scenes of action/violence grew stronger throughout the 1980s and 1990s. When *Charlie's Angels* was released as a movie in 2000, metal had become a firmly established musical "code" (following Gorbman) for representing action and violence, and the soundtrack to the film underlines this shift.

The Influence of Film

In their book *Rock on Film,* David Ehrenstein and Bill Reed examine rock music in mainstream cinema up to 1982.[37] They observe that rock has often been associated with "bad boys" or evil/sinful characters, but they do not identify rock music as a common signifier of action, adventure, and violence. While their work creates a historical context for popular music in cinema soundtracks, the exclusion of metal bands and music that emphasizes distorted guitar power chords from their consideration reveals the distinct absence of metal in movies of this period. In fact, the authors point out that rock music soundtracks in war films, like the Rolling Stones' "Satisfaction" in *Apocalypse Now* (1979), appear "at an appropriately nervous lull in the bloody proceedings."[38] It is only after the early 1980s that film begins to play a major role in the growing connection between scenes of action/violence and metal music.

In the soundtrack to the 1986 movie *Top Gun*, the influence of hard rock and metal is clearly discernible, and the plot features action and violence associated with life in the military. In the film, a young naval aviator, Pete "Maverick" Mitchell, trains to become an elite fighter pilot in the navy. As a subplot, Mitchell is haunted by the memory of his father, who was a fighter pilot shot down in the Vietnam War—yet another example of the military background often given to these characters. One of the songs from the movie's soundtrack, "Danger Zone," written by Giorgio Moroder and Tom Whitlock and performed by Kenny Loggins, was a major success and reached #2 as a single in the Billboard charts. "Danger Zone" appears in the opening sequence to the film, which shows F-14 fighter jets being prepared for takeoff on the deck of a naval aircraft carrier. Just as one of the jets launches from the ship, the music shifts from a slow, synthesizer-dominated melody to the hard rock beat and distorted electric guitar of "Danger Zone." The sequence involving the song continues for about ninety seconds, and there is no spoken dialogue. Scenes of sailors on the deck of the carrier preparing the jets and coordinating signals for takeoff and landing are punctuated by F-14s catapulting into flight from the ship or snaring the landing rope.

The hard rock/metal influences are prominent in "Danger Zone." The song is dominated by a distorted guitar timbre, power chords, and a riff in E Aeolian mode. A single, sustained E power chord accompanies the verses. The song demonstrates another important signifier of metal music in the form of a semi-virtuosic distorted guitar solo. Robert Walser, author of *Running with the Devil: Power, Gender and Madness in Heavy Metal Music*, believes that the guitar solo is "virtually required by the conventions of the [metal] genre," and the solo in this song clearly references this style.[39] The movie creates a strong connection between the music ("Danger Zone") and military action, and provides an important example of the growing relationship between metal-influenced music and action scenes.

In the afterword to *Unheard Melodies*, Gorbman makes an interesting comparison between *Top Gun* and another movie, *The Blue Max* (1966). *The Blue Max* is often considered a precursor to *Top Gun* based on plot similarities. *The Blue Max* tells the story of a German fighter pilot in World War I and, like *Top Gun,* is celebrated for memorable scenes of fighters in flight and action. Gorbman observes that the music accompanying the scenes in *Top Gun* is very different from *The Blue Max,* but still highly effective in communicating meaning:

> The first clip showed the takeoff and flight of the vintage airplanes in *The Blue Max* (1966), for which composer Jerry Goldsmith had written "soaring" orchestral music of Wagnerian grandeur. In the second clip, the takeoff and flight of fighter jets in the 1986 *Top Gun* had for musical accompaniment a rock song with lyrics ["Danger Zone"]. Goldsmith commented that this music served little use but as a vulgar advertisement for the rock group, the music video, and the soundtrack album. Was he right to suggest that such music has little effect on spectators (and, if this is the case, did the soundtrack play no role in making *Top Gun* the top grossing film of 1986)? Although the effect of the *Top Gun* music is certainly not "stirring" in the manner of the *Blue Max* score, it is nevertheless compelling in its high-tech, driving energy, and sexual exuberance.[40]

Contrary to Goldsmith, Gorbman contends that the score to *The Blue Max* and "Danger Zone" are equally "compelling" musical portrayals of similar cinematic scenes. Her observation of these differences reveals the historical shift in how action scenes were portrayed musically, from orchestral "grandeur" to distorted guitar power chords. In the late 1960s and throughout the 1970s, cinematic scenes of war, military action, and violence were rarely paired with metal music. *Top Gun,* however, demonstrates the increasing association between metal and such scenes. Gorbman also claims that Goldsmith described "Danger Zone" as an "advertisement." While she does not cite the source of his comment, the idea that "Danger Zone" is an "advertisement for the rock group, the music video, and the soundtrack album" seems to anticipate the use of hard rock/metal music and music videos in military recruiting. As we have seen from "The Creed," the military would eventually employ the format of a music video in its recruiting efforts and metal would play a significant role in the music of military advertising.

In retrospect, the opening to *Top Gun* resembles a mid-1980s version of the navy's "Accelerate Your Life" advertisement (video example 5). Both videos show sailors in action sequences with music as the only sound element and project the message of action and excitement through metal-influenced music. Goldsmith's description of "Danger Zone" as an "advertisement" and "music video" in 1986 now seems like a prediction that has become fully realized in the twenty-first century as military advertisements have synthesized metal music and images of military action in the format of a music video.

An excellent counterpart to *Top Gun* is the 1986 film *Iron Eagle* and its sequel, *Iron Eagle II* (1988).[41] While these films never achieved the popular success of *Top Gun* and are highly stylized with cinematic conventions of the 1980s (now cheesy cult favorites), they further illustrate the relationship between metal and scenes of action and violence. In *Iron Eagle,* the son of an air force fighter pilot, Doug Masters (Jason Gedrick), attempts to rescue his father who has been shot down and is being held captive in an unidentified Middle Eastern country. A continuous theme throughout the movie is Masters's fondness for listening to hard rock music while flying. At one point in the movie he recollects flying with his father, who scolds him, "These are training maneuvers, Doug, not auditions for the Thunderbirds. It's not a rock concert." Most scenes depicting Masters in flight are accompanied by a hard rock soundtrack, including the final action sequence where he destroys an enemy airfield while listening to a heavy metal song on his portable cassette player.

The popular *Terminator* trilogy offers another example of the increasing connection between metal and action/violence, specifically the original *Terminator* (1984) and *Terminator 2: Judgment Day* (1991) soundtracks. In *Terminator,* a cyborg (Arnold Schwarzenegger) is disguised as a human and sent from the post-apocalyptic future to kill Sarah Connor (Linda Hamilton). The movie overflows with graphic violence as the remorseless Terminator kills anyone, including civilians and policemen, who stands in the way of his objective, a total of twenty-seven deaths. The soundtrack to the action scenes mainly consists of synthesizer-based music, not metal. In fact, the only music demonstrating a metal influence occurs when Connor enters a dance club to make a telephone call. The Terminator tracks her to the club, where people dance to the song "Burnin' in the Third Degree," by Tahnee Cain & Tryanglz. The distorted power chord guitar riffs and virtuosic guitar solo of the song reference the metal style. However, as the scene builds in suspense and the Terminator approaches Connor, pointing his gun at her, the song slowly fades out and synthesizer brass, strings, and effectual sounds become the primary music. These timbres continue in the ensuing gun battle and chase scene. In this case, the metal-influenced music is gradually displaced by synthesizer sounds at the culmination of the violent action.

On the other hand, the second movie in the trilogy, *Terminator 2,* reveals a closer relationship with metal music. Renowned for its theme song, Guns n' Roses' "You Could Be Mine" (*Use Your Illusion II,* 1991), *Terminator 2* depicts sixteen deaths by violent act. One of the most popular hard rock/metal bands of the late 1980s and 1990s, Guns n' Roses has sold approximately 90 million albums worldwide, and "You Could Be Mine" is their second-best-selling single. The album cover to the single shows Schwarzenegger on a motorcycle holding a shotgun with the text "Guns n' Roses, You Could Be Mine, from *Terminator 2: Judgment Day.*" The song appears in the movie during the end credits as well as during opening scenes with thirteen-year-old John Connor (Edward Furlong), one of the main characters. (In one scene, Connor's friend wears a Guns n' Roses T-shirt.) The music video for "You Could Be Mine" (video example 13) provides further evidence of metal in action/violence sequences. The video alternates between action scenes from the movie and footage of the band playing live in a club. As a subplot within the video, the Terminator appears in the club where the band is performing and targets Guns n' Roses for termination. The video concludes as the Terminator approaches the band after the concert and determines that terminating them would be a "waste of ammo."

The film version of *Charlie's Angels* (2000) offers another constructive point of comparison because the television series, while not as graphically violent as the movie, presents scenes that include guns and gunfire but does not pair these scenes with metal music. The movie, on the other hand, consistently references metal music in action sequences. In the opening scene, two characters negotiate an exchange of diamonds for a bomb aboard a commercial airplane. One of the characters, an undercover "angel," grabs the man strapped to the bomb and tackles him out of the emergency exit. At the moment she grabs him, the music changes from a mellow, hip-hop-influenced groove to the distorted, power-chord guitar riff of Mötley Crüe's "Live Wire."

The final action sequence unfolds to a soundtrack of metal music and builds intensity through the use of progressively heavier, more aggressive, metal subgenres. As each "angel" engages in hand-to-hand combat with different villains, the music begins with "Breathe" by Prodigy, a techno/

electronica band. The song layers distorted power-chord guitar riffs over techno/electronica beats. The action continues and the music shifts to "Song 2" by the alternative metal band Blur. This song is more typically grunge and Nirvana-influenced with its predominant distorted power-chord guitars and hard rock backbeat. At the peak of the fighting, the music changes to the opening of "Blind" by the nü metal band Korn. The detuned, distorted guitars and guttural utterances of "Are you ready?" at the beginning of "Blind" signal the heaviest of the three metal subgenres. Thus, metal serves as a musical "code" for action and violence in the film *Charlie's Angels,* and metal subgenres appear to be carefully organized such that progressively intense fighting is musically depicted through progressively heavier songs. Other movies, among many, demonstrating the relationship between metal and scenes of action/violence include *The Last Action Hero* (1993), *Escape from L.A.* (1996), *The Matrix* (1999), *The Marine* (2005), *The Devil's Rejects* (2005), and *300* (2007).

The increasing association of metal music with action, adventure, and violence through the 1980s, 1990s, and to the present day was largely influenced by film and television, but these are not the only developments that forged this musical connection. Other mass media helped establish and perpetuate metal timbres as signifiers of these features. Examples include video/computer games such as Castlevania: Symphony of the Night (1997) and sports shows such as ESPN's *X Games* and WWF/WWE professional wrestling, all of which frequently reference metal music. These two influences merge in sports video games, where metal and hip-hop/rap are two of the most widely utilized musical genres.[42] Steve Schnur, executive of music and marketing for EA Worldwide, a major video game company, said, "It's just great music to game to. Especially if you're pounding someone's flesh in or crashing someone's car, nothing beats heavy metal."[43] "Song 2," which appeared on the *Charlie's Angels* soundtrack, was licensed by EA in the 1998 soccer game *FIFA 98: Road to World Cup,* and in the Microsoft Xbox 360 action game *Test Drive Unlimited.*[44] The song has also been played at the home games of National Hockey League teams such as the Boston Bruins and Ottawa Senators and Major League Baseball teams such as the Boston Red Sox, Texas Rangers, and Washington Nationals. Blur claims that the U.S. military tried to buy the rights to the song in 1999 for its new stealth bomber commercials, but the band denied the request.[45]

The Influence of MTV

MTV strongly influenced the use of metal music in military advertising and propaganda videos. Although music videos predate MTV, the success of the network through the 1980s and 1990s as one of the highest-rated cable television networks resulted in stronger bonds between televised visual imagery and music. The music video format became infused in mainstream American culture, and metal music played a prominent role in MTV programming. Andrew Goodwin, author of *Dancing in the Distraction Factory: Music Television and Popular Culture,* identifies 1983–85 as a crucial period when the network tried to establish supremacy among cable competitors and "programmed heavy metal with a vengeance."[46] Metal music videos received considerable airtime on MTV, and the visual imagery of these videos reinforced associations between action/violence and the music. Recent studies of violence in music videos observe that the genres of metal and rap most frequently accompany violent images. In a study by Stacy L. Smith and Aaron R. Boyson, they estimate that violence was prevalent in approximately 29 percent of rap videos and 27 percent of metal videos.[47] This clearly distinguishes these genres within popular music: rock (12 percent), R&B (9 percent), and Adult Contemporary (7 percent).[48] To illustrate this point, let us consider three metal videos, Metallica "One" (. . . *And Justice for All,* 1988), Megadeth "Holy Wars" (*Rust in Peace,* 1990), and Slayer "Bloodline" (*God Hates Us All,* 2001).

One of the most popular metal bands in history, Metallica released their first music video, "One," in 1989 (video example 14). The video alternates between black-and-white scenes of the band performing and excerpts from the 1971 movie *Johnny Got His Gun.*[49] In the film, a World War I American soldier, Joe Bonham, is severely wounded by an artillery shell and loses his arms, legs, and most of his face. As a result, Bonham is blind, deaf, mute, unable to smell, and kept alive by machines. He communicates by tapping his head in Morse code and pleads for death.

The video begins with silence and close-ups of singer James Hetfield, followed by film scenes of Bonham ducking for cover in a trench as an artillery shell explodes nearby. The music begins. The images of the shell exploding around Bonham repeat throughout the video, and excerpts from the film portray the mental torment he suffers as a result of his injuries. Dialogue from the movie is interspersed in the video, which concludes, like the film, with Bonham lying in bed, still wishing for death in his world of psychological and physical anguish. The video for "One" not only demonstrates a correlation between metal music and violence, but it musically portrays violence and mental torment in a radically different way than the original movie soundtrack. The soundtrack to the movie is primarily composed of orchestral timbres, and there is no music in the combat scenes. This sharply contrasts the metal music in the video of Metallica's "One," produced eighteen years later.

Formed in 1983, Megadeth is one of the leading bands of the thrash metal subgenre, which emphasizes speed and aggressive guitar distortion. Along with Metallica, Slayer, and Anthrax, Megadeth is commonly known as one of "the Big Four" of thrash metal. The video for "Holy Wars" (video example 15) alternates between scenes of the band performing and footage of civil unrest, beatings, and combat in the Middle East. The violence in this video, however, is far more explicit than that shown in "One." Among the graphic violence in "Holy Wars," we see missiles fire, machine guns shooting, explosions, casualties on stretchers, and men mopping blood off the ground. There are also direct political allusions in the video as the faces of Palestinian leader Yasir Arafat and Libyan leader Muammar al-Gaddafi flash on the screen. The overtones of war extend into the scenes of the band performing in which singer/guitarist Dave Mustaine wears a belt of machine-gun rounds.

My final example of violence in metal videos is Slayer's "Bloodline" (video example 16). The video mostly shows the band performing in a room and moves among different portrayals of the band: they perform dressed in suits, their "street" clothes (mostly black jeans and T-shirts), and their street clothes covered in blood. The scenes of the band in black jeans and T-shirts and dripping with blood dominate the video. A priest is introduced toward the end of the video, and the scene suggests that he takes off his belt to beat a young girl after offering her a communion wafer. While this is the only violent act in the video, the close-up images of singer Tom Araya covered in blood create a strong implication of violence.

While "One" and "Holy Wars" clearly connect music with images of wartime violence, "Bloodline" demonstrates a more general association between metal and violence. An interesting issue arises here. The videos do not seem to promote violence or the military. In fact, they might even be said to protest or oppose violence—many of the musicians and fans of thrash and death metal claim that the subgenres attempt to expose the realities of war in an effort to promote peace. What these videos clearly reinforce, though, is an association between metal and portrayals of violence.

My goal in this discussion is to examine the factors that contributed to the use of metal music in military recruiting. The introduction of metal around 2003 in the advertising of almost all branches of the armed services represents a dramatic shift in the musical styles of military advertisements and propaganda videos. As I have shown, this change resulted from the association between metal and visual images of action, adventure, and violence that developed within American mass media since the 1980s. Television, film, MTV, and a variety of other influences, like computer/video games and sports television, began to depict action, adventure, and violence with metal music and metal timbres. While not all scenes utilized metal, the genre was rarely referenced before the early 1980s and slowly became associated with these images over two and a half decades. By 2003, metal had become a widely accepted musical "code" for such scenes, and therefore complemented the military's advertising strategy of portraying military service as an opportunity for action, adventure, and excitement. It would logically follow that a musical genre that had become associated with these characteristics would then be featured in recruiting efforts.[50]

MTV had an added effect on metal in military advertisements because, as McLaren observes, the network lowered the age of the average music consumer and made imagery more essential to popular music.[51] As younger viewers were making a greater association between what they saw and heard, metal became an obvious choice for military advertisements and propaganda videos. Metal is largely consumed by white, male, 17- to 25-year-olds of the lower-middle and middle class, and this is the key demographic for military recruitment. At least during the 1980s and 1990s, this demographic was also a major audience for MTV. The military appears to have chosen music that became associated with the characteristics of military service (action, adventure, and excitement) it wanted to project in an attempt to attract recruits.

The impact of metal music in military recruiting is also reflected in the proliferation of music videos created by soldiers to express their wartime experiences. The web site Grouchy Media (www.grouchymedia.com) broadcasts dozens of military music videos created by American soldiers. These videos, including many metal songs, incorporate images taken by soldiers from the combat field, primarily Iraq and Afghanistan. Soldiers pair metal songs like "Bodies" (Drowning Pool), "Die MF Die" (Dope), "Hit the Floor" (Linkin Park), and many others with imagery of military action and scenes of violence. Specialist Colby Buzzell said that listening to music in the combat field was like a movie soundtrack: "It is having your own soundtrack to your own movie to your own war. If you watch a movie, and you have a war scene or shoot-'em scene, it is not the same without some cool music dubbed on top of it."[52] His comments reveal the importance he places on music in scenes of war, and he makes an explicit connection between "war scenes" or

"shoot-'em scenes" and "cool music." As evident from Grouchy Media, soldiers often choose metal music for their music video-inspired depictions of
war. In fact, many soldiers find these videos highly motivating. On a recent
post on the Grouchy Media discussion forum, a combat rescue swim instructor said that it was not uncommon "to show the videos in class between
breaks for a motivation factor."[53]

The first Grouchy Media video, "Taliban Bodies," set to "Bodies" by
Drowning Pool, dates from 2001—the only video it produced that year
(video example 17).[54] The sequel to "Bodies," "Die MF Die" by Dope, appeared on Grouchy Media as the only video from 2002, followed by another
video in 2003. But in 2004, thirteen videos were produced, followed by six
in 2005, twelve in 2006, thirteen in 2007, and fourteen in 2008. While the
founding of Grouchy Media corresponds with the beginning of the war in
Afghanistan (October 2001), the surge of videos in 2004 could be explained
in part by the start of the Iraq War in March 2003 and the increased mobilization of American troops. Another reason might be that the military
began using metal music in its recruiting efforts around 2003, and the genre
became an acceptable way for the military to portray itself. It is most likely a
combination of these two explanations, enhanced by the availability of new
technology that made creating music videos much easier than in previous
conflicts. Grouchy Media demonstrates that metal music significantly affected how soldiers themselves depict war. This genre had been codified by
mainstream American mass media to portray action, adventure, and violence, and the military began employing it in recruiting advertisements and
propaganda videos in order to attract recruits by portraying these aspects of
military service. Through Grouchy Media, it is clear that soldiers use metal
as a soundtrack to war footage, and this choice seems to be made apart from
any official efforts or prompting of the military.

We have seen some of the important roles of music, particularly metal, in military recruiting. As mentioned, the military devotes a significant
amount of money to its advertisements in order to attract soldiers. While
these advertisements are intended to stimulate an interest in the military
among possible recruits, they do not seem to be the determining factor in a
recruit's propensity to join. In my interviews, I asked soldiers to comment on
why they joined the military. While their reasons were different and multi-
faceted, many, like Buzzell, C. J. Grisham, Stephen Johnson, and others,
mentioned the role that recruiters played in their enlistment. This is not to
downplay the importance of military advertisements and the music within
them; the advertisements seem to represent a vital first phase of recruiting in

which appeals to honorable duty and excitement are used to initiate interest for possible recruits. Recruiters, however, appear to take the primary role of convincing them to join.

MUSIC IN BASIC COMBAT TRAINING

Having discussed the role of music in military recruiting and the influences upon it, I would now like to diverge briefly to the subject of music in Basic Combat Training (BCT). When recruits decide to join the military, they attend BCT in their respective branch of the armed services. In the army, for example, a recruit is sent to a ten-week training period at one of the army's BCT facilities, like Fort Benning, Georgia, or Fort Jackson, South Carolina. During this time, all personal items are put in storage, including any music or music player. Music is almost completely absent from this first stage of soldier life. (Recruits have been known to sneak in iPods with their personal effects, however. If caught, the iPod is put in storage and push-ups tend to follow immediately afterward.) The purpose of this separation from outside distractions, such as music, is to create a focused environment for recruits.[55] As Specialist Jennifer Atkinson, who served a one-year tour in Iraq (2005) as a photojournalist/public affairs specialist with the Third Infantry Division, explained, "In basic training, there is no music except for marching cadences and if you go to church on Sunday. . . . Basic training is a very controlled environment. Basically, anything that is your personal property with the exception of religious books and letters is put into storage for you. And you can have it when you graduate basic training, but what they do is, they very much refocus you into doing everything the way the Army wants you to. CDs and music like that is distracting, so they don't allow you to have it."[56]

Music in BCT primarily involves running and marching cadences that are intended to build morale and camaraderie among recruits, and intended to assist in physical training exercises. During cadences, drill sergeants sing short call-and-response melodies to their trainees. On long running exercises, for example, the singing helps recruits endure the training. Documentary Recordings (www.militaryrecordings.com) has been producing field recordings of military running and marching cadences for forty years. The CDs are recorded on location at various training facilities with drill sergeants and recruits from different branches of the military, like the Army Infantry, Special Forces Green Berets, and the Marine Corps.

According to Documentary Recordings, the lyrics of call-and-response melodies are unique to each drill sergeant: "Each caller employs his own distinct style and lyrics. This collection reflects that rich, informal diversity [so that] . . . every cadence [is] wonderfully unique."[57] Drill sergeants may compose their own cadences, but they are also taught numerous cadences during their own training. The texts typically revolve around the military and aspects of training, but some topics are completely foreign to military life. Cadence titles include "Soldier, Soldier Have You Heard," "Pilot Flying Low," "Here We Go, Easy Run," "Run Me Some More . . . Hey," "My Old Granny, She's 91," "When I Say Rhythm," and "Ahab Had a Camel." The lyrics below are to "We're Airborne Rangers"—a marching cadence sung in Airborne Ranger training.

> Hey, all the way
> Rangerin' every day
> We're Airborne Rangers with the black berets
> We're kamikaze killers and we earn our pay
> We're jumpin' out of airplanes, runnin' through the swamp
> Uncle Sam gets in trouble, 75th gonna stop
> Our minds like computers, our fists are like steel
> If one don't get you, then the other one will
> We do push-ups every morning and my body's a rock
> We'd run to Alabama but we'd wear out our socks
> Hey, all the way
> Rangerin' everyday

The environment of BCT is concentrated on the process of shaping soldiers, without unwanted distractions, like music. The military believes that this limitation keeps recruits mentally focused on training and does not introduce unwanted interference in transforming recruits into soldiers. After graduating from BCT, a soldier is sent to Advanced Individual Training (AIT), where he or she learns a specific skill; there the policy on personal music is relaxed. During this time, soldiers return to many of the amenities of typical daily life and can listen to music according to their personal preference. Upon completion of AIT, fully trained soldiers begin their specified jobs in the military. The following chapters examine some of the roles of music in soldier life during deployment.

2 | Music as an Inspiration for Combat

Throughout history, music has often inspired soldiers for combat. Plato believed that music could directly affect human behavior and that certain musical modes, like Phrygian, were likely to arouse emotion and incite aggressive behavior. The war or battle cry is possibly the earliest form of music as an inspiration for combat. In this genre, members of a group sing, chant, or yell words and melodies to prepare for war or during battle itself. Soldiers of almost all cultural backgrounds have sung battle cries. Spanish soldiers, for example, shouted, "Santiago y cierra, España" (Saint James and attack, Spain) during the Reconquista; Finnish cavalry warriors, Hakkapeliitat, cried, "Hakkaa päälle" (Cut them down) in the Thirty Years War (1618–48); and Japanese pilots screamed, "Banzai" (Ten thousand years) as a battle cry in World War II. Certain musical instruments, like bagpipes, have historical roots in inspiring soldiers for combat. In *The Piper in Peace and War,* historian C. A. Malcolm claims that pipers Allester Caddell and William Steel were commended by Scottish military leader Alexander MacNoughton for their playing that inspired archers in a 1627 battle against France.[1]

American military history also demonstrates how music has motivated soldiers. In the Revolutionary War (1775–83), drum and fife performers rallied troops for battle and entertained soldiers after combat.[2] George Washington felt that music was so vital to the morale of his troops that he ordered drum and fife majors to improve the quality of music or suffer a deduction in wages: "The music of the Army being in general very bad; it is expected, that the drum and fife Majors exert themselves to improve it, or they will be reduced, and their extraordinary pay taken from them. Stated hours to be assigned for all the drums and fifes, of each regiment, to attend them and practice—Nothing is more agreeable, and ornamental, than good music; every officer, for the credit of his corps, should take care to provide it."[3] Musicians accompanied soldiers as they marched into the combat field and sometimes performed during the fighting. This practice continued in the American Civil War (1861–65). Although music often signaled commands in the battlefield, like when to attack, fire, or retreat, it also appears to have made a dramatic impact on soldiers. A regimental historian of the Fourteenth Connecticut Volunteer Infantry wrote, "With shot and shell crashing around all about them, they played 'The Star-Spangled Banner,' 'The Red, White, and Blue,' and 'Yankee Doodle' and then repeated them for fully twenty minutes. They never played better . . . its effect upon the men was magical."[4] After reading, music making and listening to music ranked as the second most popular pastime among Civil War soldiers.[5]

In the twentieth century, developments in audio technology significantly influenced how soldiers used music as an inspiration for combat. With the invention of radio, music became far more present in the lives of soldiers— one of the first uses of music on military radio was as entertainment for wounded World War I soldiers during their recovery in military hospitals.[6] In World War II, German military radio stations broadcast music to inspire troops in the combat field. Guy Sajer, a German soldier, claims that officials broadcast Wagner's "Ride of the Valkyries" over shortwave radio to motivate soldiers during many of the last battles of the war. His book *The Forgotten Soldier* describes a scene where he stands next to German tanks, which play Wagner's "Ride" from their radios, before an attack in Memel (Lithuania).[7] American World War II veteran Bruce Brown suggested that this was a common practice for German soldiers in the months before Germany's surrender in 1945.[8]

American soldiers of the Second World War, however, apparently did not have inspirational music played for them before or during combat. More often, music was employed by the U.S. military to boost morale rather than to explicitly motivate troops for war.[9] In 1942, the War Department established Armed Forces Radio, which later came to include television, to play popular music for soldiers. Its goal was to provide "a touch of home" to servicemen and women.[10] Live music was also a part of the efforts to boost morale. Glenn Miller's American Band of the Allied Expeditionary Forces (AEF) traveled to Europe to perform for troops on 7 June 1944, the day after D-Day. Extremely popular among soldiers, the AEF performed, according to Miller, eighty-nine separate shows in August 1944.[11] Many of these performances were sponsored by the USO, a private, non-profit organization founded in 1941. The USO's mission was "to provide morale, welfare and recreation-type services to our men and women in uniform. The original intent of Congress—and enduring style of USO delivery—is to represent the American people by extending a touch of home to the military."[12] Although some of this music may, as a secondary effect, have motivated soldiers for war, its main purpose was to reconnect soldiers with American life.

During the Vietnam War, radio stations like the Armed Forces Vietnam Network (AFVN) continued to be closely tied to soldier life, and many Vietnam veterans recall that the AFVN was their primary source of music in the war.[13] As new forms of audio technology, such as tape players and stereos, gradually became a part of American culture, some soldiers obtained such devices and were able to listen to their personal preference of recorded music. "Dagger X-Ray," an Operation Desert Storm combat veteran, said that he knew of occasions in Vietnam where "some units played music over horns as they went into battle."[14] Before leaving the military camps to go on missions, some soldiers may have listened to rock music to psychologically prepare for combat, though evidence for this is elusive; most Vietnam veterans in fact said that they did not use music in this way.[15] Certainly using rock music for this purpose before combat was not a widespread practice.

For American soldiers who served in Operation Desert Storm, the greater availability of portable audio devices, like small tape players, provided the opportunity for music to play a more prevalent role as an inspiration for combat. On a recent www.Desert-Storm.com discussion forum, "Dagger X-Ray" wrote, "As my track passed through the breach, I had AC/DC 'Are you ready' and 'Thunderstruck' playing over the track intercom system. Kinda made for a good atmosphere/feeling for all of us with headphones on. Officers inside the track didn't mind cuz it wasn't cluttering up the unit comms. . . . Much of the music I listened to at the time was to get myself wound up . . . amped up so that I was ready for anything at that point. Being on an adrenalin rush felt good and having some AC/DC or some Megadeth accompanying it was even better."[16] These devices allowed music, in this case hard rock and metal, to be heard in settings like military vehicles. Another Desert Storm veteran, "achevyfan," recalls wearing out a Megadeth tape, and many Desert Storm soldiers identified hard rock/metal bands as favorites before combat (Metallica, Skid Row, Guns n' Roses, Judas Priest, Faith No More, and others).[17] While Desert Storm demonstrates a precedent for how soldiers in Iraq motivate themselves for possible combat through music, audio technology of the early 1990s did not allow personal music to be as readily accessible. CDs, portable CD players, and mp3 players were not yet the primary media for audio consumption, and to a certain degree this limited the development of music as a factor in soldiers' lives. "Achevyfan" commented, "Sure wish we had iPods then."[18]

SOLDIERS' ACCOUNTS FROM IRAQ

Music has become a significant source of combat inspiration for American soldiers in Iraq. The relationship between music and soldier life seems more intimate in this war since new technology allows music to be a part of soldiers' lives on and off the battlefield in unprecedented ways. Erik Holtan explains that "the sheer fact that music is globally accessible made it so much easier for it to play a role while deployed. Personally, I had my laptop filled with all different kinds of music, for whatever situation I was in. I used my iPod for when I traveled as well as to put me to sleep at night. Sometimes to cover up the sounds of where I was, i.e. helicopter, mortars, IEDs [Improvised Explosive Devices], etc."[19] Most soldiers listen to music daily on portable music devices like laptops, CD players, mp3 players, or iPods. Tanks, Strykers, and Humvees are equipped with audio and communication systems that allow soldiers to construct improvised sound systems to listen to music while on patrol; in this context, music is played within the vehicle, not broadcast outside to Iraqi civilians. C. J. Grisham describes how he and his fellow soldiers created a surround-sound system in their truck:

We took those lansing-type of computer speakers—the big bass-y ones— we took those, we mounted them up. We created this little webbing on the top of our truck out of 550 cord. We tied up in the webbing these speakers, we did four of them, so kind of like a surround-sound system in our truck. Then, we had a laptop and CD player with all my mp3s on it and we just plugged the outlets into the laptop. And then we had a converter that you could plug the speakers into, so that was our power—that was our sound system in the truck. It looked like crap but it sounded good.[20]

The practice of constructing sound systems in military vehicles appears not to be isolated, and many soldiers say that they listened to music while on patrol. Colby Buzzell recalls, "Our vehicle had a CD player hooked up to the radio, so sometimes we would just listen to music from the speakers inside the vehicle," and Neal Saunders explains that "guys have music wired up in the back of their Bradleys, or through the communication systems in their tanks. In the Humvees, you have a little CD player with a speaker and try to turn it up as loud as you can."[21]

Given the technology that allows music to be heard more frequently and in a greater variety of settings, like military vehicles, music's role as an inspiration for combat seems stronger than in previous wars. Almost every soldier I interviewed said that they listened to music before leaving the military bases to go on patrols or in vehicles while on patrol during some point in their deployment. Within these listening contexts, metal and rap emerge as the predominant musical genres of choice. In the following interview excerpts, soldiers describe their experiences.

Jennifer Atkinson (speaking about her husband's platoon):

My husband was there with Fourth ID (Infantry Division), which was one rotation prior to mine. They were in the shit a whole lot more than I was. They would go out and before they would go out, he said he remembers listening to a song [Lil' John's "I Don't Give a Fuck"]. They would listen to it over and over and over again, and they called it their "getting crunked" song. "Getting crunked" is just getting right with whatever you have to do, and getting in the right mindset. They would play it, and it had a refrain in it . . . and they would just chant that over and over and over again until they were pretty much screaming it. I understand because it takes a lot to get amped up to go out there because you can go out and you don't know what's going [to] happen. You have to be really kind of hyped up and ready for anything. It was just this loud, crude refrain that they could just repeat over and over and over again until they were ready to go out.[22]

Buzzell:

Sometimes we would go out on patrols and we'd be sitting in the back, bored and a couple of us would have our headphones on listening to music, some of us would have mp3 players, some of us would have CD players. . . . Right about when we're about to go out on a raid or a mission or something, I'd listen to Slayer to get all into it. Its kind of a surreal experience listening to Slayer out there, I can't think of a, it's just weird. It kind of got me in the mood for it, it just gets you pumped up for it. The feeling of the music, it's whatever puts you in whatever mood. . . . Sometimes when we were getting the vehicle ready right before going on a mission, our TC, which is the guy in charge of the vehicle, would play some music out of the speakers, and we'd listen to it. Or sometimes on an observation post, when we got the setup, we would play some music. One time we went out on a mission—it was a joint mission with us and the Iraqi police and it was just a patrol. We had these military intelligence guys with us and they had speakers on their Humvee—propaganda speakers so when we go in their town they'd have an interpreter say, "Hey, we come in peace," kind of thing. When we left the gate for that mission one of the MI [Military Intelligence] guys had an mp3 player and he played the theme song from "Rocky." What is that song they always play on parades? I forgot how it goes. It doesn't have lyrics, but every fourth of July you hear that song. And the theme from "The Good, the Bad and the Ugly," and when he played the music, when we [were] getting ready to go out beneath the wire, everyone was just charged. Even the Iraqis who probably had never heard those songs before, were all getting totally pumped up to go out on the mission. It just gets you ready to go. Because sometimes your motivation is down and you're like, "I don't want to play soldier today, I don't want to do this." But then you hear "The Good, the Bad, and the Ugly" theme song and you're like, "Fuck yeah, hell yeah, I'll go out on a mission today."[23]

Grisham:

The Eminem "Go To Sleep" song, it kind of got us pumped up because every time we left that camp, there was a firefight. The thing is, my job is to go out and try and make friends with people and try to convince them that it is in their best interest to tell me where the bad guys are. I'm not going out there looking for a fight, I'm not breaking down doors and all that kind of stuff. So, that kind of wears at you and you finally get yourself into that mentally that, you know what? I'm going to have to shoot at someone today, so might as well get pumped up for it. So that Eminem song, "Go To Sleep," when we got to Fallujah was kind of our anthem and before every mission we'd blare that and we'd all scream the lyrics out. Now crossing the border [from Kuwait into Iraq], Metallica was the big push, and generally on the patrols, Metallica was a big patrol one. . . . Usually it was "Seek and Destroy," was a good one, "The Four Horsemen," "One" which is a great song, and "Sanitarium," because we all felt a little crazy. It seemed like there was a Metallica song for just about every mood. . . . At night time it was quiet, whenever we do a night mission. But generally during the day we'd listen to it [in the truck]. We just didn't want to listen to it loud when we were off base because we didn't want to offend anybody.[24]

Joshua Revak:

In the communication system, there's a place where you can put in—it is like an input where you can plug in. I think it used to be for a phone and when the tanks would sit in a small group, in like a defensive position or something, the tanks would be spread out. I don't know how far apart, but they would run a landline to each tank with a phone that you crank the phone, then it rings, and they would hook it up in the communication system. And I think that's the way they would be able to hear if they had their helmets on. So instead of hooking the phones up to that, we'd take a pair of headphones and cut the wire and just hook each side of the wire up to there—all the communication systems you could plug a CD player into it. That actually helps a lot when you are on long missions. . . . A lot of people couldn't even roll out without music, it soothed them or prepared them mentally. A lot of guys would listen to Drowning Pool and gangster rap to try and get really pumped up, like predator kind of music, I guess, things like that, metal, hardcore, Linkin Park, stuff like that.[25]

William Thompson stated that the infantry soldiers in his battalion would listen to metal and rap, or what he described, like Revak, as "predator music," before going on patrol.[26] Arkansas National Guardsman David (JR) Schultz, who deployed to Baghdad in 2004, stated that Drowning Pool's "Bodies" was popular among the infantry soldiers in his battalion.[27]

Many documentaries of the Iraq War, like *Occupation: Dreamland*, *Gunner Palace*, and *Soundtrack to War*, offer further evidence of metal and rap inspiring soldiers for combat.[28] In *Occupation: Dreamland*, a film about the Alpha Company of the 2nd Battalion of the 505th Parachute Infantry Regiment in Fallujah, soldiers watch and listen to a music video of Slayer's "Bloodline" while they put on Kelvar vests and goggles before going out on a security mission. *Gunner Palace*, a documentary by Michael Tucker, who lived with the 2-3 Field Artillery for two months in one of Uday Hussein's weekend palaces in Baghdad, features a sonic backdrop of metal and rap music provided by the soldiers. In *Soundtrack to War*, multiple soldiers make the analogy that "war itself is heavy metal," and in fact, the original version of George Gittoes's documentary was titled *War is Heavy Metal*. Bing West's *No True Glory: A Frontline Account of the Battle for Fallujah* provides a report of troops listening to Drowning Pool's "Bodies"—a song popular among soldiers interviewed in *Soundtrack to War*—as preparation for combat, "before jumping off into attack, McCoy had the habit of gathering troops and playing at full blast [Drowning Pool's] 'Let the bodies hit the floor.'"[29]

While many soldiers inspire themselves for missions with metal and rap, Botelho took a different approach. He listened to music that was indigenous to Iraqi culture instead of music to make him aggressive before going out of the military camps.[30] This selection was based on his specific duties. Ronald Botelho collected information from Iraqis and said that he listened to indigenous music as a way to inform himself about local culture. He aimed to establish a connection of trust with the people:

I listened to a lot of the cultural music to try and get into the rhythm, particularly the rhythm and how people spoke and their body language. I had to use a translator all the time because I don't speak Arabic or Persian Farsi. And so if you have, at least in my mind, if you have an idea of how the language flowed, musically—I think I may have mentioned a couple of Arabic singers, and when I did, people's face would light up. It's, "Oh, you know something about it, not some stupid American." I would get a little bit more forthrightness from them, a little bit more information. A lot of it is useless, but nonetheless, I would get something. So music in my field helped bridge the gap between knowing nothing and cultural awareness. . . . If I could say anything else, it is bridging the cultural divide that is the most important for me. And if I think about it even harder, music played a key role in that. That is not the case for a lot of people, for most of the soldiers and what they do. It is in what I do because my job is getting information.[31]

Botelho admits that his experience was not typical. In a scene from *Soundtrack to War*, soldiers discuss the rap artists they listen to in their vehicles and someone mentions singer-songwriter Diana Krall. One of the soldiers then says, "We support you, Diana, but we just can't listen to you when we roll."[32]

Some soldiers explained that metal and rap music was effective as an inspiration for combat, even though they did not listen to this music before deploying to Iraq. Specialist Mark Miner, who served in an Infantry platoon in Baghdad from September 2004 to 2005, said, "We used to play rock in our room to pump us up before patrols. . . . Before I went I never really liked heavy metal. When I was there, however, I listened to certain songs that just fit well with my moods at times."[33] One woman I spoke with said that since her brother came back from Iraq, he listens to death metal constantly even though he was not a dedicated fan before his deployment.[34] While most soldiers prefer metal and rap within the context of combat inspiration, I was curious as to what happens if a soldier does not enjoy these styles of music. Buzzell commented that these soldiers often times are unable to avoid the music, since it is played inside a vehicle or within the helmets of the crew in a tank. He recalled a situation during Christmas 2003 when his fellow soldiers played music that was not to his liking:

One time at Christmas, we were in Samarra, and one of the guys ordered a Chipmunks Christmas CD with Alvin, Simon, and Theodore singing Christmas carols. And he put that in the CD player in the vehicle and I couldn't take it, I'd be like, "Turn that shit off." I fuckin' can't stand that shit because we'd be listening to it for hours and hours. And he got a big kick out of it, driving around Iraq listening to the Chipmunks. Yeah, you are screwed if you don't like what is playing. God, I still cringe when I think about that.[35]

SOCIAL ORDERING AND PRE-COMBAT MUSIC

In the process of inspiring themselves for combat, soldiers also participate in pre-mission rituals involving specific music. As mentioned in the previous interview excerpts, soldiers sometimes gather before leaving a base to listen to songs. In the scene from *Occupation Dreamland,* for example, the soldiers put on their military equipment while listening to Slayer; Grisham mentioned that "Go To Sleep" was their "anthem" in Fallujah; Atkinson noted that "I Don't Give a Fuck" was the pre-mission "getting crunked" song for her husband's platoon. All of these situations involve aspects of ritual where soldiers come together and participate, either by listening or singing/yelling along with the lyrics, in organized, pre-combat actions. Many times these actions are repeated before each mission or patrol. In this way, metal and rap are a means of creating aspects of social ordering. The soldiers psychologically prepare themselves for the possibility of combat through the shared experience of music. Tia DeNora has observed that music has the capacity to function "as a device for clarifying social order, for structuring subjectivity (desire and the temporal parameters of emotion and the emotive dimension of interaction) and for establishing a basis for collaborative action."[36] DeNora's description accurately reflects what happens in soldiers' pre-combat rituals. The music has a collective effect on the soldiers and operates as a "pre-text" for action.

Music also enhances the feeling of community within these rituals. By singing/screaming the lyrics of a song or listening to a song within the same physical space, soldiers create a sense of community through their common act in preparation for a common objective. Music is a means of establishing the identity of the group and supports the feeling of togetherness through a ritualized musical experience. Many soldiers claim that music helped form social groups within the military. Soldiers would frequently create and sustain friendships around their mutual enjoyment of particular popular music genres. Buzzell explained, "The kids that would listen to country music would all be a clique, and the kids that listen to gangster rap would all be a clique, and the kids that listen to punk would be a clique. It is sort of like, if you're at a party or with a group of people and you listen to punk, or metal, or whatever, and you meet another person that is into punk or metal, at least you have something in common. You can start talking to them and kind of relating and forming maybe a friendship, rather than somebody who listens to something entirely different or doesn't know anything about it. It was kind of interesting how the different cliques all kind of were into the same music."[37]

To a certain extent, soldiers are pre-conditioned for this type of ritual and community building. The musical environment of running and marching cadences in Basic Combat Training involves soldiers collectively singing responses that are intended to develop camaraderie. Soldiers in BCT are taught the importance of teamwork and oneness that is vital to military service, completing a mission, and, in some cases, survival. The soldiers' pre-mission rituals may be considered extensions of these types of activities. The tendency of soldiers to come together around music and to sing or yell the lyrics together seems to have precedence in aspects of BCT. Even military advertisements and propaganda, such as the army's "Army of One" campaign and many of the videos discussed in chapter 1, highlight ideas of community and togetherness within military service.

Grisham's account of music as an inspiration for combat suggests another function of music while on patrol. He recalls that his group would listen to music during missions and that the music in this setting was beneficial to soldier concentration: "It was always still there keeping us alert. For some reason, when we had the music on in the truck, there was less talking and more you were paying attention to your sector. You were on your guard a little bit more, because you were able to sustain your horizon, and you didn't have to keep up with the conversation. You just focus on the music, and focus on your sector, and make sure that you weren't getting shot at."[38] DeNora observes that music has the power to operate as "a device with which to configure a space such that it affords some activities—concentration—more than others. . . . Music affords concentration because it structures the sonic environment, because it dispels random or idiosyncratic stimuli, aesthetic or otherwise."[39] In Grisham's case, the music replaced the silence that was likely to stimulate conversation among the soldiers, and thus helped to direct their attention back to the duty at hand. Conversely, other soldiers believe that music heard while on duty, particularly in combat zones, could distract soldiers or limit their ability to hear. The effect of music in these circumstances—its ability to enhance or disrupt concentration—appears dependent on context and individual response.

Soldiers' accounts confirm that metal and rap music most often functions as an inspiration for combat, but not during combat itself. The music is a "pre-text" for action, not a soundtrack to the fighting. Every soldier I interviewed said that any music they listen to before combat does not continue in their minds as a real-time accompaniment to combat. Saunders commented, "As soon as guns start firing and you're fighting your way out of an ambush, or those tanks starts going off, or those RPGs [Rocket-Propelled Grenade] start going off, you don't fuckin' hear that music. It's all just instinct, man. It's all what you got inside of you that starts coming out."[40] The soldiers' survival instinct and trained reactions block out sounds that are not immediately useful or relevant to combat. Buzzell, in fact, suggests that the sounds of combat become the music. Although he senses a relationship between Slayer's music and the sounds of war, the music is decidedly not in his ears during combat: "In combat? No. You know why? Because the explosions and the machine guns, and the shooting that's going on, that's the music. It's kind of like listening to Slayer, like that sort of shit. Listening to a 240 [machine gun] fire off rounds, or a TOW missile hit something, that's music to your ears kind of. And that sounds all twisted and wrong, but that's music in itself."[41] Similarly, Grisham points out that even if music was playing in a tank or Humvee during combat, the music seemed to disappear from the soldiers' perception: "When shots started firing, we didn't hear anything. It's like it stopped for a little while."[42]

Interestingly, metal music as an inspiration for combat is not limited to American soldiers. I had the opportunity to interview former Israeli Defense Force (IDF) sergeant Ziv Shalev, who commanded a ten-member intelligence team located on the northern border of Israel. Shalev recalled that listening to metal music when preparing for combat was a common practice among certain Israeli soldiers. In fact, he said that his team would listen to Metallica and hard rock/metal songs before ambushes or missions, and identified Metallica's "One" as a popular song in pre-mission listening. As mentioned above, "One" was also popular with Grisham and his tank mates during the initial invasion of Iraq. Shalev's description pointed to certain similarities between the listening practices of American and Israeli soldiers. Both groups listen to the music with the intention of psychologically preparing themselves for the possibility of combat; the same aspects of ritualization and sense of community occur among soldiers; and they listen to the same musical genres—even the same songs. These similarities suggest that metal music is codified in comparable ways in American and Israeli societies.

My findings with regard to pre-combat listening practices of American soldiers led me to consider how the opposing forces to the U.S. military in Iraq might use music for recruitment and/or combat preparation. In the following chapter, I offer an introduction to the music of anti-American and anti-Israel groups in Iraq and the Middle East as counterpoint to how American and Israeli soldiers interact with music. While this move is intended to complement my consideration of U.S. military forces, it may make some readers uncomfortable. I was unable to speak with anyone involved with these groups or with the production and dissemination of this music (although I spent a considerable amount of time on internet forums with fans of this music). One may contend that if I have not been there and have not spoken to those who produce the videos, I should not write about it. On the other hand, much of the music I examine exists in the form of media texts, like videos broadcast over the internet. I was able to find this music because it was posted on the internet and could only engage it as music in media. In this way, the limitations of my approach are similar to my engagement with music of U.S. military recruiting. My requests to speak with those who create the music in advertising of the U.S. military were denied or ignored, so I did not have that basis for my analysis of the music either. I approach the music of anti-American and anti-Israel movements through a methodological framework similar to my approach to the music of U.S. military recruiting, by understanding the music as part of a "symbolic contract" between sound and image in the context of media texts.

3 | Looking at the Opposing Forces

AN INTRODUCTION TO THE MUSIC OF ANTI-AMERICAN AND ANTI-ISRAEL MOVEMENTS

Having discussed how music figures prominently in military recruiting and the ways in which it motivates U.S. soldiers for combat, it is now appropriate to turn to the question of how music is utilized by those fighting against the U.S. forces in Iraq. Limiting the question to strictly anti-American militia groups is problematic, however, because much of the anti-American propaganda under discussion targets Israel as much as it does the United States. Israel and the United States are closely linked in these propaganda videos to the extent that the two countries are sometimes depicted interchangeably.[1] This linkage is largely due to the support that the United States is seen to extend to Israel, both in having helped the nation come into existence as well as in enhancing its military strength. Thus any discussion of Iraqi militant groups' anti-American music should consider anti-Israel music as well.

Another factor complicating my research of music in the Iraq War is that there was no way for me to verify where anti-American and anti-Israel music videos were actually made. In the case of the Islamic State of Iraq (ISI), a Sunni group, possibly linked to al-Qaeda and the Mujahideen Shura Council, many of the images contain combat footage from Iraq, but it is not clear if the final videos, which are edited to include slogan graphics and overdubbed musical soundtracks, were made in Iraq by Iraqis using Iraqi music. In fact, much of the music comes from artists outside Iraq, such as the Saudi nasheed singer Abo (or Abu) Ali. Furthermore, the primary form of dissemination appears to be the internet, so the geographic sitedness of these videos is not clearly specific to any single country. Because these videos sometimes contain graphic images, they do not appear frequently on television, but circulate on internet video web sites. All these factors made any attempt to limit consideration to Iraqi videos problematic. The extension of my focus beyond Iraq, however, should not be confused with suggesting that these videos are indicative of broad cultural sentiments within the entire Arab world. To the contrary, the following discussion of music is primarily isolated to what would be considered fundamentalist movements.

The music I discuss appears in videos produced by movements such as Fatah, Hamas, Hezbollah (Hizbullah), and the ISI. Among the objectives of these movements is the removal of any American presence from the Arabian Peninsula and the Middle East, and repossession of all territory held by Israel, including land held since Israel's birth in 1948 and the subsequent Arab-Israeli war that year, as well as land captured in the Six Day War of 1967. Specifically, these groups call for either the total elimination of Israel or the establishment of a sovereign Palestinian state while returning Israel to roughly its pre-1967 borders as outlined in UN Resolution 242. Of course, the goals of these movements are multi-faceted and complex, but their propaganda largely focuses on these aims.

MUSIC AND DIFFERENT PRACTICES OF ISLAM

The music of anti-American and anti-Israel videos reflects how different political movements interpret the role of music within Islam. These groups are deeply rooted in the Islamic faith, and their interpretations of Islamic teachings act as a guide for their military and political actions. The majority of music I examined references Allah, verses from the Qur'an, Hadith, or other aspects of the Islamic faith.[2] Groups like Hezbollah and the ISI have flags or insignias that include religious slogans. Hezbollah, or "Party of God," places a quote from the Qur'an on its flag: "Then surely the party of Allah are they that shall be triumphant" (Qur'an 5:56), and the first paragraph of its statement of purpose reads, "Hizbullah is an Islamic freedom fighting movement founded after the Israeli military seizure of Lebanon in 1982, which resulted in the immediate formation of the Islamic resistance unit for the liberation of the occupied territories and for the expulsion of the aggressive Israeli forces."[3]

Although the majority of music in this media references aspects of Islam, the status of music varies considerably among Muslims.[4] Some moderate interpretations of the religion permit music and musical instruments, while others claim that music is only permissible if the texts praise Allah and are accompanied by percussion instruments or drums. Still more conservative practitioners of the faith prohibit music entirely. These conservative Muslims view music as a catalyst that excites the passions and obscures the clarity of Allah's message. As such, music is outlawed. Nasheeds (nashid, nasyid in Malaysia), however, are permissible sacred recitations that embody the spiritual essence of religious devotion to Allah.[5] Even though they may resemble sung melodies or chants—many adopt polyphonic textures—they are not considered music.[6] Amnon Shiloah, author of *Music in the World of Islam: A Socio-Cultural Study,* describes the background of nasheeds and explains how nasheeds blur the distinction between music and sacred recitation:

> The magic and rhythm of word that epitomized classical poetry was enhanced by the chanting that underscored public recitations. This kind of recitation was given a special name: *inshad,* which originally meant raising the voice—*nishda*—from which is derived *inshad al-shi'r,* a protracted poetical recitation delivered in a loud voice. This meaning obviously gave rise to *nashid,* a term that at a later period designated various musical forms. Originally this term also referred to the raising of the voice; its extended musical connotation probably derived from the melodious reciting of poetry in public as practiced in pre- and post-Islamic times.[7]

Nasheeds developed such that the differences between recitation and music were obscured. While there seem to be aspects of "musical connotation" within the genre, it also has been associated with poetic recitation with a raised voice. This latter understanding is the interpretation adopted by conservative Muslims. For them, nasheeds are not "music," but sacred recitation—a permissible form of melodious expression. In his counterintelligence work, William Thompson found that many Muslims do not categorize the unaccompanied, vocal melodies of nasheeds as "music," but as "prayers."[8]

In recent years, the nasheed genre has undergone dramatic changes, and in some cases has become highly popularized and westernized. As music scholar Margaret Sarkissian has shown, nasheeds (nasyids) in Malaysia reference Western popular music styles and images.[9] In fact, they are commonly sung by pop performers who adapt aspects of the Western popular music vocabulary with Islam-oriented lyrics in Arabic, English, Indonesian, and other languages. Sarkissian has called nasheeds "a marker of Islamic youth culture in Malaysia," and this designation can be extended to a significant part of the global Islamic youth community.[10]

Although some Muslims welcome the popularization and westernization of nasheeds, conservatives disapprove of this trend. In internet discussion forums, the status of music, traditional nasheeds (those without instrumental accompaniment), and popularized nasheeds are fiercely debated.[11] For example, the following exchange appeared in comments posted on YouTube for the video "Mercy Like the Rain," by the pop nasheed group Shaam (emphasis and misspellings in the original):

> **Gokerrumesysa:** according to what you think that music is haram [forbidden]. if it doens't include any bad or haram things why is it haram? Also if it includes some words for glorify to Allah how you can say it is haram???? if you explain me i will be realy happy.
>
> **Amrica06:** MU.S.IC IS ALWAYS HARAM NO MATHER WHAT,
>
> **EmAZet:** No it isnt, music without instrumental isnt haram. Mohammed (s.a.w.s.) sang songs himself, so music is allowed, if its done only by voice of us.
>
> **XlostWithoutYewX:** NO IT ISN'T!
>
> **mishcutie42090:** yes, it is

In reference to the pop nasheed "This is Islam" by Mustaqiim Sahir, big-dtv123 protested the title "This is Islam Song" given to the video.

> **bigdtv123:** There are no "Islamic songs," my brother. If you wish to call your songs, simply "songs," then go ahead, but please don't call them "Islamic songs," the reason is Prophet sallallaahu alaihi wa sallaam [Muhammad] never came with songs, so barakallaahu feek [blessings of God], don't ascribe them to Islaam. Shukran [Thank you].

Traditional nasheeds have a passionate following and subculture. Like pop nasheeds, they are part of an active recording industry, and artists such as Abo Ali, Abu Abdul Malik, Meshary Rashid al Afasy, and many others release a variety of nasheed albums. Many postings in online discussion forums request links to particular nasheeds or artists and provide information on where to obtain recordings on the internet.[12] This global community expresses an interest in sacred recitations on a variety of topics, from peaceful reflections on Allah to war/jihad nasheeds about Chechnya, Iraq, and Palestine. The inclusion of instrumental accompaniment frequently appears as a topic of discussion. While there is a general consensus regarding the *haraam* (forbidden) status of pop nasheeds, the use of drums is a source of considerable debate. For example, in a discussion forum on www.ummah.com, Jangli Zemaryan responded to the question of drums in nasheeds:

EVERYONE READ THIS . . . ALL MUSICAL INSTRUMENTS ARE HARAAM. . . . THESE
NASHEEDS WITH INSTRUMENTS IN ARE HARAAM AND YOU SHOULDN'T LISTEN TO
EM INSHA'ALLAH! [God willing]. A quote from the Prophet Muhammad peace and
blessings of Allah be upon him from the Hadith Shaih Al-Bukhari: "There will be
people of my Ummah [community or nation] who will seek to make lawful: fornica-
tion wine-drinking and the use of ma'aazif [musical instruments]."[13]

A reader then asks, "Since when was a drum harram?"[14] Some online music
retailers, like www.mshoppe.co.uk, that sell these albums include a product
overview indicating the "drum free, approved" status of nasheed recordings.
Although nasheeds have provoked widespread debate in online forums
about the role of music in Islam, conservative Muslims have generally held
a negative view of instrumental music and the development of the nasheed
genre beyond unaccompanied recitation. Given the diverse perspectives that
Muslims have on music, there are a variety of soundtracks in anti-American
and anti-Israel propaganda.

MUSIC IN ISI VIDEOS

The U.S. Department of Homeland Security proposes that the ISI may be an
umbrella label for all al-Qaeda and Sunni militant movements in Iraq; clear
distinctions among different movements are often hard to assess as groups
typically join forces around the common objective of war with the United
States and Israel when their mutual interests or lands are threatened. ISI
videos primarily depict Improvised Explosive Device (IED) attacks, suicide
missions against American military forces, or celebratory events associated
with the movement. These videos document the continuing violence and
instability in Iraq and show successful attacks against U.S. soldiers. Most
often, the video is filmed by a member of the organization with a handheld
camera.

ISI videos are professionally produced by the al-Furqan Foundation, the
media production arm of the ISI created in November 2006, and promoted
as "alternative news/media reporting" to gain support within the region and
to attract recruits. In video example 18, the ISI rebroadcasts an al-Jazeera
television news report of their "show of force" in the Iraq city of Ramadi,
emphasizing their control of the city and the public support they obtained.
The video shows masked men dressed in black or white driving cars and
motorcycles through the main streets of the city, holding AK-47 assault rifles and waving flags. At the beginning of the video, two men hold a banner

which reads, "Council of the Mujahideen." While the original sound track of the reporter's voice is still audible, a distinct sonic feature of this video is that the ISI has overdubbed the traditional, unaccompanied nasheed, "Qom," as an additional soundtrack.[15]

"Qom" (Rise Up)[16]

Chorus: Rise up and leave off resting
It is Islam, (it has) returned
In the path of Allah, we have walked
And announced Jihad
(repeated three times)

We have returned with a machine gun
Possessing leadership today
We have followed the awakening of this generation
Groups and individuals
(repeated twice)

We have not known life
Except with vehemence and endurance
(Chorus, repeated twice)

The gathering of believers has sprung
With the genuine youth
In the nights of affliction they have walked
Behind the elucidating Qur'an
(repeated twice)

They do not care about oppression
Between the jaws of years
(Chorus, repeated twice)

Give glad tidings to the people of a morning
Aglow with lucidities
And with which the conquest is manifest
In the depths of darkness
(repeated twice)

And of one row united
In guidance, by the hands of the obedient
(Chorus, repeated twice)

Oh, the (fateful) night of the unjust
Oh, the humiliation of the jesters
Oh, the waste of years

The clear warning has arrived
(repeated twice)

We have come to you with a machine gun (rata-tat-tat-tat-tat)
And an elucidating Qur'an

Although information regarding the date of composition is unclear, "Qom"
is a contemporary war/jihad nasheed by Abo Ali, and an internet posting
claims it is from his recent "an-Nuheim" album.[17] The nasheed is a religious
call to duty, asking Muslims to "awaken" their Islamic duty of unburden-
ing the years of oppression and "affliction." The intentional addition of this
nasheed seems to underscore the importance that the ISI places on the recitation, and the religious call to duty of the text coupled with images of the
ISI celebration of control in Ramadi encourages others to "rise up and leave
off resting." Through the addition of the nasheed, this video recasts the al-
Jazeera news report in religious terms as a call to duty.

"Qom" also appears in other ISI videos; it is the soundtrack to another
video showing an IED attack on an American Humvee in Baghdad (video
example 19).[18] (Before viewing this video, one should be aware that video examples 19–22 contain violent footage that some readers might find disturbing.) The structure of most ISI videos is uniform, consisting of a slogan in an
introductory graphic, an overdubbed war/jihad nasheed, and images of an
IED attack. For instance, video example 20 presents another IED attack on
an American Humvee. Here, the overdubbed nasheed is "Kllna alqool qool"
(The word is the word), also by Abo Ali. The lyrics follow:

Chorus: The word is the word of the sword until the wrongs are righted[19]
The despicable ones have even wronged
The messenger of the people of strong will
(repeated three times)

Solo: our sanctuaries would not have been desecrated
Had the lions surrounded them
The filthiest of bandits have attacked us
So where are the swords?
They have forgotten that we are the defiant ones
Who defend like lions
We are those who trampled with our steeds
The thrones of the empires
The thrones of the empires
(Chorus, repeated twice)

We are those who built our forts out of skulls

Which we brought from the lands of the tyrant
By force and on top of the booty
Our messenger is the one who made us
Noble builders of glory
Our messenger is the sun of truth
Who lit the face of the world
Who lit the face of the world
(Chorus, repeated twice)

He lit the lamp of a light
Black from misguidance
And created from a few people
A generation coming with the dawn
So they destroyed a head of aggression
And humiliated every oppressor
War against every aggressor
And peace for every peaceful one
And peace for every peaceful one
(Chorus, repeated three times)

Like "Qom," this nasheed is a call to duty based on invaders who have "desecrated our sanctuaries." It promotes a rise to action ("where are the swords?") in defense of Islam.

In addition to the soundtrack of "Kllna alqool qool," the ISI video of this IED attack includes another musical component. As the vehicle approaches the IED, the man holding the video camera repeatedly chants, "Allahu Akbar." His chanting intensifies as the explosion occurs. Thompson confirmed that "Allahu Akbar" is typically chanted in videos where attacks are carried out: "I've seen a lot of those videos in my line of work—where some guy's in a vehicle somewhere, and they're videotaping the whole thing and they pull the trigger and the thing explodes. They get all excited, and start yelling, 'Allahu Akbar,' doing it before it happens too."[20] This phrase, shortened from "Allahu Akbar min kulli shay," meaning "God is greater than everything," is common in Muslim cultures; its use ranges from greetings to battle cries. As a war cry, Muslim warriors have chanted "Allahu Akbar" (God is greatest) for centuries to invoke the power and favor of Allah, and the ISI videos illustrate this chant still being employed as an inspiration for battle.

Further examples demonstrate the widespread appearance of traditional nasheeds and "Allahu Akbar" in ISI propaganda.[21] For instance, video example 21 depicts an IED attack on a Humvee with an overdubbed nasheed. One can hear the cameraman murmuring "Allahu Akbar" as the Humvee approaches the point of IED detonation. The nasheed continues as the images switch from documentation of this attack to a display of the items recovered from the wreckage—a helmet, papers, pictures of a soldier's wife and children, and part of a human foot. The lyrics below present two war/jihad nasheeds, "Sanakhudu Ma'arikana Ma'ahoum" (We will venture to battle with them—by Tariq Jabir [originally a Palestinian nasheed, but also used by the ISI]), and "Asad al-Fallujah" (Lions of Fallujah—artist unknown), used in ISI videos; like "Qom" and "Kllna alqool qool," these nasheeds express the textual themes of Islamic duty to expel invaders of their homeland.[22]

"Sanakhudu Ma'arikana Ma'ahoum"

We will venture to battle with them
We will march in congregations toward their bases
We shall return the stolen rights
And with full strength shall topple them

With the relentless weapon of truth
We shall liberate the land of the free
We shall return purity to Al-Quds [Jerusalem] once again
After humiliation and disgrace

Thunderously we shall infiltrate their hiding shelters
With boisterous stance that distresses them
We shall erase dishonor with our hands
And with full strength shall penalize them

We will not yield to accept an occupied fraction [of land]
We will not leave a hand-span to oppression
For the land will revolt to scorch them
As within the land are raging volcanoes

"Asad al-Fallujah"

Attack, O Lions of Falloojah [Fallujah]
Destroy for me a crooked head
My cavalry long ago bowed
In humiliation, with gashed bellies

Strike the invaders of Iraq
For their proofs have become exposed
Raise your head, O brave hero
For my split forehead is bleeding

Your sons taught my sons
By the whizzing of bullets singing

Teach me, so that I become a man
Fighting the disbelievers and infidels

Fallujah became a hope for me
A sister for distressed Jenin [a city in the West Bank]
Never fear an invader
Their bravest men fear chickens

Sons of Mu'aadh [a messenger of Muhammad] and al-Qa'qaa' [an Iraqi weapons
    facility]
The shine of dawn has appeared
Sons of Iraq, do not lose hope
Be firm, sons of al-'Oojah [Fallujah]
For the steeds of Allah have dashed forth
In the morning, for glowing honor

MUSIC IN FATAH AND HAMAS VIDEOS

Other movements, like Fatah, a faction within the Palestinian Liberation
Organization, similarly produce and promote videos with traditional nasheeds. Video example 22 is a short documentary of Al-Moayad
Bihokmillah Al-Agha, a suicide bomber who killed five people in a 12
December 2004 attack on Israel. It shows him training and saying final
prayers before going on the suicide mission. Al-Moayad speaks to the camera before killing himself in the attack: "We will destroy you, and reach you
everywhere. We will teach you lesson after lesson, attack after attack." The
video concludes with footage from the attack—a massive nighttime explosion. As in the ISI videos, the soundtrack to the scenes of Al-Moayad is a
traditional nasheed.[23]

Former Fatah member Walid Shoebat claims that nasheeds were not
only a part of recruiting and inspirational videos, but were often composed
and sung by members of Fatah.[24] At the age of sixteen, Shoebat was initiated
into Fatah and sent on a mission to bomb a branch of an Israeli bank, Bank
Leumi, in Bethlehem. He threw an explosive device on the roof of the bank
but was never successfully prosecuted for his actions. He sang the following
two nasheeds, among others, as a member of Fatah.[25]

"SHARPEN MY BONES"

Sharpen my bones and sharpen them
And make them into swords

Fill me up a Molotov cocktail
We are a nation of blood
Who break through the night
And transforms their flesh into bombs

"KOSHER BLOOD"

[Jews] O killers,
your blood is halal/kosher to us
Where will you hide from us in that day?

Shoebat asserts that nasheeds and war/jihad songs are learned from child-hood and taught in recruiting efforts to indoctrinate children into move-ments like Fatah.[26]

While my consideration of nasheeds is limited to those used by spe-cific anti-American and anti-Israeli movements, which typically convey war/jihad themes, it is important to reinforce that many nasheeds express peaceful messages of religious reflection.[27] Moreover, the religious indoctri-nation of children is by no means isolated to Islam. In the 2006 documen-tary *Jesus Camp*, directors Heidi Ewing and Rachel Grady reveal a church of Evangelical Christians who use music in religious services to transform children into "soldiers in God's Army." Pastor Becky Fischer is acutely aware of the similarities between their intense religious indoctrination and the in-doctrination of children in fundamentalist Islamic movements. She largely sees the urgency and intensity of their Evangelical Christian practices as needing to match that of fundamentalist Islam. The similarities between these two groups, who appear to stand opposed to one another, could be an interesting area for further research as their musical practices have much in common.

The practice of teaching war/jihad songs to children appears in certain parts of the Middle East. On 22 May 2007, Hugh Riminton of CNN reported on the status of a Baghdad kindergarten.[28] In addition to showing the educa-tional difficulties faced by Iraqi children in violent surroundings, he docu-mented the songs these children learn in school. In one case, a five-year-old girl sings, "I give a knife to my father to slaughter the chicken, and he gives me a machine gun and a rifle. Now I'm a soldier in the Liberation Army."[29] The class, as a group, sings a song taught by their teachers: "I swear, I swear, on my parents, on the blood of the martyrs, I will defend my homeland." In a subsequent interview, Headmistress Suhailah Ibrahim clarifies that the defenders of the "homeland" and "Liberation Army" fight in opposition to U.S. forces in Iraq.

Anti-American and anti-Israel songs are also taught and promoted to children for recruiting purposes in television programs produced by the Palestinian movement Hamas.[30] The children's show *Tomorrow's Pioneers* has aired on Hamas-sponsored Al-Aqsa television since April 2007. The show is hosted by a young girl, Saraa, who wears a hijab (veil or woman's head covering), a man dressed as a Mickey Mouse-inspired character, Farfour, and the moderator, Hazim Al-Sha'arawi.[31] The child host, the costume mouse who speaks in a high-pitched voice, and the brightly colored background set clearly suggest that the show is intended for children. *Tomorrow's Pioneers* includes a segment in which viewers can call in to the show. Video example 23, a collection of excerpts from *Tomorrow's Pioneers*, presents a sequence from 30 April 2007 in which an eleven-year-old named Harwa calls in and sings a song: "The people firmly stand, singing this to you. Rafah [a town in Gaza] sings, 'oh, oh.' Its answer is an AK-47. We who do not know fear, we are the predators of the forest."[32] Farfour dances as Harwa sings, and he mimics throwing stones and pointing a rifle. Likewise, Farfour dances when twelve-year-old Muhammad calls in and sings, "Oh Jerusalem, we are coming. Oh Jerusalem, it is the time of death. Oh Jerusalem, we will never surrender to the enemy and we will never be humiliated. It is beloved Palestine that taught us what to be, and taught us to be the soldiers of the Lord. We will destroy the chair of the despots. It is the time of death, we will fight a war." Farfour's comments at the beginning of the example also reflect the interchangeability of the United States and Israel in propaganda, referencing both American and Israeli officials: "Allah willing, Allah willing, this country, its children, its men, its women, and its elderly will win. We will win, Bush! We will win, Sharon!—Ah, Sharon is dead. We will win Mofaz!—Mofaz left. We will win, Olmert! We will win. We will win, Condoleezza!" *Tomorrow's Pioneers* operates as a vehicle for propaganda and recruitment. The songs are a means of indoctrinating children with Hamas principles from an early age. The recruitment strategy aims to instill specific values in children so that they will be sympathetic to the goals of Hamas as adults, and more likely to join. The songs on *Tomorrow's Pioneers* are an important tool in this process and represent war/jihad nasheeds used in propaganda disseminated to children.[33]

Traditional nasheeds, however, are not isolated to anti-American and anti-Israel propaganda. They sometimes inspire Muslim men for combat against rival Islamic sects or signal attack orders. Thompson described one night in Baghdad when Sunni and Shi'a militants began fighting while nasheeds were being broadcast over the speakers from a mosque:

The mosques, in the middle of the night, one or two of them start blasting their calls, their prayer calls, and then you hear gunfire. You realize that there is a battle going on. . . . We realize that it is all AK-47 gunfire, so it is Iraqi vs. Iraqi, Sunni/Shi'a probably. These mosques play music—this was explained to me by an Iraqi actually—at times they'll play this music over their loudspeakers as almost like a soundtrack to battle. Now I don't know how much truth that is from their point of view, but that is what an Iraqi had told me. And it makes sense, either that or a lot of times they are signals for certain things to happen. They use it that way. And also they use it, I believe, as an inspiration. They see fighting as they're going to die, and they're going to go to heaven if they die in combat. So they're listening to this music, and . . . what they say when they kill people is, "Praise God."[34]

An Iraqi explained to Thompson that the nasheeds signaled when to attack, but also that the chants had the power to inspire these Muslim fighters for combat based on the commonly held conservative Islamic belief that dying in jihad guarantees salvation. Warriors achieve "shahid" (or "shaheed," martyrdom) status if they are killed in jihad and are granted entry to heaven by Allah. Jihad, though, is not limited to fighting against American or Israeli military forces; it can apply to all perceived threats, even fellow Muslims. Certain Sunni militants, for example, view the Shi'a fighters as a corrupt, detrimental influence on their practice of Islam, and vice versa.

Moreover, Jason Sagebiel suggested that in noncombat situations the nasheeds played on mosque loudspeakers were employed to attract Muslims to specific mosques. Mosques would raise the volume level of the recitations in order to overpower the recitations being broadcast from the others: "All of these mosques seem to compete with one another. I remember I was in a building doing overwatch security for a unit of Marines who were a block or so away. There were three mosques within a four hundred meter radius and one would turn on. They'd start their recitations and that would come up, the other would start, and the other one would start, and they were tweaking their volume trying to drown out the others. They were trying to attract more people."[35] These examples demonstrate how nasheeds can operate as both an inspiration for combat and an attempt to attract Muslims to a mosque.

LESS TRADITIONAL MUSIC IN VIDEOS

Most of the soundtracks to the videos I have discussed up to this point are perceived by conservative Muslims as sacred recitation. The music of anti-American and anti-Israel movements is not, however, limited to traditional nasheeds. Musical instruments and Western-style music videos exist in this propaganda as well. Video example 24, for instance, presents an excerpt from a cartoon, aired on Hezbollah Al-Manar TV in June 2002. The video shows young boys casting stones at Israeli soldiers until one of the soldiers shoots a boy. The music of this sequence is sung by men, with accompaniment provided by strings and percussion instruments. The pitch structure, rhythm, and style of the vocal part recall traditional nasheeds; the singing is punctuated by spoken text. As the boys prepare to chase the Israeli soldiers with stones in their hands, the singing and music begin: "You are the aim and the concern, let your stone pour out blood. Your land is your honor and is what matters. It is your promise and your friend." The music continues over the following spoken dialogue: "My book has turned into a stone. With it I repel the treacherous. It is small like [the boy] but its effect is great." The men's singing resumes: "Purify yourself, pray and set out. Your blood perfumes the soil of your land. Your name will be engraved on Heaven's doors." Then, the boys begin throwing stones at the Israeli soldiers and the spoken dialogue enters: "I swear my loyalty to you, Al-Aqsa. I swear my loyalty to you, Jerusalem. I may miss a lesson, but my love for you itself is a lesson." The boys run after the soldiers and the singing returns: "Come out of every tunnel, window and door. Join your stone to mine. Shooting doesn't scare us." At this moment, the music stops and an Israeli soldier fires at one of the boys. As the boy is shot and falls to the ground, a solo female voice enters with a vocalise. The vocalise quickly fades and an image of the Al-Aqsa mosque appears with the spoken text: "The dear [child] has fulfilled his desire, achieving the honor of Martyrdom. He is not considered dead, he who dies for his country."

Scenes of Israeli soldiers targeting and killing children are common in anti-Israel video propaganda. Typically, the children are portrayed as playing peacefully and only acting against the soldiers, such as by throwing stones, when they feel that an injustice has been committed. In video example 24, the scene before the song may depict an atrocity against Muslims. Like *Tomorrow's Pioneers*, the recruiting strategy is to make children sympathetic to the cause and activism of the movement in order to increase the likelihood that they will join as adults, and songs are an important way of transmitting and promoting the movement's message. The music of this animated video, however, demonstrates a more permissive stance on music within Islamic practices. While the text and message are based on religious calls to duty, as are all the videos discussed in this section, the inclusion of musical instruments illustrates a less conservative interpretation on the position of music. Here again I reiterate that songs encouraging people to sacrifice their lives for their homeland are by no means unique to nasheeds or songs from the Middle East. Svanibor Pettan observes that in the Croatian war of the early 1990s, "the textual motif of giving one's life for the homeland was quite common. In one example the singer offered his life to God in return for the life of his homeland."[36]

In some instances, the music in videos of anti-American and anti-Israel movements resembles Western music videos. Video example 25 was aired on Palestinian Authority TV from March 2002 to October 2004, showing a young woman dressed in fatigues singing to the camera in an MTV-inspired video format. The scenes shift from her singing with background dancers dressed in black to images of (presumably) Israeli soldiers in the field—one of the soldiers is wiping blood from his nose. Not only does the structure allude to music videos, but the music is pop-influenced. While her singing style recalls some of the vocal inflections of traditional nasheeds, the music includes a syncopated drum/percussion backbeat, bassline, and full range of synthesizer sounds. The style is clearly pop with a message about activism and Islam. She sings, "What is dearer to us than Al-Aqsa, shake the earth, raise the stones. You will not be saved, oh Zionist, from the volcano of my country's stones. You are the target of my eyes. I will even fall as a shahid. Allah Akbar, oh young ones." The idea of raising stones in defense of Al-Aqsa is the primary subject of video example 24, and the sacrifice of one's life as a "shahid" (holy martyr) appears in almost all the videos. Within the context of video example 25, it seems appropriate to suggest that the phrase "Allah Akbar, oh young ones," which appears after "I will even fall as a shahid," references the common battle cry uttered as an inspiration for combat by many of the cameramen in ISI videos before attacks. Although this example articulates the message of action against Israel through popular music, in contrast to the ISI videos it demonstrates a far more permissive position on music. This video might be considered a nasheed due to its religious content, but the musical instruments, pop-influenced music, and music video format of video example 25 gesture toward more permissive attitudes about music in Islam.

CONNECTIONS TO THE MUSIC OF
U.S. MILITARY RECRUITING

These video examples reflect the diverse perspectives on music by anti-American and anti-Israel movements, and nasheeds appear to be an important component. While members of groups like the ISI would most likely object to my claim that their videos employ "music," the soundtracks of traditional nasheeds play a significant role in their propaganda. Given the highly debated position of music within Islam and the frequent prohibition of music by conservatives, one can assume that the intentional addition of nasheeds to video footage is a conscious decision and that nasheeds are believed to communicate or signify something that is not implicit within the sound of the video. In this way, the addition of these sacred recitations creates the "symbolic contract" described by Michel Chion between sound and image. The nasheed soundtrack "adds value" to the images and establishes an important association between what is seen and heard. It reinforces and creates meaning in the message of anti-American and anti-Israel videos.

Nasheeds are an important part of recruitment. If we examine the ISI videos, for example, there is nothing within them that calls the viewer to action. By overdubbing the nasheed, however, the video images receive added value that sends a specific message. Instead of documenting a successful IED attack, the nasheed lends meaning to the actions of the video and calls upon Muslims to join in jihad efforts. But, in addition to the texts, the type of musical texture employed (with or without instruments) references a particular view of Islam and music. Like the honorable duty music of U.S. military recruiting, the music of anti-American and anti-Israel recruiting efforts reinforces the images of the video through culturally specific calls to duty. Honorable duty music draws upon signifiers of honor, country, and duty within U.S. culture, while the overdubbing of nasheeds invokes Islamic calls to duty. A principal difference is that the music of U.S. military recruiting appeals to a sense of country without the direct religious connotations that are important in anti-American and anti-Israel recruiting efforts. The nasheed texts in these videos appeal to a sense of religious nationalism, or reference aspects of country and honor based on disputed territories occupied by Israel or the U.S. occupation of Iraq. As evidenced by Article Fifteen of the Hamas Covenant 1988, this call to defend one's country is almost always framed within the context of Islamic duty: "The day that enemies usurp part of Moslem land, Jihad becomes the individual duty of every Moslem. In the face of the Jews' usurpation of Palestine, it is compulsory that the banner of Jihad be raised."[37] In both cases, the recruiting strategy of honor, country, and duty proves effective. From the information I collected, it appears that most Muslim combatants join different movements for these purposes, and in *Evaluating Military Advertising and Recruiting: Theory and Methodology*, the National Research Council suggests that "duty to country" is one of the most important factors in U.S. soldiers' propensity to enlist.[38]

While the primary reason that U.S. military recruits and potential Muslim combatants join up is not because of their respective propaganda but because of the impact of personal recruiting, the idea of national duty resonates strongly in both groups, and the music of their propaganda draws upon signifiers of this meaning. In this way, these videos may be highly effective. The culturally specific messages projected by the music forge an initial bond between duty to country and service in either the military or combatant movements. If duty to country and/or religion is one of the principal reasons recruits join a military or combat group, it then follows that propaganda would attempt to strengthen this connection, and both the U.S. military and Islamic combatant movements appear to use music to achieve such goals.

Further similarities exist between the uses of music by anti-American and anti-Israel movements and by the U.S. military. In chapter 2, I described how U.S. soldiers listen to metal and rap as an inspiration for combat. As Thompson's explanation of Sunni/Shi'a fighting illustrates, nasheeds appear to have similar effects on certain Muslim combatants. The traditional nasheeds played from the mosques not only sounded a signal to attack, which is a longstanding use of music in combat, but continued during the battle to motivate the fighters. Additionally, many of the U.S. soldiers I interviewed adopted pre-mission rituals involving specific songs and sang with the music until, in some cases, they were screaming or yelling the lyrics. This act inspired them for possible combat. On the other hand, "Allahu Akbar" served as a common pre-attack chant for many of the combatants in ISI videos. As the time or position of attack came closer, the Muslim cameramen would begin chanting, which intensified until it resembled shouting or screaming. This practice demonstrates a degree of parallelism with the U.S. soldiers who scream or yell words to specific songs. Chanting "Allahu Akbar" is meant to invoke the power and favor of Allah during battle, which lends a sense of inspiration to the person(s) chanting. The U.S. soldiers attempt to accomplish the same goal of inspiration for combat through screaming or yelling the words to songs. The words of pre-mission songs operate similarly to a battle cry, and the process of interacting with the music in an increasingly intense way to the point of screaming is akin to how Islamic combatants chant "Allahu Akbar."

There is also an analogous component of defining group identity. We have seen how U.S. soldiers promote a sense of community or group-ness through pre-mission rituals and collectively yelling the music. The shared experience of shouting the music is one way of sonically defining the identity of the group. In some instances, the "Allahu Akbar" chant represents one Muslim (or Muslims) chanting for divine inspiration for the acts carried out by others. Those who repeat "Allahu Akbar" are attempting to invoke the spirit of Allah to assist their fellow soldier in battle, and this creates a distinct group defined by the combatants and the person(s) chanting. While obviously very different, in both instances, the act of chanting or yelling sonically establishes a connection or sense of shared purpose among combatants.

The final point of comparison I would like to make involves utilizing music to appeal to specific audiences. In chapter 1, I documented the profound musical change in U.S. military recruiting videos to include metal. I analyzed this change as a product of television, cinema, and MTV depictions of action, adventure, and violence through the 1980s, 1990s, and to the present day, but I also showed that the fan base of metal music corresponds with the main demographic of U.S. military recruiting, 17- to 25-year-old white males. The musical instruments and westernized/popularized music appearing in the videos of anti-American and anti-Israel movements might be interpreted similarly. The incorporation of pop-influenced music and MTV-style formats can be seen as an appeal to Islamic youth culture. The primary recruiting pool for these movements consists of young Muslim men, many of whom have been exposed to Western music and television, particularly in areas of the proposed Palestinian state. The more permissive stance on music within these videos suggests that these musical styles are intended to appeal to Islamic youths. Video example 25 might be considered a popularized nasheed, and the message of the video seems purposefully framed within the context of Western music videos in order to appeal more broadly to the target audience of this movement. Video example 25 could thus be interpreted, to a certain degree, within the same framework as the New Jersey National Guard video "The Creed" (video example 7). "The Creed" is a music video with a metal song soundtrack, composed specifically as a recruiting tool; recall that the words to "The Creed" were based on the U.S. Army's "Warrior's Ethos." The recruiting strategy of the metal music is to depict military service through a genre that appeals to the key demographic. Video example 25 seems to function similarly. The MTV video format, which is also the structural format of "The Creed," and pop-influenced music are the vehicles through which the anti-Israel message is communicated. These are intended to appeal to an audience of Islamic youths who would be the primary consumers of pop music.

In my research on the music of anti-American and anti-Israel movements, I was surprised to find some unusual selections of music. In one case, the Islamic Jihad Army released a video that employs background music of slow, chorale-style textures and timbres resembling the honorable duty music found in U.S. military recruiting (video example 26). This music is almost interchangeable with some of the Marine Corps or Army recruiting advertisements of chapter 1. The video also contains narration in English, suggesting it is intended for English-speaking audiences. The use of honorable duty music may be intended to create a degree of parallelism with U.S. soldiers. Honorable duty music is a way to musically convey feelings of honor, patriotism, and duty within American culture, and by employing this music, the Islamic Jihad Army may be using these culturally specific codes to cast its own mission in a similar way. In this case, an opposing group to the U.S. military seems to be aware of the distinct cultural resonances of this music. Additionally, I found a curious classical music reference in a promotional advertisement on al-Zawraa TV, a Sunni television station that broadcast out of Iraq until November 2006, when it was shut down for showing anti-Shi'a propaganda and footage of attacks against U.S. forces. In a promotional lead-in to footage of attacks against U.S. military forces, an excerpt from the second movement of Beethoven's Ninth Symphony accompanies the slogan graphic for the television station. Given the conservative Sunni position of the station, it seems odd that such an iconic piece of Western classical music would be chosen to advertise jihad-endorsing Islamic television.

Finally, I would like to discuss the introduction to a Holocaust denial documentary, *Merchants of the Myth*, that aired in Iran from October 2006 to January 2007 (video example 27). The video begins with flames superimposed behind the Star of David. In the center of the star, a series of images depict combat, civil unrest, and finally what looks like the face of Adolf Hitler. The star fades into the background flames as the title of the documentary appears. The music accompanying this introduction consists primarily of distorted electric guitar, bass, drums, and synthesizer. The style is influenced by hard rock/metal and seems to allude to a nü metal type of guitar riff. Considering that the documentary asserts that the "Zionist regime" created the "myth" of the Holocaust and perpetuated it through the American cinema industry, the choice of a Western musical style, and particularly metal, seems peculiar for the introduction. I interpret this in two ways. The music could suggest that metal music is indicative of Israeli culture, and as I learned from my interview with Ziv Shalev, metal is a common musical genre in Israel. This soundtrack couples the Star of David with music that is symbolic of unwanted Western and Israeli influence. Or, perhaps, the music is intended to be the soundtrack to the scenes of combat and civil unrest appearing within the Star of David. In this case, metal music accompanies scenes of violence. I argued in chapter 1 that metal has become associated with depictions of action, adventure, and violence, and this example supports the idea that metal has been codified in these ways across national and cultural boundaries.

In this chapter, I have introduced the music of anti-American and anti-Israel movements to show how music is used as an inspiration for combat and recruiting. My goal here is to provide counterpoint to chapter 2, which showed how American soldiers in Iraq employ music as an inspiration for combat, and chapter 1, which analyzed music in U.S. military recruiting. Even though these two groups are involved in day-to-day fighting against one another and their musics are dramatically different, there appear to be similarities in how music operates within the contexts of recruiting and as an inspiration for combat. The following chapter continues the exploration of music within an experience of military service. Having discussed music in recruiting and in preparation for combat, I now examine how music operates in the combat field against an enemy, specifically music as a psychological tactic.

4 | Music as a Psychological Tactic

Psychological tactics are an important component of military operations. The ability to demoralize, intimidate, or influence an enemy without physical engagement is one of the most effective tactics of warfare. In *The Art of War*, Sun Tzu (sixth century BC) writes,

> To capture the enemy's entire army is better than to destroy it; to take intact a regiment, a company, or a squad is better than to destroy them. For to win one hundred victories in one hundred battles is not the acme of skill. To subdue the enemy without fighting is the supreme excellence. Thus, what is of supreme importance in war is to attack the enemy's strategy. Next best is to disrupt his alliances by diplomacy. The next best is to attack his army. And the worst policy is to attack cities.[1]

Sun Tzu argues that causing an enemy to surrender before conflict begins is one of the most desirable means of waging war and can be achieved through psychological tactics. This type of warfare has been employed throughout history, operating typically as the first form of attack because of its capacity to increase the perceived strength of an army and conserve its resources.[2] Even when hostilities begin, the conflict can end much sooner through a psychological rather than a military arsenal.

The first use of music as a psychological tactic is difficult to pinpoint. The beating of drums or trumpet calls might have once struck fear in military opponents, but this music may also have been intended to inspire soldiers, to signal commands, and maneuver troops. Dan Kuehl, professor of information operations at Fort McNair's National Defense University, offers insight into the background of music in psychological operations: "[Music] plays a role especially in the realm of one of the five core competencies of information operations as we now define it in the U.S. military—psychological operations. And in that sense, it has been used since the beginnings of warfare. I would suggest that, unless you are a biblical literalist, Joshua did not make the walls of Jericho fall down with his trumpets, but he psychologically dislocated the defenders with that operation. And we've seen that all the way up to the modern times."[3] In many cases, the distinction between music that was intended to motivate troops for combat or psychologically threaten an adversary is blurred. For instance, the playing of bagpipes, an early instance of music inspiring soldiers for combat, was also used by Scottish clans as a psychological tactic.

One possible example of music employed as an intentional psychological tactic comes from the battle of the Alamo during the Texas Revolution (1835–36). According to retired army major Ed Rouse, a twenty-year veteran of psychological operations (PSYOPS) and psychological warfare (PSYWAR): "In our own American history, the Mexicans under Santa Anna, played the dreaded 'Deguello' [no quarter to the defenders] throughout the night and into the chilly, pre-dawn hours of March 16, 1836 as columns of Mexican soldiers attacked and overran the Alamo. The 'Deguello' is considered so emotional that many Texas schools still ban the playing of the song at sporting events even today."[4] Even in this instance, though, there is little documentation that the strategy was solely employed to psychologically intimidate or disorient the defenders of the Alamo, and throughout history, there seems to be degrees of overlap with music as an inspiration for combat and signals for tactical maneuvers. The nasheeds broadcast from the mosques during the Sunni/Shi'a fighting demonstrate the dual functionality of music as an inspiration for combat and a signal for attack.

The invention of radio introduced new ways for music to function in psychological operations. During World War II, radio hosts like "Tokyo Rose" (Japan) and "Axis Sally" (Germany) broadcast popular American music in an effort to attract their target audience, and then interjected propaganda messages between songs. The Japanese attempted to demoralize American troops serving in the Pacific through radio broadcasts in which announcers, usually women, proclaimed the inevitable defeat and demise of the Americans. These efforts, Kuehl says, appeared to backfire: "They played American music, which was spectacularly unsuccessful. In terms of what she was trying to do, which was to demoralize the American soldiers with the news of, 'Today, we sank five of your battleships off the coast of

Okinawa.' And everyone could say, 'what a bunch of horse pucky.'"[5] Hitler's radio propaganda program, "Axis Sally" (Mildred Gillars), which was aimed against British and American troops, achieved comparable results—many of the soldiers ignored the anti-Jewish propaganda and enjoyed the music.[6]

On the other hand, it appears that Allied forces were able to launch a somewhat successful radio campaign in Germany. From May to September 1940, the British suspected a German naval invasion across the English Channel and began a BBC radio program that taught English phrases to would-be German invasion forces. Rouse cites the following excerpt as an example from a broadcast (spoken in German):

> And so it will be best if you learn a few useful phrases in English before visiting us. For your first lesson, we take "die kanaueberfahrt." The channel crossing. Now, just repeat after me: "das boot sinkt." The boat is sinking. The boat is sinking. "Das wasser ist kalt." The water is cold. "Ser kalt." Very cold. Now I will give you a verb that should be very useful. Again, please repeat after me: "Ich brenne." I am burning. "Du brennst." You are burning. "Er brennt." He is burning. "Wir brennen." We burn. "Ihr brennt." You are burning. "Sir brennen." They are burning.[7]

These Allied broadcasts were intended to perpetuate rumors spread throughout Europe that the British had developed a way to set the English Channel on fire, and many Germans believed this was true. The propaganda seemed to be effective as documents discovered after the war reveal that Nazi officials considered the British capable of this defense strategy.[8]

The loudspeaker was another important technological development within psychological tactics and has been employed since World War II to project propaganda, messages intended to cause an enemy to surrender, or noises aimed at disorienting an enemy. In *The Art of Military Deception*, Mark Lloyd claims that noises were broadcast over loudspeakers by both the Japanese and Americans in World War II, and by the Japanese against the British Fourteenth Army.[9] The purpose of this tactic was to unnerve opposing forces: "Under certain circumstances loudspeakers may be used to transmit disorienting noise in the direction of the enemy. If the enemy is confident this will have little effect. If, however, he is apprehensive perhaps in anticipation of a coming assault, it will deprive him of sleep, prey upon his already frayed nerves and reduce his willingness and ability to fight."[10] In Vietnam, the United States broadcast messages via loudspeakers at the Viet Cong based on the folk tradition of the "wandering soul." It is believed by some in Vietnamese culture that a person must be buried in their homeland or their soul will wander in pain and suffering.[11] The U.S. military attempted to use this belief in order to get the opposing forces to surrender. Soldiers with loudspeakers and helicopters with speakers bolted on the sides played messages based on the premise that the Viet Cong would desert their mission because they did not want to risk dying away from their homeland and thus become a "wandering soul." Retired sergeant major Herbert A. Friedman, the American representative to the International Psychological Warfare Society, provides an example of what was said on these loudspeaker messages:

> **Girl's voice:** "Daddy, daddy, come home with me, come home. Daddy! Daddy!"
> **Man's Voice:** "Ha! [his daughter's name]. Who is that? Who is calling me? Oh, my daughter? My wife? Daddy is back home with you, my daughter! I am back home with you, my wife. But my body is gone. I am dead, my family. I . . . tragic, how tragic. My friends, I come back to let you know that I am dead! I am dead! It's hell, hell! It is a senseless death! How senseless! Senseless! But when I realized the truth, it was too late. Too late. Friends, while you are still alive, there is still a chance you will be reunited with your loved ones. Do you hear what I say? Go home! Go home, my friends! Hurry! Hurry! If not, you will end up like me. Go home my friends before it is too late. Go home! Go home my friends!"[12]

While loudspeakers were an important part of projecting spoken messages and have been a part of military and law enforcement operations for decades, music was rarely a part of these broadcasts. More often, music was employed in radio programs to attract listeners, who would then be exposed to propaganda. In these cases, music was not truly the operational psychological tactic; it was a means to appeal to the audience for whom the spoken message was intended. Even in the present battlefield of Iraq, loudspeakers are more frequently utilized to project spoken messages rather than music.

In December 1989, however, a key event defined music as a highly effective psychological tactic within military operations. Operation Just Cause was an attempt by the U.S. government and President George H. W. Bush to arrest Panamanian dictator Manuel Noriega. As U.S. troops invaded Panama, Noriega sought asylum in the Papal Nunciatura (the Vatican embassy). Soldiers surrounded the Nunciatura and negotiations between Monsignor José Sebastian Laboa and Panamanian general Marc Cisneros began for Noriega's release. Ronald Botelho was deployed on this operation in support of the 3rd Battalion, 75th Ranger Regiment, and 4th PSYOPS group in Panama. He recalls that one of the PSYOPS goals was to limit communication: "Someone came up with a great idea. We knew where Noriega was holed up and he was asking for asylum in different places. One of the ways in which we wanted to limit his communications, both with the outside world, vis-à-vis him coming on a platform and talking, and internal communications from within that, what was it? The Pope's House—was to just limit communication outreach. And one of the ways in which we did that was to play music."[13] Because of the embassy's proximity to hotels and residential buildings, it was also feared that reporters with powerful microphones would be able to overhear the sensitive talks. With this in mind, U.S. forces created a musical barrier by playing hard rock/metal music, such as AC/DC, Mötley Crüe, Metallica, Led Zeppelin, and others, through loudspeakers surrounding the Nunciatura.

While some accounts claim that the music was played to boost the morale of American troops (a claim that even here demonstrates the overlap between psychological tactics and inspiration for possible combat), it had, regardless of original intent, a powerful side effect. When Noriega commented that the music was irritating him, the Marines increased the volume, playing the music continuously: "The young PSYOPS soldiers discovered that Noriega, an opera lover, hated rock music. The result? Led Zeppelin and Martha Reeves and the Vandellas 'Nowhere to run, nowhere to hide.'"[14] As Kuehl noted, "I'm not sure if that upset him more or the residents around him. Anything you can do that will create a psychological reaction on the part of a targeted audience is a valid operation."[15] The relentless blasting of hard rock/metal music had such a powerful impact that Monsignor Laboa considered sleeping outside the embassy. The music was soon replaced by less controversial noise-jamming signals to prevent reporters from eavesdropping on negotiations, and Noriega from publicly communicating to audiences outside. But one of the possibilities of music as a psychological tactic had been discovered. Ben Abel, spokesman for the U.S. Army's psychological operations command at Fort Bragg, North Carolina, cites Operation Just Cause as one of the defining events for the use of music as a psychological tactic: "Since the Noriega incident, you've been seeing an increased use of loudspeakers. The Army has invested a lot of money into getting loudspeakers that are smaller and more durable."[16] Operation Just Cause is important to any historical consideration of psychological tactics because it is one of the first instances where music, not sounds or spoken messages, was tactically employed in a major military operation. Certainly in contemporary times, Operation Just Cause is a seminal event in the practice of utilizing music as a distinct psychological tactic.

MUSIC AS A PSYCHOLOGICAL TACTIC IN IRAQ

In the Iraq War, American military forces employ psychological tactics involving music in two principal ways: music played from loudspeakers in public areas (as in Operation Just Cause), and music used privately in detainee interrogation. As we have seen, the majority of psychological operations involving loudspeakers project a spoken message rather than music, and this still holds true in Iraq. The army has developed special PSYOPS speaker trucks (as described by Abel) that travel throughout cities broadcasting messages, mostly in Arabic.[17] The speakers are large and can be heard from hundreds of meters away. The messages are controlled from inside the truck via a small mini-disc player or a microphone, and generally play propaganda recordings about the peaceful intentions of American soldiers and ask Iraqi civilians to cooperate with efforts to capture insurgents. David Schultz said that when he went on joint patrols in Baghdad with PSYOPS soldiers before the Iraqi elections in January 2005, an interpreter spoke messages through the loudspeakers urging citizens to vote.[18] These speaker trucks also play recordings of instructions to surrender. Grisham explains that if insurgents hide in a building and refuse to come out, American soldiers sometimes order them to surrender with these speaker trucks. He paraphrases one such message: "This is the American Army. We've got you surrounded. We've got overwhelming firepower aimed right at you. Come out with your hands up."[19]

In specific circumstances, however, these trucks are part of sensory deprivation and irritation/frustration operations. Soldiers may engage in these tactics in the event that the instructions to surrender fail and insurgents remain in a building overnight. Sensory deprivation via music and/or noise prevents the insurgents from sleeping and detracts from their ability to fight, as Lloyd suggests. In this way, music provides a source of irritation and frustration, not because there is anything specific to music, but because music is part of a sonic arsenal that includes any annoying or unwanted sound. The music played in these situations is considered to be irritating or frustrating to the intended audience, and the degree of effectiveness will vary depending on age, gender, sociocultural background, and other factors.

If music is employed, soldiers often play hard rock/metal and rap because these genres are thought to be the most immediately irritating to insurgents in Iraq. The selection of hard rock/metal is also based on the success of this music against Noriega in Operation Just Cause. Botelho comments that these genres were chosen because they were the "music that could be irritating to most people. Now, I'm not a big hard rock fan, myself. But nonetheless, anything [within the hard rock genre] probably would have worked. My guess is that if we played classical, we may have put half of Panama to sleep and someone could sneak up and probably take our heads off as well. Jazz probably would not have worked because Noriega would probably get on the horn and ask for more. Hard rock has a very limited and dedicated clientele. And so rock it was. Loud, hard, and fast."[20] The goal is to irritate and frustrate insurgents, or "smoke them out," in order to detract from their ability to fight and increase the possibility of their surrender without engaging in combat.[21] Typically, the speaker trucks constitute only one form of sensory deprivation tactics and might operate alongside lighting trucks that project extremely bright beams of light on a target.

One of the most publicized events of the war took place in Fallujah on 31 March 2004, when four private military contractors were dragged from their car and executed. Their corpses were burned, mutilated, and hanged from the top of Fallujah's bridge over the Euphrates River, and the event was videotaped and received worldwide coverage. In response, the U.S. military began operations to retake control of Fallujah. As part of the strategy, large speakers were bolted on Humvees' gun turrets to play hard rock/metal music as the soldiers surrounded the city. The army does not have an official playlist and the choice of music is left to the soldiers, but the genre selection seems limited to hard rock/metal or rap.[22] Abel describes the psychological purpose of playing hard rock/metal and rap at insurgents in Fallujah: "It's not so much the music as the sound. It's like throwing a smoke bomb. The aim is to disorient and confuse the enemy to gain a tactical advantage. If you can bother the enemy through the night, it degrades their ability to fight. Western music is not the Iraqis' thing. So our guys have been getting really creative in finding sounds they think would make the enemy upset. These harassment missions work especially well in urban settings like Fallujah. The sounds just keep reverberating off the walls."[23]

Bing West's *No True Glory: A Frontline Account of the Battle for Fallujah* is a firsthand report of the military action in Fallujah based on several months' travel with the battalions that regained control of the city. His reporting provides another example of the use of hard rock/metal and rap directed at the insurgents, but with an interesting twist. The music was played so relentlessly into Fallujah that the Marines nicknamed the city "LalaFallujah" (a reference to the day-long summer festivals of mostly rock and rap music that were popular in the mid- and late 1990s). However, the insurgents responded with loudspeakers of their own: "The Marines were mocking the city as 'LalaFallujah' (after the popular stateside concert Lallapalooza) and cranking out 'Welcome to the Jungle' by Guns n' Roses and 'Hell's Bells' by AC/DC. Not to be outdone, the mullahs responded with loudspeakers hooked to generators, trying to drown out Eminem with prayers, chants of *Allahu Akbar,* and Arabic music."[24] In this instance, a sonic battle was waged between Marines' attempts at psychological intimidation, harassment, and sensory deprivation against insurgents inside Fallujah who tried to drown out the metal and rap with their own music, most likely nasheeds broadcast from mosques.

The idea of projecting music during war as a psychological tactic is famously depicted in Francis Ford Coppola's 1979 Vietnam War movie *Apocalypse Now,* ten years before the U.S. military used music in Operation Just Cause. In the film, Colonel Kilgore (Robert Duvall) has speakers mounted on helicopters and then blasts Wagner's "The Ride of the Valkyries" at the North Vietnamese Army because, he says, Wagner's music "scares the hell out of the spooks." While there does not appear to be any evidence that music was used this way during the Vietnam War, the movie may have been the inspiration for later military tactics.[25]

Among soldiers in the Iraq War, this scene from *Apocalypse Now* is well known, and the military has, in fact, played Wagner's "Ride" in much the same way as in the movie. C. J. Grisham was part of a team involved in "thunder runs," a type of mission first used in the Vietnam War that aimed to demonstrate military power by fighting aggressively in a designated area and then pulling out. During a "thunder run" into Baghdad, Grisham said they blasted Wagner's "Ride" on the outside of their truck as they attacked, as in the movie.[26] The purpose was twofold. First, the music was motivational for the American soldiers who knew the scene from the film. Second, according to Grisham, Saddam Hussein liked old American movies and Wagner's "Ride" is referenced in some of these as an attack song. By referencing the music associated with attacks—music Hussein may have known from his fascination with old American movies—and particularly a famous movie scene depicting a successful American invasion, the team aimed to hasten the Iraqi forces' surrender through psychological intimidation. As Grisham noted, "Hopefully to try to get the enemy to think, 'Oh my God, these guys are freaking insane, look at the music they are playing. They know they're going to win.'"[27] Although this psychological tactic has not been typical of U.S. military operations, other music has been used in the same way elsewhere. A Marine adopting the pseudonym, "Major Pain," who served eight months in Afghanistan and one year in Ramadi, Iraq, recalled that "in Afghanistan,

I did an attack on a village as an Army PSYOPS section hummer with me played the Taliban song from Toby Keith as we attacked."[28]

The second principal way music operates in psychological tactics involves the handling of detainees. Music in interrogation is not the only way in which music has been used during captivity. Svanibor Pettan writes that music was used to humiliate prisoners during the war in Croatia in the 1990s, documenting instances where prisoners were forced to sing the patriotic and supremacist songs of their captors and beaten if they refused.[29] Within U.S. military operations, Adam Piore reported in May 2003 that American interrogators played metal and American children's songs to break the will of uncooperative captives in Iraq.[30] Piore claimed that if prisoners refused to answer questions, they were often exposed to metal or children's songs for prolonged periods. According to Sgt. Mark Hadsell of PSYOPS, this tactic was intended "to break a prisoner's resistance through sleep deprivation and playing music that was culturally offensive to them. These people haven't heard heavy metal. They can't take it. If you play it for 24 hours, your brain and body function start to slide, your train of thought slows down and your will is broken. That's when we come in and talk to them."[31] Among the metal songs chosen for interrogation were Metallica's "Enter Sandman" and Drowning Pool's "Bodies"; one of the children's tunes played in this manner was the purple dinosaur Barney song "I Love You."

It does not appear that the use of music in interrogation originated in the government-funded experiments of the second half of the twentieth century. Rather, the practice of interrogating detainees with music appears to be new. When I asked Kuehl if he was familiar with any historical precedent for this tactic, he said that this was a fairly recent development.[32] Music scholar Suzanne Cusick claims that present detainee interrogation practices can be traced back to interrogation research funded by the Office of Strategic Services and its successor, the Central Intelligence Agency, as well as by British and Canadian intelligence services, since the 1940s.[33] Many such experiments used low-volume noises, like hissing or static, to dull the sense of sound by creating an unchanging sonic backdrop, but there is no mention of music in these studies. Background noise and soundproofing were used in research to test how the control and elimination of all sensory stimuli affected human behavior and mental processes.[34] The experiments were funded by government agencies in response to fears that Russia had developed powerful behavior modification and hypnosis techniques.[35] Even though certain aspects of the research may have suggested the use of music in interrogation, they did so only peripherally, and there are clear differences in the scope, purpose, and practice of how sound was tested in these experiments and how music is employed in detainee interrogation in Iraq. In the CIA experiments, the purpose of the noises was to dull or entirely block out auditory perception, not to sonically antagonize a person.

This difference is significant for understanding the path that led to the use of music as an interrogation tactic. The success of Operation Just Cause in 1989 suggested that music could operate as an effective form of irritation, frustration, and sensory deprivation in a very different way from the government-funded experiments that employed constant, low-level noise to numb sensory perception. Perhaps a more likely precedent for the use of music in interrogation can be found in Great Britain. On 9 August 1971, twelve suspected IRA terrorists were arrested by British agents and subjected to five "disorientation" or "sensory deprivation" techniques between 11–17 August and 11–18 October.[36] In 1978, the Plenary Count of the European Court for Human Rights (ECHR) mentioned in its ruling that British tactics in handling their prisoners included "subjection to noise: pending their interrogation, holding detainees in a room where there was a continuous loud noise or hiss."[37] Although music does not yet appear in this type of interrogation, it seems that British agents tried to agitate their detainees in much the same way as U.S. interrogators in Iraq. The noise was not intended to deprive the suspects of auditory stimuli, but to sonically overstimulate them such that they would agree to answer questions in order to make the sound stop.

In my research, I interviewed three soldiers who were involved with detainee interrogation in Iraq. Locating interrogators and securing interviews is difficult; much of the information about interrogation is classified and the soldiers are often hesitant to speak about their experiences for fear of being quoted out of context on what has become a sensitive and highly publicized topic. As mentioned in the introduction, interrogators are frequently advised to withhold any details regarding interrogation from the media because opposing forces use the media to collect, analyze, and disseminate information. From the military's perspective, a detainee who is aware of the purpose of an interrogation technique is less susceptible to it.[38] In the early stages of my research, I requested an interview with PSYOPS personnel at Fort Bragg, North Carolina. They asked me to send my questions in advance as part of my formal request. I did so but was nevertheless refused. I was unable to obtain even e-mail responses to basic questions about the history of music in PSYOPS. Given these obstacles, I am especially grateful to the soldiers who contributed to this component of my research, and so I attempt here to provide the most complete context for their words while at the same time not compromising sensitive information.

Of the three soldiers with whom I spoke who were directly involved in the interrogation of detainees, only C. J. Grisham claimed that he used music during interrogation. As part of his duties in tactical intelligence, he was involved in the detention and interrogation of noncompliant captives in Iraq. Grisham indicated that most detainees willingly answer questions and in only 10 percent of the cases did he have to attempt to break the will of a detainee by using sounds. Metal and children's songs were a way "to get on these people's nerves so that they will break down their resistance. You just want to find some way to put a wedge between that resistance. And once you chip away a little bit of it, it starts crumbling, and so music is a just a way of doing that."[39] Grisham also said that he made a tape of babies crying; detainees usually answered questions after a half hour. He explained, however, that interrogators could not be reckless in their choice of sounds because they were required by law to listen along with the detainee. In the following interview excerpt, he describes the interrogation process:

I had tapes of babies crying that I would play. And I made them listen to Britney Spears and I made them listen to Metallica—was a big one. The only problem with that was that as long as they were listening to babies crying, I had to listen to babies crying. You can't, the purpose—it's sensory deprivation. You are not allowed to do anything to the enemy, by law, that you wouldn't do yourself. So if I'm getting eight hours of sleep, the people I'm interrogating have to get eight hours of sleep, if I'm only getting two hours of sleep, then my prisoners are only required to get two hours of sleep. We can't treat them any worse than we treat ourselves. If I'm going to treat these guys to sensory deprivation—is what we call it— we just try and get them frustrated, "I don't want to hear that anymore!" "Ok, then just tell me what I want to know." We had to sit there for hours listening to babies crying, but we know what the purpose of this is, so it doesn't really get [on] our nerves as much and we can tune it out. We used all kinds of music. I used the Slipknot [a metal band] stuff, which actually scared them a little bit. Or Mudvayne [another metal band] and Slipknot. . . . Ninety percent of interrogations aren't really interrogations, they are more like debriefings. You go in there, you ask them a question and they answer you, you ask them a question and they answer you, you ask them a question and they answer you. And then you've got that 10 percent that you have to get creative with and actually use approach techniques, and actually use things like music and sensory and sleep deprivation, things like that. And again, when I say sleep deprivation, again, that's me staying up just as long as they stayed up. There was a time when I went 48 hours and like so many minutes, it was almost exactly 48 hours without sleep because I'm forcing this guy to stay awake. Except I'm getting to jump around and scream and yell just to stay awake. When I say sleep deprivation, again, I was never investigated for war crimes because I never committed any; there is a line you don't cross, I was sleep deprived too. Mudvayne worked really well, and Metallica worked really well and really any kind of American music, except for the popular stuff. I didn't know this but walking down the street when we first get into Baghdad and all the kids, all they know is, "Michael Jackson." I'm like, "What?" I wasn't used to the Arabic dialect, the Iraqi Arabic dialect, and so it was like, "Michael Jackson." And I'm like, "What's that kid saying?" Then he started doing the little moves, the foot moves and stuff like that, and I'm like "Holy Cow!" And there is these full-grown guys walking around with N'Sync T-shirts, they just don't realize how dumb they look. I never used any of that because, you put on a Michael Jackson tape, which to me would make me talk, but you put it on for those guys and like, "Oh, Michael Jackson," and it doesn't do anything for them. But you put on the hardcore, heavy metal American music from the Deep South or wherever. They don't want to hear that stuff, they think it's Satanic.[40]

Grisham indicated that he did not have specific training for using music in interrogation.[41] In fact, Rick Hoffman, vice president of the U.S. PSYOPS Veterans Association, told the BBC's Radio 4 "Today" program that the military believes this technique has no lasting effect on prisoners.[42] Nevertheless, its usefulness in the short term is supported by Grisham's experience.

The use of music to exhaust the will of a prisoner also has numerous cinematic precedents. In a scene from Alfred Hitchcock's 1940 film *Foreign Correspondent*, Nazi spies attempt to obtain secret information about a peace treaty from a character named Van Meer (Albert Basserman). Van Meer is drugged and placed in a bed with bright lights shining directly upon him. A recording of big band jazz music is played repeatedly as one of the spies prevents Van Meer from putting his hands over his ears. Another spy comments to a man just entering the room, "It's a very attractive mess, I know, and the music a little vulgar. But it serves its purpose." While it is almost certain that Nazi interrogation tactics before and during World War II involved sleep deprivation, it is difficult to establish that music was a part of such techniques. Another cinematic example is the James Cagney comedy *One,*

Two, Three (1961). In one scene, East German officials interrogate a character, Otto (Horst Buchholz), who has been accused of being an American spy. The scene implies that they have been playing Brian Hyland's 1960 hit "Itsy Bitsy Teeny Weeny Yellow Polka-Dot Bikini" for hours in an effort to break Otto's will. Although Otto is a dedicated Communist, the repetitive music drives him to sign a confession.

THE TORTURE DEBATE AND SOLDIERS' TRAINING AND PRACTICES

The use of music in detainee interrogation has prompted significant debate in American culture. Of particular interest is whether this technique constitutes torture. Academic professional societies, such as the Society for Ethnomusicology (SEM), consider the use of music as a tool for interrogation to be torture, and thus oppose the technique categorically. On 2 February 2007, SEM issued a "Position Statement Against the Use of Music as Torture," and called for specific disclosures of instances where music is used in such a way:

> The Society for Ethnomusicology condemns the use of torture in any form. An international scholarly society founded in 1955, the Society for Ethnomusicology (SEM) and its members are devoted to the research, study, and performance of music in all historical periods and cultural contexts. The SEM is committed to the ethical uses of music to further human understanding and to uphold the highest standards of human rights. The Society is equally committed to drawing critical attention to the abuse of such standards through the unethical uses of music to harm individuals and the societies in which they live. The U.S. government and its military and diplomatic agencies has used music as an instrument of abuse since 2001, particularly through the implementation of programs of torture in both covert and overt detention centers as part of the war on terror.
>
> The Society for Ethnomusicology:
> • calls for full disclosure of U.S. government-sanctioned and funded programs that design the means of delivering music as torture;
> • condemns the use of music as an instrument of torture; and
> • demands that the United States government and its agencies cease using music as an instrument of physical and psychological torture.[43]

The society recommends Cusick's article "Music as Torture, Music as Weapon" "for further information on the American history and praxis of using music as an instrument of torture."[44] Meanwhile, government officials, such as U.S. Attorney General Michael Mukasey, have waffled on far more severe interrogation techniques, like waterboarding. In 2008 waterboarding lay at the heart of a debate on torture, with the Bush administration hesitant to classify this technique as torture, and others, including Senator John McCain, himself tortured during captivity in the Vietnam War, generally opposed. I agree with McCain that techniques like waterboarding are torture (as do the majority of Americans), and I find torture unequivocally repugnant.

To examine this issue further, I turn attention now to the question of soldiers' training and experiences. It is not my intention, however, to answer the ethical question of whether music in interrogation is torture. My research has led me to the conclusion that, even from a strictly legal perspective, there still exists much uncertainty and ambiguity regarding music employed in interrogation and its possible qualification as torture. Thus it is important to learn more about this subject by engaging in ethnography-based research with American soldiers. Particularly when one considers the consequences of claiming that music in interrogation is torture—such a claim immediately casts those who used this technique as torturers and war criminals—I think the severity of such accusations demands that we approach the topic as carefully and comprehensively as possible. At least, scholars should attempt to ask American interrogators about the issue.

Soldiers' practices and experiences are primarily shaped by international law and U.S. military policy. To provide a thorough context for this discussion, we must understand the legal frameworks of torture because these laws regulate how soldiers are trained for detainee interrogation. Torture has specific definitions according to international law and treaties. Nations have vastly different policies on torture depending on their ratification of domestic and international laws; what is torture in one country may be legal in another. And even if a country has ratified a particular covenant, they may amend it or add restrictions regarding its application. I focus only on the conventions and treaties to which the United States is a signatory and those laws that govern the interrogation of detainees in war. The best place to start is the Geneva Conventions of 1949. The United States has ratified the Third and Fourth Geneva Conventions, which outline the guidelines for the treatment of prisoners of war (POWs or PWs) and the treatment of civilians in wartime. Article 17 of the Third Geneva Convention states, "No physical or mental torture, nor any other form of coercion, may be inflicted on prisoners of war to secure from them information of any kind whatever. Prisoners of war who refuse to answer may not be threatened, insulted or exposed to unpleasant or disadvantageous treatment of any kind." Throughout the second half of the twentieth century, however, it has been difficult to clearly ascertain which specific acts constitute torture; many countries have interpreted "unpleasant or disadvantageous treatment" in different ways.

In 1949, the ten-member Council of Europe signed the European Convention on Human Rights, which was largely based on the Universal Declaration of Human Rights (UDHR) of 1948. Article 3 of the Convention maintains, "No one shall be subjected to torture or to inhuman or degrading treatment or punishment." Both Ireland and the United Kingdom were members of the council, and in the 1978 ECHR case cited above, Ireland asserted that UK officials had broken Article 3 in their interrogation of the twelve arrested men, specifically with regard to five techniques of sensory deprivation (the third of which has been cited above):

> (a) wall-standing: forcing the detainees to remain for periods of some hours in a "stress position," described by those who underwent it as being "spreadeagled against the wall, with their fingers put high above the head against the wall, the legs spread apart and the feet back, causing them to stand on their toes with the weight of the body mainly on the fingers";
>
> (b) hooding: putting a black or navy coloured bag over the detainees' heads and, at least initially, keeping it there all the time except during interrogation;
>
> (c) subjection to noise: pending their interrogations, holding the detainees in a room where there was a continuous loud and hissing noise;
>
> (d) deprivation of sleep: pending their interrogations, depriving the detainees of sleep;
>
> (e) deprivation of food and drink: subjecting the detainees to a reduced diet during their stay at the centre and pending interrogations.[45]

The court, however, ruled that these techniques did not qualify as torture:

> The Court considers in fact that, whilst there exists on the one hand violence which is to be condemned both on moral grounds and also in most cases under the domestic law of the Contracting States but which does not fall within Article 3 (art. 3) of the Convention, it appears on the other hand that it was the intention that the Convention, with its distinction between "torture" and "inhuman or degrading treatment," should by the first of these terms attach a special stigma to deliberate inhuman treatment causing very serious and cruel suffering.
>
> Moreover, this seems to be the thinking lying behind Article 1 in fine of Resolution 3452 opted by the General Assembly of the United Nations on 9 December 1975, which declares: "Torture constitutes an aggravated and deliberate

form of cruel, inhuman or degrading treatment or punishment."

Although the five techniques, as applied in combination, undoubtedly amounted to inhuman and degrading treatment, although their object was the extraction of confessions, the naming of others and/or information and although they were used systematically, they did not occasion suffering of the particular intensity and cruelty implied by the word torture as so understood.[46]

While this ruling had no impact on the official policy of the United States at the time, it called into question the nature of specific psychological interrogation techniques and stimulated international debate as to whether these techniques constitute torture. Future efforts to establish laws on torture would be influenced by the perspectives on the five techniques outlined in this ruling. The court's decision set a precedent for using sound, but not music, as a distinct interrogation technique by ruling that the former was not torture.

In 1990, the U.S. Senate ratified General Assembly Resolution 39/46 of the United Nations Convention Against Torture and Other Cruel, Inhuman or Degrading Treatment or Punishment (UNCAT), but placed restrictions on UNCAT regarding the definitions of "cruel, inhuman, or degrading treatment or punishment" and "torture":

> The United States considers itself bound by the obligation under Article 16 to prevent "cruel, inhuman or degrading treatment or punishment," only insofar as the term "cruel, inhuman or degrading treatment or punishment" means the cruel, unusual and inhumane treatment or punishment prohibited by the Fifth, Eighth, and/ or Fourteenth Amendments to the Constitution of the United States. . . . That with reference to Article 1, the United States understands that, in order to constitute torture, an act must be specifically intended to inflict severe physical or mental pain or suffering and that mental pain or suffering refers to prolonged mental harm caused by or resulting from: (1) the intentional infliction or threatened infliction of severe physical pain or suffering; (2) the administration or application, or threatened administration or application, of mind altering substances or other procedures calculated to disrupt profoundly the senses or the personality; (3) the threat of imminent death; or (4) the threat that another person will imminently be subjected to death, severe physical pain or suffering, or the administration or application of mind altering substances or other procedures calculated to disrupt profoundly the senses or personality.[47]

Thus, the Senate limited the acts that constitute "cruel, inhuman or degrading treatment or punishment" to those within U.S. domestic law as outlined in the Fifth, Eighth, and Fourteenth Amendments to the Constitution. In this way, international practices were aligned with domestic law. Torture was defined as an act deliberately "intended to inflict severe physical or mental pain or suffering"—a definition similar to Article 17 of the Third Geneva Convention—and "mental pain or suffering" was explained in four forms. This provided more specific definitions of acts that the Senate identifies as psychological torture.

It appears that these guidelines regulated allowable practices of detainee interrogation until the Iraq War. The UNCAT restrictions and Geneva Convention laws helped form some of the procedures for lawful and unlawful practices in the army's Field Manual 34–52 (FM 34–52), Intelligence Interrogation, which was revised in 1992 and provides the protocols for soldiers' training and detainee interrogation in the field. FM 34–52 offers specific examples of physical and psychological torture and proposes two tests regarding the boundaries of lawful and unlawful techniques:

> While using legitimate interrogation techniques, certain applications of approaches and techniques may approach the line between lawful actions and unlawful actions. It may often be difficult to determine where lawful actions end and unlawful actions begin. In attempting to determine if a contemplated approach or technique would be considered unlawful, consider these two tests:
>
> Given all the surrounding facts and circumstances, would a reasonable person in the place of the person being interrogated believe that his rights, as guaranteed under both international and US law, are being violated or withheld, or will be violated or withheld if he fails to cooperate.
>
> If your contemplated actions were perpetrated by the enemy against US PWs, you would believe such actions violate international or US law.
>
> If you answer yes to either of these tests, do not engage in the contemplated action.[48]

Nowhere in the manual are sound or music mentioned as tools for interrogation, nor did the army train its interrogators to use music as a technique at this time.

Once music began to be employed in interrogation, however, it became clear, as Grisham noted, that its purpose is sensory deprivation. This would violate the Geneva Convention according to some observers, or at least qualify as "cruel, unusual or inhumane treatment or punishment" under the UNCAT restrictions. Additionally, the evidence provided by the Physicians for Human Rights (PHR) in *Break Them Down: Systematic Use of Psychological Torture by US Forces*—which Cusick cites as evidence that music in interrogation is torture—mentions loud rock or rap music as a means of sensory deprivation.[49] This document goes into extensive legal detail and aims to show how psychological techniques practiced by some U.S. officials are, in fact, torture. So why is it not officially considered to be torture or a violation of international and U.S. law?

It is difficult to answer this question. The PHR study suggests that music in interrogation can qualify as psychological torture when it is abusively applied as a tactic for prolonged sensory and sleep deprivation. But Gretchen Borchelt, one of the main legal authors of the study, said that there was neither legal precedent nor firm ground on which to qualify the isolated use of music in interrogation as torture.[50] The PHR document was mainly intended to address tactics like waterboarding, hooding, food and water deprivation, prolonged sleep deprivation, dog intimidation, and other psychological tactics (such as those in the 1978 ECHR case), but not specifically music. Borchelt advises that, according to U.S. and international law, the status of music in interrogation as "torture" or "cruel, unusual, and inhumane treatment or punishment" is, at best, not clear.[51]

Unfortunately, the experiences of American soldiers involved in my study who took part in detainee interrogation are not particularly clear either. Grisham was careful in his interrogation procedures not to violate the guidelines of FM 34–52 or international law. He was trained by the army that, under the Geneva Convention and international treaties signed by the U.S. government, interrogators must experience similar conditions to those they impose on their detainees, excluding physical harm. The Geneva Convention dictates that prisoners must not be subjected to "disadvantageous treatment," and the two tests of the 1992 FM 34–52 imply that one should not apply techniques one believes would be illegal under international or U.S. law if others were to use them. If a U.S. interrogator listens to music within the same setting, is this "disadvantageous treatment"? The military did not interpret music as constituting torture or any violation of law, and this was the protocol for Grisham's interrogation practices.[52] For Grisham, the circumstance in which an interrogator experiences the same environment or techniques as a detainee, barring physical harm, did not constitute a violation of U.S.-ratified laws.

On the other hand, Thompson indicated that music in interrogation would probably have been a violation of the Standard Operating Procedures of his division. While there was no official policy against music, it would have been a questionable practice and may have fallen into the category of a prohibited "change of scenery" as outlined in paragraph 8–63 of FM 34–52. He explains:

My understanding was that that [the use of music in interrogation] would be in violation of our, at least of our, standard operating procedures. I think that we bumped that into the category of a change of scenery, which is: you can't put somebody in a blindfold, put them in a Humvee, and drive them around in circles and tell them they're in a different country, that kind of thing. There are certain guidelines you have to follow and we adhered strictly to those things. . . . Where I was, it was probably illegal, it was one of those questionable things that you would probably err on the side of caution and not do it. If you are working in a BIF, Brigade Interrogation Facility, or a DIF, Division Interrogation Facility, and you get private sections, and they find out you are doing something like that, you could go to jail.[53]

While Thompson's training did not address the issue of music in interrogation, he was instructed by his Section Sergeant that this practice would have been questionable and that the soldiers should exercise caution in situations where the field manual procedures were unclear.

These two accounts demonstrate contrasting interpretations of music in interrogation. One of the possible explanations for the discrepancy between the guidelines for detainee interrogation as practiced by Grisham and Thompson lies in the timeframe of their deployments. Grisham was part of the initial invasion force in 2003; Thompson deployed in 2004. This is significant because the psychological and physical abuses of prisoners at Abu Ghraib prison were exposed in April 2004—after Grisham returned from his service and coinciding with Thompson's deployment. Due to the international outrage at these events, the guidelines for interrogation practices became more restrictive, and American interrogators may have erred "on the side of caution" with regard to techniques that were not clearly defined as lawful or unlawful. Thompson remarked, "At the time, all this stuff is going on at Abu Ghraib, all these horrible things that people are doing in interrogations—it just makes everybody look bad. So, we had to be on our toes all the time, being super careful."[54] The U.S. Army may have responded to the public indignation at Abu Ghraib by restricting the practices of interrogation for fear of further claims of prisoner abuse.

At the beginning of the war, the army's policy on interrogation seems to have operated according to an understanding of "disadvantageous treatment" and the two tests, in which, barring physical harm, an interrogator must be subjected to the same circumstances of treatment that he or she imposes on a detainee. Particularly in relation to music and the presence of interrogators within the room, there was no clear legal ruling on whether this technique is torture, and the interpretations of the U.S. military during that time indicated that it is not. These were the guidelines for Grisham. Thompson, however, was involved in detainee interrogation as the Abu Ghraib abuses were exposed, and the army seems to have responded by placing tighter restrictions on its interpretation of questionable interrogation techniques. Thus for Thompson, music in interrogation, while not officially outlawed by the Third Geneva Convention, UNCAT, or FM 34–52, was prohibited.

The wars in Iraq and Afghanistan have brought the psychological techniques employed in interrogation to the forefront of public awareness, and the prisoner abuses at Abu Ghraib seem to have led to a revision of U.S. interrogation practices. In 2006, the FM 34–52 was revised and now provides a more detailed description of unlawful actions.[55] In addition to the two tests, the following acts are prohibited:

- Forcing the detainee to be naked, perform sexual acts, or pose in a sexual manner.
- Placing hoods or sacks over the head of a detainee; using duct tape over the eyes.
- Applying beatings, electric shock, burns, or other forms of physical pain.
- Waterboarding.
- Using military working dogs.
- Inducing hypothermia or heat injury.
- Conducting mock execution.
- Depriving the detainee of necessary food, water, or medical care.[56]

These revisions address many of the issues brought forth by the PHR study and the five techniques of the 1978 ECHR ruling, with one important exception. There is no mention or clarification regarding the prohibition of music or sound deprivation in interrogation. U.S. and international laws governing detainee interrogation by army personnel still lack a clear position on music. Even though some interrogators may now be prohibited from using music in interrogation, from all supporting documentation, the army does not consider this practice to be illegal according to ratified treaties. Ultimately, the debate as to whether this legally constitutes torture remains unresolved, but there does not appear to be precedent or legal ground for the isolated use of music in interrogation, as currently practiced by the U.S. Army, to qualify as torture.

I am not defending torture. My intention is merely to provide insight on the issue in light of soldiers' experiences and to illustrate many of the complexities surrounding this issue. My hope is that this work will provide a better understanding of music in interrogation and the laws that directly shape soldiers' training and practices. If academic professional societies such as SEM claim that music in interrogation is torture, I believe they should contextualize their position statements to account for the legal complexities of music in interrogation and those that arise from ethnographic research with soldiers. Not only will this provide a more comprehensive understanding of the issue, which is ultimately a researcher's first priority, but it would provide a more relevant and informed platform for positive social change.

Many of the interrogators themselves do not consider this practice to be torture. In fact, some are outspoken about the ineffectiveness and cruelty of the acts that clearly constitute torture. A Pentagon survey released on 4 May 2007 asked 1,767 U.S. troops about the use of torture against insurgents: 36 percent of soldiers and 39 percent of the Marines agreed with the statement, "Yes, it [torture] should be used to gather vital information," while 41 percent of soldiers and 44 percent of Marines took the position, "Yes, but only if it could save US troops' lives."[57] Although the survey was largely flawed, lacking a specific definition for torture and relying on prefabricated, multiple-choice answers, Grisham was outraged at the responses (emphasis in original):

> Brothers and sisters in the military, listen to me. **TORTURE IS NEVER ACCEPTABLE!!** The minute we begin thinking that it's okay to torture people in the HOPES that we gain some valuable insight or intelligence is the minute we have no leg to stand on the next time one of our own is captured, kidnapped, or arrested. Torture will NOT save lives. Do it enough and I'm sure we'll get something that may help us here and there, but in the long run it's only going to get MORE Soldiers KILLED!! . . . You troops who think it is okay need to pull your heads out of your collective asses and WAKE UP!! And you'd better wake up NOW before someone YOU love is put six feet in the ground. I don't care how sick, disgusting, rabid, soulless or hate-driven you think the enemy is. We **NEVER** sink to their level. By doing so, we give tacit approval to their beheadings, their tortures, and their maltreatment. I don't know who these people are voting in this poll, but if I ever find you, I'll make it my goal in life to have you removed from my military. And if I have to resort to torture to do it. . . . . I'll throw in the streets of Baghdad instead. See how far your torture gets you there![58]

A female interrogator in Iraq, "JessDawn," agrees with his disgust over the poll:

> As a U.S. Army Interrogator I fully support what CJ typed. Not only does it cause more damage than it is worth it is not a productive way to gain information. People will say what ever they THINK you want to hear if it will stop abuse. This can cause bad info getting to our soldiers in the field and in my opinion that is worse than getting no information.[59]

While Grisham strongly opposes the use of torture to try to obtain information, he does not place music in the same category as torture. JessDawn echoes Grisham's feelings about the human damage that torture inflicts, but also points out the military ineffectiveness of such a strategy. She believes that the reliability of information provided under torture is so highly questionable that she would rather get nothing.[60] In his interrogation experience, Botelho agreed that the quality of information given in torture situations tends to be compromised.

The perspectives of these interrogators highlight some of the complex issues surrounding the use of music in interrogation and its possible qualification as torture. One of the main difficulties involves a lack of consistency regarding what is permissible as an interrogation technique. Botelho points out that "there were so many different agencies who had their own interrogators working, every alphabet agency you can name, had interrogators there and not everybody, as you know, worked from the same playbook."[61] It appears that different branches of the military and government agencies have different regulations regarding lawful interrogation practices. The interrogators surveyed in my study are all army personnel, and because the army field manuals for interrogation are declassified, I was able to investigate this topic in some detail, although I certainly cannot make any claims at a comprehensive assessment. On the other hand, the CIA manuals for interrogation, which recently underwent revision, remain classified and specific allowable practices are not made known to the public.[62]

Additionally, detainees may be subjected to entirely different interrogation laws once they are transferred to Iraqi interrogators. Thompson explains that "the Iraqi interrogators—those guys don't play by the rules. They are still dealing with the mentality of Saddam's regime. It's pretty horrible."[63] Because Iraq has ratified different treaties and covenants than the United States, the international laws regarding Iraqi treatment of detainees differ considerably from those of the United States. To what extent music may have played a role in non-U.S. Army or Iraqi interrogation techniques, I do not know. It has been and will probably continue to be a difficult task to gather and corroborate evidence on this sensitive topic. We can, however, gain an idea of how music operates in some circumstances as a psychological tactic in the Iraq War. In this chapter, I have presented much of the relevant evidence for the two primary applications of music through loudspeakers in the combat field and in detainee interrogation by army personnel. The following chapter moves beyond music as an operational tactic and explores the music composed by soldiers, much of which is based on their experiences in the combat field.

5 | Music as a Form of Soldier Expression

In almost every American military conflict, it has been common for soldiers to sing songs and make music within the context of the combat theater as a means for individual as well as collective expression. While song topics have varied widely, many times the lyrics addressed aspects of war. For example, songs of the Revolutionary War, like "Hail, Columbia" and "Yankee Doodle," or Civil War songs by Henry Work Clay ("Brave Boys They Are," "Marching through Georgia") and George Frederick Root ("The Battle Cry of Freedom," "Just Before the Battle, Mother") were well known among both soldiers and civilians. In both World Wars I and II, soldiers sang the popular war songs of the time, such as "Over There," "The Rose of No Man's Land," "Remember Pearl Harbor," "There's a Star-spangled Banner Waving Somewhere," and many others. In fact, during World War I, the U.S. Army issued an official songbook containing seventy patriotic, folk, religious, and popular songs, with the slogan "A Singing Army is a Fighting Army." Military song historian Les Cleveland describes these types of songs as "military occupational songs," which comprise "any type or kind of singing or chanting that is known to have circulated among military groups and has originated either within the services or has been adapted from the resources of popular culture."[1] One might say that the American military has always comprised soldiers with a strong disposition for singing.

Soldiers, however, did not often follow the traditional verses of well-known songs, but tended to change the texts in order to reflect their wartime experiences. For instance, the World War II paratrooper song "Blood On the Risers" adopts the melody of "Battle Hymn of the Republic." Below are the first two stanzas and chorus of the original lyrics followed by the World War II parody.

"BATTLE HYMN OF THE REPUBLIC"

Mine eyes have seen the glory of the coming of the Lord
He is trampling out the vintage where the grapes of wrath are stored
He hath loosed the fateful lightning of His terrible swift sword
His truth is marching on.

Chorus
Glory, glory, hallelujah!
Glory, glory, hallelujah!
Glory, glory, hallelujah!
His truth is marching on.

I have seen Him in the watch-fires of a hundred circling camps
They have builded Him an altar in the evening dews and damps
I can read His righteous sentence by the dim and flaring lamps
His day is marching on.

"BLOOD ON THE RISERS"

He was just a rookie trooper and he surely shook with fright
He checked off his equipment and made sure his pack was tight
He had to sit and listen to those awful engines roar
"You ain't gonna jump no more!"

Chorus
Gory, gory, what a hell of a way to die
Gory, gory, what a hell of a way to die
Gory, gory, what a hell of a way to die
He ain't gonna jump no more!

"Is everybody happy?" cried the Sergeant looking up
Our Hero feebly answered "Yes," and then they stood him up
He jumped into the icy blast, his static line unhooked
And he ain't gonna jump no more.

"Battle Hymn of the Republic" was itself part of the text adaptation tradition. The words were written in 1862 by Julia Ward Howe, the wife of a doctor serving in the Civil War, but the melody is derived from a popular song of that time, "John Brown's Body," also known as "John Brown Song" or "John Brown."[2] Even more, the lyrics of "John Brown's Body" were written circa 1860–61 based on a fundamentalist camp meeting tune, "Say Brothers Will

You Meet Us." Although the authorship of "Say Brothers Will You Meet Us" is not clear, the song is sometimes attributed to William Steffe in the 1850s.[3] Thus, "Blood On the Risers" is a parody of "Battle Hymn of the Republic," which is a text adaptation of "John Brown's Body," a song itself derived from "Say Brothers Will You Meet Us"—in other words, a parody of an adaptation of an adaptation. Further examples of parody songs from the World Wars include, among many others, "The Shell Hole Rag," "I Wore a Tunic," and "D-Day Dodgers."

During the Vietnam War, text adaptation continued to be prevalent. Vietnam song historian Lydia Fish cites Joseph B. Treaster, a *New York Times* reporter in Saigon, as follows:

> Almost every club has a resident musician, usually a guitar player, whom the men crowd around, singing songs about their lives in a strange country and the war they are fighting. The songs are laced with cynicism and political innuendoes and they echo the frustrations of the "dirty little war" which has become a dirty big one. Above all, the songs reflect the wartime Yank's ability to laugh at himself in a difficult situation. The songs grow fast as first one man, then another, throws in a line while the guitar player searches for chords. The tunes are usually old favorites.[4]

In *Dark Laughter: War in Song and Popular Culture,* Cleveland provides detailed research on "the vast number of musical parodies of popular songs and adaptations of their lyrics that proliferate in the military as a vigorous part of the folklore-popular culture matrix" between the World Wars and including Vietnam.[5] He emphasizes that the military occupational song tradition is primarily adaptive.

Soldiers fighting on opposite sides of a conflict have even been known to practice text adaptation for the same song. "Free America," for instance, is a song of the American Revolutionary War. Major General Dr. Joseph Warren, an original Minuteman from Boston, is credited as the author of the text, but the melody belongs to "The British Grenadiers," a song popular among soldiers of the British Army. In World War II, Allied forces frequently heard the German song "Lili Marlene" on the radio in Europe; its popularity inspired Tommy Connor and J. J. Philips to write lyrics in English loosely based on the original. Anne Shelton and Martha Tinton each recorded "Lili Marlene" with these lyrics in 1942 and 1944, respectively. Perry Como also recorded the song in 1944, using different lyrics adapted from Connor and Philips's version. German, British, and American soldiers wrote countless parodies and text adaptations of the song, including the above-mentioned "D-Day Dodgers." A translation of the original German song by Hans Leip (lyrics,

1915) and Norbert Schultze (music, 1938), the English lyrics by Connor and Philips (ca. 1940, as recorded by Shelton and Tinton), and the "D-Day Dodgers" parody (World War II) follow:[6]

"Lili Marlene," original German translation

Outside the barracks by the corner light
I'll always stand and wait for you at night
We will create a world for two
I'll wait for you the whole night through
For you, Lili Marlene
For you, Lili Marlene.

Bugler tonight, don't play the Call To Arms
I want another evening with her charms
Then we will say goodbye and part
I'll always keep you in my heart
With me, Lili Marlene
With me, Lili Marlene.

Give me a rose to show how much you care
Tied to the stem, a lock of golden hair
Surely tomorrow you'll feel blue
But then will come a love that's new
For you, Lili Marlene
For you, Lili Marlene.

When we are marching in the mud and cold
And when my pack seems more than I can hold
My love for you renews my might
I'm warm again, my pack is light
It's you, Lili Marlene
It's you, Lili Marlene.

"Lili Marlene," Connor and Philips

Underneath the lantern by the barrack gate
Darling I remember the way you used to wait
'Twas there that you whispered tenderly
That you loved me, you'd always be
My Lili of the lamplight
My own Lili Marlene.

Time would come for roll call, time for us to part
Darling I'd caress you and press you to my heart

And there 'neath that far off lantern light
I'd hold you tight, we'd kiss "good-night"
My Lili of the lamplight
My own Lili Marlene.

Orders came for sailing somewhere over there
All confined to barracks was more than I could bear
I knew you were waiting in the street
I heard your feet, but could not meet
My Lili of the lamplight
My own Lili Marlene.

Resting in a billet just behind the line
Even though we're parted your lips are close to mine
You wait where that lantern softly gleams
Your sweet face seems to haunt my dreams
My Lili of the lamplight
My own Lili Marlene.

When we are marching in the mud and cold
And when my pack seems more than I can hold
My love for you renews my might
I'm warm again, my pack is light
It's you Lili Marlene
It's you Lili Marlene.

"D-Day Dodgers"

We're the D-Day Dodgers out in Italy
Always on the vino, always on the spree
Eighth Army scroungers and their tanks
We live in Rome, among the Yanks
We are the D-Day Dodgers, over here in Italy.

We landed at Salerno, a holiday with pay
Jerry brought the band down to cheer us on our way
We all sang the songs and the beer was free
We kissed all the girls in Napoli
For we are the D-Day Dodgers, over here in Italy.

The Votlurno and Cassino were taken in our stride
We didn't have to fight there. We just went for the ride
Anzio and Sangro were all forlorn
We did not do a thing from dusk to dawn
For we are the D-Day Dodgers, over here in Italy.

On our way to Florence we had a lovely time
We ran a bus to Rimini right through the Gothic Line
On to Bologna we did go
Then we went bathing in the Po
For we are the D-Day Dodgers, over here in Italy.

Once we had a blue light that we were going home
Back to dear old Blighty, never more to roam
Then somebody said in France you'll fight
We said never mind, we'll just sit tight
The windy D-Day Dodgers, out in sunny Italy.

Now Lady Astor, get a load of this
Don't stand up on a platform and talk a load of piss
You're the nation's sweetheart, the nation's pride
But we think your bloody big mouth is far too wide
For we are the D-Day Dodgers, out in sunny Italy.

When you look 'round the mountains, through the mud and rain
You'll find scattered crosses, some which bear no name
Heartbreak, and toil and suffering gone
The boys beneath them slumber on
They were the D-Day Dodgers, who'll stay in Italy.

So listen all you people, over land and foam
Even though we've parted, our hearts are close to home
When we return we hope you'll say
"You did your little bit, though far away"
All the D-Day Dodgers, way out there in Italy.

While text adaptation was a widespread practice, it is sometimes difficult to determine if soldiers wrote a significant amount of original music. Particularly in the wars before the twentieth century, soldiers' compositions received little documentation. Keith and Rusty McNeil, authors of the *Colonial and Revolutionary Songbook (American History Through Folksong)*, claim that "the American Revolution inspired both British and American citizens and soldiers to write songs about their differences," but there is little evidence that much of the original music composed by soldiers survives to the present day.[7] Often times, one cannot verify whether a soldier composed the music and words or rewrote words to an existing melody. For the most part, it appears that soldiers sang popular and military occupational songs with original or altered texts.

In World War II, soldiers had greater access to musical instruments, like the acoustic guitar, which was and continues to be the most common in-strument among American soldiers. Bruce Brown said that there were so many acoustic guitars on his World War II aircraft carrier that they had "gui-tars coming out of their ears."[8] Archival recordings of World War II songs held by the American Folklife Center of the Library of Congress (Gordon Collection) demonstrate that soldiers did create some original music, like a "War Song" composed by a Native American Sioux soldier in 1943.[9] Thus, it appears that original composition was a part of some soldiers' music mak-ing in World War II, but Brown told me that the predominant form of sol-diers' musical expression on his Carrier was singing existing songs or altered song lyrics. The Vietnam War saw a growing amount of music composed by soldiers, like the 1966 "Ballad of the Green Berets" by Staff Sergeant Barry Sandler and Robin Moore. During the war, the increased availability of mu-sical instruments facilitated soldiers' use of music as an expressive vehicle.[10] According to Fish, some soldiers even mail-ordered instruments, such as the Autoharp, to Vietnam.[11] Nonetheless, prior to and including the Vietnam War, it seems more common for soldiers to parody songs—there are dozens of parodies of "Ballad of the Green Berets"—or to sing existing songs than to compose original music.

Additionally, perhaps because the conflict was so short, there does not appear to be a significant amount of music written by soldiers during Operation Desert Storm in 1991. Many soldiers who served in this conflict do not recall original music being written while deployed. "Dagger X-Ray" noted, "I am not familiar with anyone writing music back at that time but then again we were always moving and nobody in my unit had time to think about anything else but what we were doing next."[12] Since the war lasted less than two months, from 16 January to the formal acceptance of ceasefire terms on 8 March 1991, soldiers may not have found the time or opportuni-ties to write any considerable quantity of music.

The military occupational folksong tradition appears to be primarily based on text adaptation rather than original musical composition. This is not to suggest that soldiers did not write their own music. Albums such as *In Country: Folksongs of Americans in the Vietnam War* feature numerous original songs written by soldiers alongside renditions of existing songs and parodies. Some soldiers were clearly composing original music during their deployment, but in terms of overall musical practices, soldiers appear to have more frequently borrowed music from popular culture or military oc-cupational songs and written their own lyrics in order to comment on their wartime experiences. Soldiers in the Iraq War continue the practice of singing existing songs, text adaptations, and parodies. However, they also seem to be pursuing original musical composition to a greater degree than in the past, and the technological possibilities of audio production are making a significant impact on soldiers' use of music for personal expression.

SOLDIERS WRITING MUSIC

American soldiers are composing, performing, and recording an unprecedented amount of original music while deployed to Iraq, largely due to the increased availability of musical instruments and technological advances of audio production. The music composed by soldiers spans a wide range of genres and styles, from acoustic guitar-based folk music to gore metal. While most soldiers say that the music they compose is inspired by their experiences in Iraq and operates as an outlet for their emotions, soldiers' lyrics explore a great variety of textual themes. Some soldiers portray their service as patriotic and heroic through folksong, while others write about the grief over the loss of a friend. Others use rap to convey their frustrations with the Iraqi people and everyday soldier life, and one soldier chose to cast his message symbolically, without lyrics, within instrumental music. The diversity of music and lyrical themes points to the broad spectrum of soldier experiences in Iraq. In this section, I document some of the music and texts written by soldiers during deployment, and then discuss how soldiers have taken advantage of recent audio recording technology to record albums within the combat theater.

Some of the music created by soldiers expresses a strong patriotic sentiment. In a scene from *Soundtrack to War,* George Gittoes interviews a soldier called "Janel" who sings an a cappella version of her song "Home of the Brave," which she composed while on a year-long deployment. The melody is in minor mode and her singing style includes pop-influenced vocal inflections.[13]

"Home of the Brave," "Janel"

Deep in the battlefield
All covered in mud, blood, sweat, and tears
We die for our country through the years
No hesitation, driving on with no fears
You know that we won't stop
Sacrifice and dedication, they give their lives with no hesitation

They give up what people take for granted every day
Go places that make the ghetto look like the States
When a war pops off they will soon meet their fate
And you know that we do it for one simple reason.

'Cause we're the home of the brave
You can't take that away from me
We fought and died for liberty
And you can't shake us, no one can defeat us
So may God guide us every day, our sweet home of the brave.

Up before the rising sun
24-7 always work to be done
Destination top secret, every mission unknown
Just hoping one day that we'll soon make it home
You know that we won't stop
Passion, drive, and determination
We fight for the rights of every nation
Just trying to survive and make the best of every day
We strive to the best cause that's how we roll
No one stands in our way, no one can stop our flow
We are the red, white, and blue, and we represent just for that very reason.

'Cause we're the home of the brave
You can't take that away from me
We fought and died for liberty
And you can't shake us, no one can defeat us
So may God guide us every day, our sweet home of the brave.

Janel explains that the song is "basically about what every soldier has to go through out here, their experiences, what they have to give up, their sacrifices, what they want, everything that they wish and hope for."[14] Her lyrics portray military service as heroic, fearless, and a sacrifice made by soldiers for their country. The title of the song references the last words of the U.S. national anthem, and the text conveys the message that soldiers perform their duties in defense of the liberties held by Americans.

In another scene from the documentary, Sgt. Jeff Knoop plays an acoustic guitar and sings a slow, major mode, folk-style song he composed, "I Pledge Allegiance."[15]

"I Pledge Allegiance," Knoop

Well she's been through a lot lately
She's been torn and burned

She's been put on trial, been cursed and spit on
But she'll wave forever in America's land.

So let's pledge allegiance, for which it stands
As she's with our soldiers in foreign lands
Yeah, she's in Iraq and Afghanistan
War torn, she's still wavin', for which she stands.

Oh, if she could talk, oh, the stories she'd tell
'Bout how some Americans have been through a living hell
Oh, she'd brag about our veterans
And the war they're still fighting, for which she stands.

So let's pledge allegiance, for which she stands
As she's with our soldiers in foreign lands
Yeah, she's in Iraq and Afghanistan
And a war she's still fighting, for which she stands.

Now she's with our veterans when our day is done
She's folded up neatly and then given to a loved one
Oh, our sons and daughters they'll carry on
The traditions of a great America, for which she stands.

So let's pledge allegiance, for which she stands
As she's with our soldiers in foreign lands
Yeah, she's in Iraq and Afghanistan
And a war she's still fighting, for which she stands.

Knoop's lyrics affirm patriotic values and symbolism. He represents the life and sacrifices of soldiers in Iraq and Afghanistan through the symbolism of the American flag. The flag is personified as a presence "in foreign lands," along with the soldiers fighting in defense of American values. Knoop's lyrics ask the listener to "pledge allegiance" to the American flag and draw upon words and phrases in the "Pledge of Allegiance":

I pledge allegiance to the flag of the United States of America
And to the Republic for which it stands
One nation, under God, indivisible
With liberty and justice for all.

The lyrics of both songs reflect many of the textual themes of "honorable duty" music used in military recruiting campaigns. The ideas of country, strength, and the army's seven Core Values (loyalty, duty, respect, selfless service, honor, integrity, and personal courage), which resonate strongly in the texts of military recruiting advertisements, emerge in the lyrics of Janel's and Knoop's songs. "Home of the Brave" speaks of soldiers' "sacrifice and determination," their strength ("no one can defeat us"), and striving "to the best" ("Be all that you can be"). "I Pledge Allegiance" asks listeners to restate the oath of loyalty to the flag and honor American ways of life. The lyrics of these songs strongly affirm patriotism and soldiers' values, which are an important part of military training and appear as themes in military recruiting efforts.

Additionally, both songs involve themes of God and country. Like "Home of the Brave," which invokes God as a guiding force for soldiers, Knoop's "I Pledge Allegiance" was inspired by his belief in God and country: "I think God helps a lot with me anyway, in helping me put down the words that I feel I need to be down. His inspiration with this here [his song] because we believe in God and country, and with the flag, the flag is part of it. I think a lot of it has to do with feelings from God and feelings from life itself."[16] While Knoop feels that sacred inspiration guided him in composing "I Pledge Allegiance," Janel asks for God's daily guidance to soldiers in the text of "Home of the Brave."

Knoop's acoustic guitar accompaniment is indicative of the prevalence of the instrument in soldiers' musical creativity. The acoustic guitar is the most common instrument used by soldiers for playing and composing music in Iraq. According to Erik Holtan, soldiers often choose to play acoustic guitar because of the instrument's frequent occurrence in popular music genres, its ease of portability, and lack of electrical needs. Many soldiers either brought acoustic guitars with them, bought them in the Post Exchange (PX) stores on camps, or had them sent from home.[17] In some instances, those with little or no experience playing guitar, like Holtan's sergeant major, purchased an acoustic guitar and instruction manuals online:

People would have guitars, they buy either over there or they would buy them online and get them sent over. And then order some guitar lessons online and order a DVD and go ahead and take lessons in their room once they had a DVD player. . . . My sergeant major and another one of the guys who was cohorts with me, they bought guitars online—acoustic guitars—and bought a bunch of instructional CDs that they wanted to learn from. They were kind of into it when I left, but I know that a lot of them [other soldiers] tried to bring guitars over. And usually they go home on leave and then bring them back off leave because you don't know what you can bring over. Then you go over there and you're like, "I can bring my guitar back." Acoustic guitars are really big because it's pretty portable. It's bigger, but it's portable. You can play it, you don't need an amp. You don't need to plug this thing in.[18]

It is a regular pastime for many soldiers to play and write music on an acoustic guitar during downtime in Iraq.

The acoustic guitar also appears as a common instrument for church services held in camp chapels. Holtan recalls that the chapels, which typically serve different religious denominations, are "well equipped with the latest gear for putting a jam band together for church, or even for fun," with musical instruments provided by the chaplains or by the military division of Morale, Welfare, and Recreation (MWR). Holtan, a drummer, occasionally played on the drum sets at various chapels.[19] The musical environment of religious services is particularly active, as various Christian denominations have their own musicians and bands. Jennifer Atkinson says that the Catholic services she attended usually had a couple of acoustic guitars and bass, while "the Protestant services, they had a lot more musical—I don't want to say they had more musical presence [than the Catholic services]—but they certainly had more people who would step up and play. They had what they called 'praise band services' where it was much more musically oriented, and you would have entire ensembles that would play. There were a lot of gospel groups that would get together. In Camp Taji, we actually had a Christian extravaganza or Christian celebration."[20] Both Holtan and Atkinson noted that many soldiers who were not religious often came to the services just to hear the live music.

Another example of acoustic guitar-based music composed by soldiers is *In the Hours of Darkness* (2007), an album by Joshua Revak. The lyrical themes of the album primarily reflect his experiences of war and include songs he wrote for soldier memorial services in Iraq. Revak stowed his acoustic guitar in a vehicle deployed with his battalion, and he would play and sing with other soldiers. When a close friend of someone with whom he performed was killed, they wrote a song in response and the battalion commander asked them to play it at the memorial service. In an interview, Revak describes how he came to perform his music at the memorial services and how the album originated (see figure 5.1).

Revak:

I brought my guitar right off from the beginning. I stuck it into the vehicle that we were deploying with. I got the off-records ok—the off-the-record ok—by my supervisor and so I stuck a guitar in there and I had it the

whole time. When we had time, I would sit around and play and a lot of times there would be people who would come and sit and listen. Then, I had a friend [Sgt. Aaron Jagger] who sang with me and we wanted to do some stuff for the battalion, you know, play music and things. We lost our first friend, we lost a real close friend—the guy that sang with me, one of his best friends—and we were just devastated, his name was Michael Woodliff. We were devastated and so we wrote a song, and the sergeant major heard it and wanted us to play it at the memorial. We ended up doing that and I've ended up playing at every memorial since. A lot of them have been close friends of mine. One of them was my best friend [Jagger] who used to play memorials with me and then he was killed, so I had to play at his [memorial service]. . . . What motivated me in the album is definitely these memorials—my friends. I've lost so many friends now that I don't even know where to start. Then, the memorials didn't get any easier, they just got harder and harder to do. Eventually it was closer and closer friends that were dying and actually the last time I saw one of my friends, was me and him played music at a memorial service. Then I got

FIGURE 5.1A–B. *In the Hours of Darkness*, album cover *(opposite)*, and Joshua Revak playing acoustic guitar in Iraq

wounded. Shortly after I got wounded, I was notified that he [Jagger] was killed, so we then ended up playing at his memorial. That right there—he was my music teacher too—so that right there, that was my motivation. It was time to do something. So I decided to do whatever it takes to do an album, and give it a shot. I'm sure that is what he would have wanted.[21]

"The Song" is a slow, major mode, folk-style song composed by Revak in memory of Jagger.[22]

"THE SONG," *IN THE HOURS OF DARKNESS* (2007), REVAK
Words can't say how much you mean to me
I wipe my face, but the tears stay
The song seems over before we play
When you went away
And always with coffee made for two
With my guitar to play a tune with you
But I wait there alone.

Don't let the song be over

I'm still trying to play along
And now they're talking about you going home
Don't let the song be over
I'll practice everything you taught, I promise
I'll try not to let you down.

And I wish I could have just one last coffee at midnight
I'd ask you how to smile in the toughest times
You showed me how to live my life on gummies and coffee grounds
I could climb a mountain out in Palmer, play with the little kids in India
Like I planned with you, but I'm alone.

Don't let the song be over
I'm still trying to play along
And now they're talking about you going home
Don't let the song be over
I'll practice everything you taught, I promise
I'll try not to let you down.

God give me peace because I don't understand
Why you let them take such good men
Give me joy because I can't smile right now
See I've forgotten how
He had the time to spend down here on earth
But it wasn't enough for me, for whatever it's worth, no.

Don't let the song be over
To live in Christ, to die is gain
I know I'll see you again.

Don't let the song be over
I'm still trying to play along
And now they're talking about you going home
Don't let the song be over
I'll practice everything you taught, I promise
I'll try not to let you down.

Many of Revak's lyrical themes serve as a means of coming to terms with the grief of losing his friends and paying tribute to their memory. Unlike "I Pledge Allegiance" or "Home of the Brave," most of the songs on Revak's album are not explicitly patriotic, but represent a way of honoring the soldiers who were killed from Revak's battalion. Revak claims that he is undecided in his views about the war: "I am not PRO IRAQ war, but not sure that I am ANTI IRAQ war, but rather undecided" (emphasis in original).[23] He hopes that fellow soldiers will find solace in the music and allow themselves to grieve for their fallen friends as a way of healing: "When we played at memorials, no one cried, no one mourned. They need to do that. Mourn your losses. Don't be ashamed to cry and mourn. . . . My purpose is to help people cry, mourn, and to heal."[24] While Revak composed most of his songs on acoustic guitar in Iraq, he recorded the larger part of the album during his recovery in Germany.

The harsh realities of the Iraq War often compel soldiers to write lyrics that graphically depict events and emotions they have experienced in the combat field. In *Soundtrack to War*, Gittoes interviews a young soldier, Bradley Corkins, who talks about his love for gore metal and plays a distorted electric guitar riff he composed based on an A harmonic minor scale. Corkins feels that the lyrics of gore metal, which primarily depict the grotesque, reflect his experiences of combat. The soldier began writing lyrics to his gore metal song after he had to remove a fellow soldier killed in an IED attack and the dead soldier's body began to fall into pieces. He says that the lyrics, "I sold my soul to thee, hell has started for me," comment on his wartime experience, "basically joining the Army, I feel I sold my soul to the Army, they are in charge of me until I get out. 'Hell has started for me' was the day we got out here to Iraq."[25]

Soldiers also express the challenges of life in Iraq through rap. Monica Davey reported for the *New York Times* in February 2005 that "freestyle" rap, a rap form with improvised lyrics, was common among soldiers.[26] She quotes *Gunner Palace* director Michael Tucker as saying that "rap has become another part of barracks culture. As far as soldiers go, rap is almost the perfect medium: they are able to say so much, to let off steam and also to have so many hidden meanings in what they say."[27] Soldiers gather in groups, sometimes in a circle, and take turns rapping mostly about the war. In many ways, rap lends itself well as a compositional genre for soldiers; it requires no instruments, and the percussive, spoken vocal style does not require the ability to sing. When compared to acoustic guitar music, freestyle rap can be performed more widely by soldiers. *Soundtrack to War* includes numerous scenes in which soldiers gather to perform freestyle rap. Private First Class Elliott Lovett, who goes by the music name "L'il E," improvised the following rap:[28]

FREESTYLE RAP, LOVETT, AKA "L'IL E"

I'm gonna tell 'em like this, this out here, this for real
Them boys don't even know what it be out here in the field

Its boys gettin' killed, and it's like everyday
But I let them boys know, up top, these boys don't play
They comin' with AKs, we comin' with M-16s
Our boys know, up top, shootin' and they means in they spleen
Expert marksmanship, I shot them straight in their lip, I'm fully equipped
Fuck with my battle, rattle with my hip
And I tell just like this, I don't play with nobody
Fuckin' with L'il E, I come just like John Gotti
Y'all niggas can't fuck with me, I'm on another level
Y'all boys don't know, I'm like the fuckin' devil
I'm the rebel, I'm the answer, I'm like black cancer
Y'all niggas, here we go, I'm like a black panther
Doin' dirty like, I'm damn near dynamite
Can't fuck with my skills, because my shit be tight
I'm out here every day and I'm goin' on God
This life is so hard, I'm on my knees at night prayin' to God
I'm like, "oh my Lord," cause it get deeper than ever
Y'all boys be listenin' to my lyrics, shit, stay clever
Stayin' on my mind, my baby girl, my pearl
Thinkin' about my wife, my life, this is my world
Up in Iraq, oh, we got to have each other's back
Because if you muthafuckin' get respect, let's turn it off.

From the opening phrases, Lovett states that he is going to explore the realities of soldier life in Iraq and reveal aspects of daily existence that are not generally known. He contextualizes the forthcoming words as an exposition of "real" soldier life.

Lovett's lyrics cover a range of topics, from the stress of combat and violence to missing his wife and child. He expresses feelings of violent superiority and animosity toward his enemies in the combat field, but then quickly shifts his focus to prayer for strength and thoughts of his family. The diversity of lyrical themes in his freestyle rap reflects a spectrum of intense emotions, and this is largely consistent with how soldiers describe their day-to-day existence. Many soldiers I interviewed said that they felt anxiety about possibly being killed in combat and the heightened awareness necessary on combat missions. But they also dwelled on thoughts of family and home within the more peaceful and secure setting of military camps. Lovett's rap captures the range and intensity of emotions felt by many soldiers.

In response to the considerable amount of music written by soldiers, the Dallas Songwriters Association (DSA) sponsored an amateur popular songwriting competition in 2006, in which military personnel were invited to submit original songs. The winners in each category of submission (pop, inspirational, jazz/world, country, hip-hop/rap, novelty, and instrumental) contributed their compositions to a CD released by the DSA, *Songs from the Soul of Service: A Collection of Songs Written by US Soldiers, Sailors, Airmen, and Marines.* Like the songs discussed in this section, the CD demonstrates a wide variety of thematic and musical content. Songs range from pop hits about soldiers in Iraq, like Mike Corrado's "On my Watch," to a hip-hop/rap song, "Ballad of the Hot Mic" by Billy G. Robertson Jr., that does not explicitly reference the war.[29]

Popular music, however, is not the only musical style through which soldiers express themselves. Jason Sagebiel studied classical guitar and music composition at Loyola University in New Orleans before being deployed. While in Iraq, he completed a piece of contemporary classical art music, "Salvation," for two sopranos and classical guitar based on a poem he had written. The poetry is accompanied by Sagebiel's program notes for the work:

"Salvation," by Sagebiel

Ah, Lingering, Have we ceased to move?
And slowly we here begin again.
But how shall we go again when our Traditions
Did die in war?
Not knowing why it was that we were, our
Future will be just as bleak.
And human progress will be undone,
Unless we pray to God and seek to know.

Program Notes

This piece, though begun in 2002, was formally completed in May of 2003 when I was serving in Iraq. My text explores the relationship of faith in the Divine to the understanding of the mundane world. It captures the melancholy I felt knowing that the world can be such a violent and terrible place, but offers a bit of hope based on trust in the Eternal. I once was distraught about our worldly situation and felt a bit apocalyptic about the status quo, but I now believe that "'twas ever thus," for whatever consolation that is worth. Since violence and war have been the history of the world, the harmony of the piece functions as a passacaglia, remaining unchanged throughout its entirety. As time and the piece progress, the harmony recurs manifesting itself in different ways (transposition or inversion) until the final statement of the passacaglia where a single note is added to the harmony. It is to say that though this has been our history, perhaps we can add just something small to make it better. A friend of mine, a musician who also had some military experience, knowing he would lose his American citizenship, volunteered to fight in one of the many rebellions in Africa, but was turned down by the group he approached because they thought he could make more of a difference as an artist by bringing light and awareness to their situation. They believed that his voice could do more for their cause than he could do with a single gun in his hand, and a knife on his side. It is enlightening to understand that some fighting men believe that fighting is not the solution but have no alternative. My prayer is that this piece can be that alternative, that something more, however small it might really be. May we be that one note added to the harmony, that bit of change, that bit of hope added to the history of the globe.

Sagebiel was one of the few classically trained soldier composers I encountered in my research. Unlike many other soldiers, though, he was musically limited to what he could acquire in Iraq. His experience with music was unique due to his job as an assistant scout-sniper team leader. The large amount of equipment he and his team had to keep with them restricted the comfort gear, such as musical instruments and music players, they could carry: "We're allowed to have things, I guess, if I wanted to bring music I probably could, we just had so much operational gear. All of the duties of an infantry squad, which is thirteen people, were now reduced down to three people, so you might have gear and communications equipment you have to carry, so it's just prohibitive."[30] But this did not prevent him from pursuing music-related activities. In one instance, he broke a loading palette and whittled it into the shape of a guitar neck. Adding parachute cord, he constructed a semi-functional guitar. Although it made no sound, the instrument allowed him to practice fingering patterns.[31] Sagebiel also made his own music paper by drawing staff lines on pieces of paper, including on official Saddam Hussein government letterhead.

Most significant, during his time in Al-Kut, in the eastern Wasit province, he was able to study 'ud, a stringed instrument somewhat smaller than a guitar, popular in the Middle East and other parts of the world, with an Iraqi teacher, Ali. Upon hearing that Ali was a gifted 'ud teacher, Sagebiel went to the municipal building in Al-Kut where Ali worked as a computer programmer and asked to study with him. When he had free time, Sagebiel would take 'ud lessons from Ali and also studied Arabic music, scales, and composition. Figure 5.2 presents a set of Arabic scales written by Ali to assist Sagebiel in his 'ud studies, and a document on official Saddam Hussein government letterhead that Sagebiel wrote for Ali to help him understand the structure of diatonic modes in Western classical music.

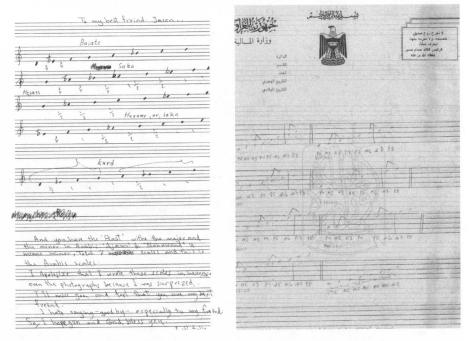

FIGURE 5.2A–B. Arabic scales by Ali, and diatonic modes by Jason Sagebiel

SOLDIERS RECORDING MUSIC

Recent advances in audio technology now allow soldiers in Iraq to record their music with greater ease and quality. Software programs like GarageBand, Fruity Loops, and ACID Pro provide recording platforms for small laptop computers, enabling soldiers to easily record, mix, and edit their music with a single microphone. Such was the case when Arkansas National Guardsmen Nick Brown and David Schultz began writing acoustic guitar songs during their free time. When members of their battalion expressed an interest in obtaining recordings of their songs, Schultz downloaded an audio program, n-Track Studio, from the internet.[32] Then he borrowed a plastic microphone originally intended for internet voice communication from one of the other soldiers and started recording songs. Brown and Schultz compiled their songs into an album, *Iraq Unplugged* (2005; see figure 5.3).[33]

The highly varied, original music on the album is thematically based on their experiences in Iraq. "All I Really Miss is You," for example, reflects

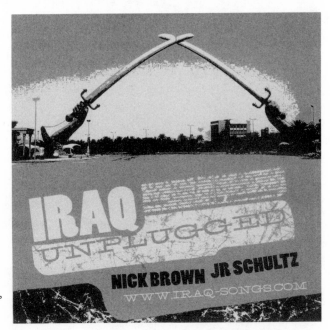

FIGURE 5.3A–C. Nick Brown, David (JR) Schultz, and the *Iraq Unplugged* album cover

upon missing one's spouse during deployment, and "When Daddies Don't Come Home" is about the children of men killed in Iraq. "The Ballad of Ahmed Razooki" tells the story of an Iraqi man trying to raise his family in the violence of war, while "Blame It On the ING" is a humorous song about the difficulties of working with the Iraqi National Guard (ING). Schultz said that the album is intended to cover the wide spectrum of emotions that soldiers experience in Iraq.[34] While *Iraq Unplugged* expresses a diversity of lyrical themes, the album transmits these messages through a single stylistic genre, acoustic guitar folksong. Below, Schultz describes the inspiration for the album.

Schultz:

He [Nick Brown] had written some songs, so we played them for each other and that was early in the deployment. From then on, every time we would get together and play, one of us would have started one, or had written a song. We got to playing them back and forth, and some people would come by and listen to us play and that's kind of how it got kicked off. Every time one of us would get inspired by something, we would sit down to write a song and that's kind of how it got started. We had basically written all of our songs during the first six months of deployment. . . . We didn't have any plans on making an album out of it—we were just kind of passing the time. We really didn't have any plans on recording it until some guys would hear it and they'd say, "Man, I need a copy of that, you should find out a way to record that." It wasn't until then that I got online one night and found some digital recording software and down-loaded it to my laptop. We had a little plastic microphone, a ten-dollar microphone that a guy bought at Best Buy before he came over—he thought he might be able to use it for voice chat on the internet. That's what all our recording went through, a program called n-Track studio and a plastic microphone.[35]

While the majority of music on the album is original, these soldiers continue the long-standing military tradition of parody songs with "Mortaritaville," a parody of Jimmy Buffett's "Margaritaville."

"Mortaritaville," *Iraq Unplugged* (2005), Brown and Schultz

Livin' on pound cake, while my MRE bakes
All of my gear is covered in dust
Strummin' my six string, under the palm trees
Smell hadji comin' from a mile away.

Wasted away again in Baghdad
Searching for my plane ticket home
Some people say that Saddam Hussein is to blame
What do you think Junior? "I think it's all Rumsfeld's fault."

We don't know the reason, we're missin' deer season
Nothin' to show but a turban or two
We're just national guard, we like to drink and play cards
How we got here, we ain't got a clue.

Wasted away again in Baghdad
Searching for my plane ticket home
Some people say that Saddam Hussein is to blame
What do you think about it Brown? "I think it's all Cheney's fault."

Stepped out of the Humvee, stepped in some dookie
Now I got shit all over my boots
I don't know if it's hadji's, could be a donkey's
But it really stinks and I don't know what to do.

Wasted away again in Baghdad

Searching for my plane ticket home
Some people say that Saddam Hussein is to blame
But we know, "It's all Bush's fault."

"Salam alaikum," think I'm going to choke him
He says one more word I can't understand
He thinks it's funny, I think he's talkin' about me
Yeah, at least I don't wipe my ass in my hand.

Wasted away again in Baghdad
One weekend a month, yeah, my ass
I'd like to kick my recruiter straight square in the teeth
But I know, "It's my own damn fault."

The lyrics of "Mortaritaville" could be interpreted in different, possibly con-flicting, ways. For instance, some conservatives may take umbrage at the attacks on Bush, Cheney, and Rumsfeld. Others might find the portrayal of Iraqis as unclean to be offensive.

While it is understandable that some listeners could be offended by the sentiments expressed in "Mortaritaville," the song appears to belong to the repertoire of barracks humor, another long-standing tradition of military musical practices (besides parody) in which controversial topics are treated with humor and a deliberate lack of sensitivity. As the title implies, in *Dark Laughter* Les Cleveland provides numerous examples of songs that mock-ingly criticize political leadership, military leadership, and the opposing forces with what might be described as distasteful lyrics, but are intended to be humorous reflections on soldier life and a way of coping with soldiers' surroundings. In World War II, for instance, Cleveland noted, "A favorite marching song of British and Commonwealth troops [to the tune of 'Colonel Bogey'] claimed that the Nazi leadership was sexually abnormal: "Hitler has only got one ball, Goering has two but very small, Himmler has something similar, But poor old Goebbels has no balls at all!"[36] During the Vietnam War, Australian troops sang "Saigon Warrior II" and added the verses below to the song "Saigon Warrior" by U.S. infantry soldier Herschel Gober:[37]

Oh the rules of engagement are something else too,
You can't shoot a dink unless he shoots at you,
For all of the murders we'd like to commit,
We end up with footprints all over our dick!

After considering the various interpretations of "Mortaritaville," I asked Schultz about his intentions when writing the lyrics and the possibility that listeners could be insulted. He was thankful that I posed this question be-cause he felt that others had misinterpreted the song, and he wanted to situ-ate "Mortaritaville" within the tradition of barracks humor songs. In an e-mail, he explained:

> The lyrics to Mortaritaville are completely meant to be taken as a joke and not a political stance of any kind. The knocks at our country's leadership just made an easy target at the time and fit so well with the theme of the song we had to include it. Although I think all soldiers can identify with the lyrics, I wrote them more through the eyes of a reserve soldier (as I was) to reflect the transition from the pre-9/11 mindset of reservists which is best summarized by a quote from my recruiter back in 1997: "The National Guard is only deployed for Tornados and you get money for college." That being said, we were all eager to answer the call and have a great deal of pride in our service. I think we made such a swift transition from civilian life to war in Iraq, that sometimes we found ourselves wondering, "How did I get here?" and I think it comes out in the song. . . . The mention of the Iraqis in the song is just a generalization that many who have been there understand. Of course it doesn't apply to all and isn't meant as an attack on their character. I happen to have worked daily with the Iraqi National Guard and came to have great respect for several of the soldiers, including the interpreters who worked with our unit.[38]

The range of interpretations and reactions to "Mortaritaville" also points to one of the many challenges of not being able to pursue onsite fieldwork. Like most military institutions, the U.S. military is a distinct culture with its own set of social norms separate from civilian life. In fact, many sol-diers speak about the difficult transition to civilian life after leaving the military, and the government has established service programs, such as the Department of Veterans Affairs Transition Assistance Program (TAP), to help soldiers adjust to the differences of life as a civilian. These differences are even more profound in the context of deployment; soldiers' lives in Iraq are part of a unique barracks culture. Understanding this barracks culture would provide a more in-depth context for "Mortaritaville," but unfortu-nately, I cannot offer insights based on experience about the barracks culture in Iraq or even engage in detail the important differences that seem to exist between non-deployment military life and civilian life. My research was lim-ited such that I was not only a non-participant/non-member of the group I was studying, but was unable to assume the role of direct observer. This is not to make excuses for what some readers may find to be objectionable and offensive lyrics; rather, knowing barracks culture would have proven invaluable to this book in many ways, and the interpretative framework of "Mortaritaville" is a good example of how onsite fieldwork would have allowed me to gain much-needed insight into some of the important contexts that frame some soldiers' music making.

Another instance of soldiers recording music is *Baghdad Music Journal* by William Thompson. Thompson studied piano and jazz at the University of New Orleans and was a professional musician before being called to active duty. Knowing that he would have limited or no access to a piano during his tour, Thompson explored other options for musical creativity in Iraq. He bought a Mac Powerbook G4 and music software, which he used to compose electronically. Using the voice recorder on his iPod to record sounds from the field and his surroundings, Thompson incorporated these samples into an electronic style of music composition. "Follow Our Orders," for instance, takes Arabic dialogue samples from a CD that was given to the soldiers by the U.S. Army to help them learn common Arabic phrases. Thompson looped a sample from this CD and also incorporated a recording of his conversation with an Iraqi man about the war. These samples were then arranged against a musical backdrop of repetitive piano, percussion, and computer-generated sounds with a free, almost atonal, piano improvisation produced through his MIDI keyboard (www.wativ.com). In "Post Election News," Thompson recorded radio static and sound samples from an Iraqi radio broadcast on the night of George W. Bush's reelection in 2004. The static and radio broadcast samples weave in and out of the musical texture, consisting mainly of a low underlying drone, a repeated percussion sound, and a "free," Vibraphone-sound improvisation, which is based on his transcription of the speech patterns (see figure 5.4).

Much of the music on *Baghdad Music Journal* reflects Thompson's training as a university-educated musician. In addition to the influence of improvisation derived from his profession as a jazz pianist, his compositions seem to fall into the category of "computer music" as understood in the Western classical art music tradition. Thompson's music falls outside of conventional popular genres, and his creative perspective is informed by a John Cage-like aesthetic on the relationship between music and sound: "I think that everything in nature has a pattern; why wouldn't also the sounds that come from it have a pattern? So in my opinion, everything in sound is music."[39] The circumstances of being a soldier in Iraq seem to have influenced him into adopting this compositional perspective because his instrument of musical expression, piano, was not available. Thompson admits not being familiar with computer-based, or electronic music, before being deployed, but he developed an interest in this musical style because it provided possibilities for creativity and expression in Iraq as recorded music.

Like Schultz and Brown, Thompson wanted to express the range of his

Figure 5.4a–b.
William Thompson
and the *Baghdad
Music Journal*
album cover

experiences in the music he composed. However, unlike these soldiers, he says that the artistic statement behind his music does not explicitly express personal views on politics, patriotism, or aspects of military life. Thompson's views, analogous to the textual themes in the other soldiers' music, are symbolically cast within the music, and his pieces musically express the complexity of issues surrounding the war:

My idea from the beginning was to convey one soldier's experiences in the Iraq War for an audience to interpret freely. I had no political agenda. If you buy the record and read any of it, there is nothing in there that says anything about whether the political situation—the war is good, or the war is bad. Obviously, we all know that all war is bad, but whether we should be there or not? I have my own opinions of course, but I wanted to let people listen to the music. I think that somebody can listen to the music and be opposed to the war, and also be for the war. The bottom line is that I just wanted people to try and get the idea without me having to say anything. I definitely have opinions and they are definitely in the music, but that [people listening to the music] would be ideal.[40]

One of the most intricate examples of soldiers recording music in Iraq can be seen in the case of 4th25, a group of soldiers led by Neal Saunders, including Sgt. Edward "Greg-O" Gregory, Staff Sgt. Terrance Staves, Specialist Michael "Paperboi" Davis, Sgt. Ronin Clay, and Specialist Michael Thomas. With the exception of Staves, these soldiers were part of Taskforce 112 of the 1st Cavalry Division at Fort Hood, Texas, and deployed to Iraq in March 2004. They were stationed in Camp War Eagle near the Baghdad neighborhood of Sadr City for one year. While in Iraq, Saunders wanted to produce a rap album about soldiers' experiences. He describes 4th25 not as a "rap group," but as a collection of soldiers who came together to record an album around his creative vision.[41] Saunders spent his military paychecks on recording equipment, and after a retail music store, Sam Ash in Philadelphia, agreed to send him the equipment, he set up a small studio and taught himself how to use the software and hardware. Saunders lived in a 30×30 room with eight or nine other soldiers and arranged an 8×4 booth in the corner of the room. So as not to disturb his fellow soldiers who had given up their own space for Saunders's improvised studio, he and the other members of the group created a makeshift soundproof booth using foam padding from shipping packages and old, flower-adorned exercise mats. Once the studio was ready, Saunders and the rest of the group began recording songs and produced a fifteen-song album, *Live from Iraq* (figure 5.5).

Below, Saunders describes how the motivation for the album arose from his personal transformation upon experiencing the Iraq War as an American soldier.

Saunders:

[It] started out as a necessity. It wasn't anything we wanted to do, it was something we felt like we had to do . . . me personally, like before we were going I'd be like, "You know, hey, if I die in service to my country that's a wonderful thing. That's good." And that's just you pretending, that's you basically holding your breath, telling people that it will be ok, or you ain't afraid to die or some shit. But to be honest, yeah, you can say all that but as soon as we got there and I started seeing how these people are dying, and the ways that they're dying, it's like, "Fuck that, I do not want to die, not like this." It puts you in a situation where that survival mode kicks in. And then it's nothing like what you ever thought it was ever going to be. There's a lot of emotion in that, there's a lot of power in that. And that is really what we wanted to get. And that's really what made me want to do this, because I had one set of beliefs before I left and then just as I got there, just everything that I knew constantly changed every day. So it was like an awakening over there for me. Probably after the third or fourth ambush we got in was really bad—in comparison, they're all bad, but the third or fourth, something was a bit more like, "Yes, today might be the day kind of thing." And that's when I was really like, "You know what? Fuck it, we've got to do this album."[42]

The songs on the album provide an in-depth look at the challenges faced by Saunders and the other soldiers while serving in Iraq, from the emotions of saying goodbye to loved ones before leaving ("The Deployment") to spousal infidelity while deployed ("Dirty"). The lyrical themes of the album explore many of the difficult aspects of soldier life in a way similar to Lovett's freestyle rap or Corkins's gore metal song. For example, in "24 Hours," Saunders addresses the contradictions of his mission as a soldier, his frustrations with the U.S. Army and the Iraqi people, and his perspectives on the problems of the U.S. occupation of Iraq. He feels that soldiers are governed by unrealistic and contradictory guidelines that limit their ability to fulfill their duties.[43] Saunders explains that he was sent to Iraq as a soldier, but was asked to smile and act like a cultural ambassador to the same Iraqi people who were exploding IEDs against him and other soldiers. The song also reveals Saunders's view that the Iraqi people have not taken responsibility for themselves. He feels that some members of the civilian population

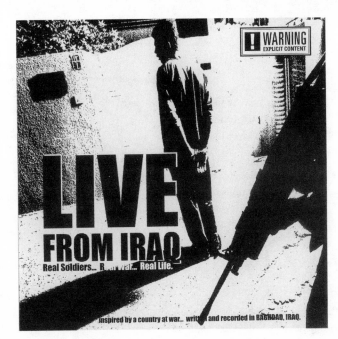

FIGURE 5.5.
Live from Iraq
album cover

assist and lie for the benefit of the insurgents, and he considers them responsible for their actions, not innocent bystanders. Saunders believes that because Saddam Hussein ruled in such a brutal way, Iraqis are not willing or able to assume responsibility, and he feels that the only way to establish order in Iraqi society is to revert to a Hussein-like "iron fist," where stability was created out of fear of violence and death.

"24 HOURS," 4TH25, *LIVE FROM IRAQ*

You people complain about the way things are now
You have no idea how lucky you really are
If I had this motherfucker for 24 hours
There would be things that would change.

Everybody's responsible, there's no more outs
Withhold information, takes to see 'em out
I don't feel for this nation, nor give fucks about 'em
They shoot from a mosque, then I'm blowin' 'em out it
No sympathy here, behind it they hide
Now either they calm down, or everyone dies
There is no in between, no neutral side

So when co-axles flyin', please don't ask me why
When we kick in your door, there is no alibi
Everybody is guilty until proved otherwise
Cause they know when to close and open their eyes
Yeah, they know when to run before their enemy ride
And at times their women be right by their side
Their kids in the streets lightin' tires on fire
Regardless of sex or age, I'm gonna retire 'em
In 24 hours, this place will be fine again.

Though I'm asking a lot, but please give me this one thing
Then one day I promise a million things will change
No problems, I swear, they'll throw in their towel
Just give me this country for 24 hours.

IEDs in the street, who shot me in front of 'em
Burn this shit to the ground, 'cause you got to know somethin'
Population in the millions, but no one knows nothin'
Light 'em up 'til they talk, if they won't talk, fuck 'em
They too will change, when you kill enough of 'em
Police, they own shit, and we will not fuck with 'em
Either that, or we reach out and touch 'em
So speak out against it or be part of the problem
Me, I hold everyone liable, there is no exceptions
Especially when you lie for 'em
They run the streets and I will let you die for 'em
Peek around through the door from the house they're hidin' in
Fuck all what's around, nothing's collateral
Damage was done when you let them live around you
Keep launching mortars, artillery pound you
For 24 hours, 'til we force the peace out of you.

Though I'm asking a lot, but please give me this one thing
Then one day I promise a million things will change
No problems, I swear, they'll throw in their towel
Just give me this country for 24 hours.

'Cause right now they got us feedin' the same motherfuckers that's bleedin' us
I don't know, it's like a game to them, it's not a game to me
I'm takin' this shit ever so seriously
Some of you will probably never know how seriously I'm takin' it.

These lyrics may strike some readers as overwhelmingly violent and hostile to the Iraqi population, and one may be shocked at how Saunders advocates crushing noncompliant resistance, creating peace through violence and fear. I asked Saunders to comment on these lyrics to better understand the context of his words.

He reemphasized that the motivation for "24 Hours" came from a variety of frustrating and contradictory situations experienced during his deployment. For example, he recalled a night when a curfew was issued and members of his unit were overwatching a main supply route to guard against attacks, but when they noticed a man digging at night, the sergeant major decided not to pursue action against him. The next day, an IED attack was exploded against a convoy. Incidents such as this compelled Saunders to write the song; in the following interview excerpt, he explains many of the circumstances of his deployment that inspired the attitudes expressed in "24 Hours."

Saunders:

There is so much shit happening here, so much bullshit behind what is happening. I mean, it's like, shit will blow up or some shots will get popped and everyone will just stand around looking. You just want to shoot, it's just a natural response. You want to shoot anybody you can see because you know that somebody just tried to kill you. And you see so many people and you're just like, "I don't know who it was, but everybody's going to fuckin' die for it." And sometimes, honestly, you feel that way. But then they start telling you, "If you don't see a weapon, you can't shoot." . . . Being there and actually seeing that shit first hand, you see that these people don't take responsibility for themselves, and only because Saddam beat that shit out of them. But as a result, now we have to put that responsibility back in them. So "24 Hours" is huge. It's like, you can't send me over there with a gun and then tell me not to shoot anything, and these people need to be expecting that if they do anything I don't like, I'm going to fuckin' shoot them. You almost have to have that same iron fist, I think, that Saddam had over them. They wouldn't do shit for fear of their life. But now these dudes will come out and do coordinated strikes on us? I just feel like we had to do something and my hands were being tied behind my back. They won't let me shoot, but these guys keep coming at us. So yeah, you give me this place for 24 hours and I'll make people act right, and a lot of people are going to die behind that shit. And it would work, I don't care what nobody says. I've seen it first hand, so people can do all the studies that they want to do and ask all the people in a relatively sane environment, "Would this work? Would this be effective?" And it's all bullshit because the bottom line is that once those guns start popping off and people start falling, and there's blood everywhere, motherfuckers start paying attention then. That's when they do what you tell them to do.[44]

The song's violent attitudes appear to come from Saunders's reaction to his surroundings where he feels, among others things, limited in his ability to defend himself and frustrated with those who aid the insurgency. He pointed out that the severity of his position is largely shaped by the life or death consequences he faced when performing his duties in Iraq.[45] Even if one has difficulty understanding Saunders's perspectives, "24 Hours" provides a unique look into the complex experiences of a soldier's life in Iraq.

For the soldiers of 4th25, the music also serves as a symbolic tribute to the men and women in the military who presently serve or have been killed. While none of the songs directly honor the memory of fallen soldiers in the same way as the music on Revak's album, *Live from Iraq* is dedicated to soldiers, both living and those killed in action. The album liner notes contain no names or photographs of individual group members, lyrics, or credits. Rather, the liner notes display graphic photographs of people killed in the war, photographs of soldiers at memorial services, and a single line of text written by Saunders: "Death? The vehicle through which we preserve our own life." He explains that a photograph in the album insert, which shows a tear on a soldier's face, expresses the remorse of a soldier as he looks out upon the carnage he has created, "because he doesn't want to have to do it, but the quote then tells us how it is that he can turn into what he needs to turn into."[46] After returning from Baghdad, the group had the album mastered, printed, and duplicated, and currently promotes it through web-based vehicles like myspace.com, iTunes, and CD Baby.

Although clearly diverse, these lyrical themes addressing the war and musical styles of soldiers' compositions share a common thread. The soldiers suggest that their motivation to write music comes from their experiences of war, and the act of creating music is a way for them to express their feelings, frustrations, and emotions. While Janel's "Home of the Brave" differs greatly from Lovett's freestyle rap in terms of musical style and textual content, both provided an emotional release for the soldiers' feelings about the war. In reference to freestyle rap, Specialist Javorn Drummond says it "is the one place where you can get out your aggravation—your anger at the people who outrank you, your frustration at the Iraqi people who just didn't understand what we were doing. You could get out everything."[47] Revak said that working on *In the Hours of Darkness* became a vital outlet during his recovery process. In June 2006, Revak was injured when a 120mm mortar shell landed close to where he was standing in Ramadi, and he was sent to Germany to recover from his injuries:

It's been huge, I don't know what I would do without it [the album]. Because the album has been my life since I was on convalescent leave—I can't walk very good. If it weren't for that, I don't really know what I would do. The idea of this album has been huge. It's just a way to get everything off my chest, you know? And a good half of the album is memorial songs. So I just really wanted to get it off my chest. Music has always been an outlet for me.[48]

Many soldiers feel that writing or recording music is a necessary act of expression or something they must do to handle their experiences in war. For Schultz, writing and recording his songs helped him express emotions that he would not have otherwise communicated. His family was surprised to find out that he had written music because he says that he is not a particularly expressive person.[49] The song "The Day You Were Born" was especially meaningful to his family since the lyrics reflect upon his absence at the birth of his son due to his deployment in Iraq.

In these ways, one might consider the songs written and recorded by soldiers to be a form of audio journaling or audio blogging. Many of the songs are inspired by their daily experiences and operate as vehicles through which soldiers express their feelings and reactions to events in Iraq. The title to Thompson's album, *Baghdad Music Journal,* reflects the idea that the music is a diary of his personal experiences expressed musically. Albums like *Live from Iraq* and *Iraq Unplugged* demonstrate a widely varied textual focus and sonically document a broad range of soldiers' emotions and experiences. And given the rise of soldier blogging, which has gone through various phases of censorship by the U.S. military, writing and recording music allows soldiers to present their own perspectives of the war apart from officially sanctioned or monitored discourse.

Music as a form of soldier expression appears to be more prevalent in the Iraq War than in previous American military conflicts. Soldiers are writing and recording music using recent technological advances in audio production, which allow music to be recorded, edited, and mixed with only a laptop and a microphone. Perhaps for the first time in history, soldiers are expressing their experiences related to war in the form of recorded songs, and entire albums are now being created within the context of the combat theater. The tradition of adaptation, which was an important part of soldiers' musical practices in previous conflicts, now exists alongside a much greater output of original music composition.

6 | Metal and Rap Ideologies in the Iraq War

The musical genres of metal and rap figure prominently in the lives of some American soldiers serving in Iraq. From the advertisements employed in military recruiting to the psychological tactics, personal expression, and pre-combat rituals characteristic of the deployment period, metal and rap appear to be an integral part of many soldiers' experiences.[1] The salience of these genres and their varied uses in the Iraq War are the result of many social, cultural, and political factors. The systems of ideas, or ideologies, expressed through these genres shape their reception and position within popular culture. In this chapter, I explore the ideologies of metal and rap in order to clarify how and why these genres came to play such important roles in the context of the Iraq War.

Throughout history, the term "ideology" has carried diverse meanings for scholars in different fields. For instance, Karl Marx described ideology, generally speaking, as the "production of ideas, of conceptions, of consciousness," which operates as the "ruling ideas" of a society and creates the structure of dominant cultural power relationships.[2] Many scholars have built upon this understanding of ideology.[3] Political scientist Mostafa Rejai believes ideology is

> an emotion-laden, myth-saturated, action-related system of beliefs and values about man and society, legitimacy and authority, acquired as a matter of routine and habitual reinforcement. The myths and values of ideology are communicated through symbols in a simplified, economical, and efficient manner. Ideological beliefs are more or less coherent, more or less articulate, more or less open to new evidence

and information. Ideologies have a high potential for mass mobilization, manipulation and control.[4]

Given the varying definitions and complexities involved in these concepts, many music scholars have limited the definition of ideology to suit their specific objectives, or adopted a somewhat flexible description. Joel Crotty and Kay Dreyfus, for example, understand ideology "to mean a set of ideas that attaches itself to music in its social and political context," a suitable definition for my purposes.[5] When I speak of metal or rap ideologies, I refer to the systems of beliefs and sociopolitical ideas represented and projected, respectively, by these musical genres.

METAL AND RAP IDEOLOGIES

At first glance, presenting a collection of beliefs that comprehensively represents metal or rap ideology may seem an impractical endeavor. These genres are highly diversified with a variety of often-opposed subgenres. In fact, the tensions among subgenres can be strong and rhetorically violent. Metal scholars Bruce Friesen and Jonathon Epstein point out that fans of thrash/death metal (Megadeth, Metallica, Slayer) typically consider fans of pop metal (Bon Jovi, Def Leppard, Whitesnake) to be "poseurs" who "have not developed an appreciation for the true aesthetic of metal, and must therefore be accorded less prestige with the subculture."[6] Likewise, Adam Krims outlines numerous rap genres, like "party rap," "mack rap," "jazz/bohemian," and "reality rap," each with its own distinct set of sociocultural contexts and musical characteristics.[7] The idea that there exists a set of aesthetic principles embodying all metal or rap music may not be sensible. Consequently, I contextualize my understanding of metal and rap ideologies in order to account for different subgenres and focus on specific aspects of these subgenres that play important roles in soldiers' musical practices in Iraq.

While metal music is rampant with hyper-individualism and conflicting subgenres, Robert Walser observes that the genre "now denotes a variety of musical discourses, social practices, and cultural meanings, all of which revolve around concepts, images, and experiences of power."[8] In her book *Heavy Metal,* Deena Weinstein examines the sociocultural aspects of metal music and similarly claims that "the essential sonic element in heavy metal is power, expressed as sheer volume. Loudness is meant to overwhelm, to sweep the listener into the sound, and then to lend the listener the sense of power that the sound provides."[9] The music operates not as a dominating force over the fan, but as an empowering agent. Throughout the metal literature, scholars like Jack Harrell, Robert L. Gross, Robert Pielke, and many others identify power as the most important concept that unifies otherwise opposed metal subgenres.[10]

The power element of metal can be discerned in a variety of ways within the music, such as the degree of guitar distortion and aspects of musical structure like vocal articulation. While power is a unifying principle shared by different forms of metal, scholars have primarily focused on musical characteristics and thematic content as a way to distinguish subgenres.[11] Walser describes metal in terms of musical features: volume, vocal timbre, mode and harmony, rhythm, melody, and guitar solos.[12] Friesen and Epstein differentiate pop metal from thrash metal according to many of Walser's categories: pop metal emphasizes a semi-vibrato vocal articulation, blues-derived harmony or Aeolian/Dorian modes, moderate-fast tempos, and syncopated guitar/bass parts; thrash metal features guttural growls and screams, Phrygian/Locrian modes, very fast tempos, little or no harmonic motion, and less syncopated guitar/bass parts.

The music and sound of metal then ascribe power to the lyrical themes of the music, which Weinstein divides into two opposing categories, "Dionysian" and "Chaotic." Dionysian themes involve "sex, drugs, and rock and roll," and focus on forms of physical gratification and ecstasy. Conversely, chaotic themes rebel against social norms and reveal a fascination with conflict, violence, and death. Pielke claims that metal songs demonstrating themes of chaos express an "attitude of negation, with its emphasis on the images of death, Satanism, sexual aberration, dismemberment, and the grotesque," to which Harrell adds images of war, destruction, decay, disillusion, pain, torture, vengeance, blood, murder, chaos, confusion, insanity, and weapons, among others.[13] Weinstein's categorization of metal lyrical themes certainly risks oversimplification, but it is useful to this study because it highlights a significant trend in metal music that is concerned with elements of war, death, and destruction. As I will show, metal subgenres that emphasize chaotic themes and more aggressive musical features, like high levels of guitar distortion and rapid, forceful bass drum and guitar/bass performance, operate more prominently in the topics I have considered.

Rap scholars have also found it helpful to distinguish among subgenres according to lyrical themes and musical features. Krims creates a method for rap genre classification by examining sociocultural function, musical styles, "flow" (rhythmic vocal delivery), and lyrical topics.[14] This framework allows

Krims to identify four main types of rap: party, mack, jazz/bohemian, and reality. Party rap, for example, consists of foregrounded rhythms for dance, consistent pitch and timbre combinations, and lyrical topics of romance, sex, celebration, pleasure, and humor; reality rap comprises more innovative rhythmic patterns, timbral "hardness," and textual themes related to difficult aspects of urban life, racial discrimination (particularly from the African American perspective), politics, religion, and didactic topics.[15] While there does not appear to be a single unifying aesthetic idea expressed among these rap genres, like power in metal, they share a common musical characteristic involving a distinct form of vocal articulation based on rhythmically driven spoken words. Some fans and enthusiasts describe rap as an acronym for "Rhythmic American Poetry," "Rhythm and Poetry," "Rhythmically Applied Poetry," or "Rhythmically Associated Poetry." These acronyms suggest that rap music texts and the style of their delivery ("flow") are critically important; Tricia Rose summarizes rap as "a form of rhymed storytelling accompanied by highly rhythmic, electronically based music."[16]

For the purpose of analyzing soldiers' musical practices in relation to my areas of study, soldiers tend to listen to "gangsta rap," a subgenre within the larger category of reality rap. Krims emphasizes that while reality rap "undertakes the project of realism, in the classical sense, which in this context would amount to an epistemological/ontological project to map the realities of (usually black) inner city life," gangsta rap "describes gang life, or more generally, life in the ghetto from the perspective of a criminal (or liminal, transgressive) figure."[17] Reality rap refers to any lyrical theme that depicts the difficulties of human existence, usually from an urban, African American perspective, but gangsta rap tends to isolate focus on lyrical themes that emphasize a "survival of the fittest" attitude in which the violence and death of the "other" (often contextualized in street life, gang life, or inner-city existence) are seen as fundamental components of one's survival. Gangsta rap's rhetorical position is typically associated with criminal or deviant behavior, misogyny, and violence in the form of murder with a firearm; the glamorization of violence and romanticization of gun culture are distinguishing features of gangsta rap within the larger category of reality rap.[18] Gangsta rap ideology also engages a power element, the power of an individual to survive and wage violence against anyone or anything that threatens survival. The texts of gangsta rap often express power through threats to destroy an enemy, and power is channeled musically through the rhythmic articulation, which tends to be the most aggressive of all rap genres. The worldview expressed in the lyrics seems to demonstrate the nihilistic attitudes Cornel

West describes as a "numbing detachment from others and a self-destructive disposition toward the world."[19]

Some aspects of gangsta rap ideology intersect with those of metal ideology. The concept of power, for example, is important to both genres, albeit in different ways. Gangsta rap often expresses power through the content of its lyrics, while power in metal is typically produced by the sound and timbres of the music itself. This is not to suggest that the timbral "hardness" of rap does not play a role in the genre's articulation of power. In his analysis of "Fight the Power" by Public Enemy, Walser proposes that the sounds of rap are an important factor in conveying power, but while timbre and sound may operate in this supportive way, many scholars have focused on the song texts as the primary manifestation of power in rap music.[20] Additionally, there is a correlation between the lyrical themes of gangsta rap and the chaotic themes of metal to the extent that they address aspects of violence and death. While gangsta rap expresses violence in terms of street life and urban struggles for survival, metal's chaotic themes engage violence in terms of war, murder (though not from a gang or inner-city rival perspective), blood, and destruction. Indeed, the textual themes of gangsta rap and chaotic metal, respectively, tend to be the most graphically violent and controversial of all popular music genres.

Because both musical styles explicitly address such topics, and in some cases glorify violence and deviant behavior, both metal and gangsta rap have been targeted by censors and restrictive legislation. In September 1985, the lyrics to songs by metal bands AC/DC ("Shoot to Thrill"), Judas Priest ("Beyond the Realms of Death"), Ozzy Osbourne ("Suicide Solution"), and others were the subject of congressional hearings initiated by the Parents Music Resource Center (PMRC). Although these hearings were intended as a fact-finding endeavor and calls for self-censorship by the music industry, many fans, musicians, and those involved with metal music interpreted the proceedings as threats to their rights of free speech. When South Carolina senator Ernest Hollings began the hearings by describing metal music as "outrageous filth, suggestive violence, suicide, and everything else in the Lord's world that you would not think of," the neutrality of the congressional panel's intentions seemed questionable.[21] The testimony given during the hearings addressed chaotic themes of violence, suicide, and death, as well as dionysian themes, such as the objectification of women and sexual exploitation, which the PMRC labeled "porn rock."[22]

After its emergence in the late 1980s, gangsta rap achieved success in mainstream popular music in the early 1990s and soon encountered legislative efforts to restrict album dissemination based on lyric content. Rap became the subject of highly publicized censorship in 1990 when 2 Live Crew's album *Nasty As They Wanna Be* was declared "obscene" by a federal judge in Broward County, Florida, for sexually explicit lyrics, particularly the song "Me So Horny." The violent themes of gangsta rap were not far behind in these censorship campaigns as a Tennessee judge later ruled that *Nasty As They Wanna Be* and NWA's (Niggaz With Attitude) *Straight Outta Compton* (1988)—one of the seminal gangsta rap albums—were obscene under state law. Since the 1990s, gangsta rappers like Ice Cube, Ice-T, Tupac Shakur, and many others have been targeted by social groups for explicitly violent and misogynist lyrics, and numerous music retailers have refused to sell their albums. Like metal, gangsta rap earned its own set of congressional hearings in 1994 to address explicit lyrical content. Kansas senator Bob Dole, former secretary of education William Bennett, and political activist C. Delores Tucker were highly critical of what they viewed as moral corruption within gangsta rap, especially during Dole's 1996 presidential candidacy.[23] A Senate hearing in 1997, "Music Violence: How Does it Affect Our Children," focused extensively on the impact of metal and rap music in relation to acts of violence.[24]

Metal and rap have generated the most controversy and public outcry in recent popular music history. Certainly the chaotic themes of metal and gangsta rap lyrics have been the focus of censorship more so than the themes of other popular music genres. Interestingly enough, soon after metal and rap became the center of the music censorship debate, the two genres began to fuse. In 1991, Public Enemy and Anthrax remade the Public Enemy song "Bring the Noise," synthesizing the rap vocal articulation (Krims's "flow") with the musical structure of metal. Other examples of such collaborations during this time include Ice-T's *Body Count* (1992), Biohazard and Onyx's remake of "Slam" (1993), and songs from the *Judgment Night* movie soundtrack (1993), which feature original songs (not remakes) performed by rap groups and metal bands such as House of Pain and Helmet, Living Colour and Run-D.M.C., Sonic Youth and Cypress Hill, Slayer and Ice-T, Biohazard and Onyx, and Faith No More and Boo-Ya Tribe. Although the idea that the two genres were the focus of censorship is not the only reason for their fusion, it certainly seems to have played an important role. In 1993, for example, the rap-metal band Rage Against the Machine expressed their own protest when they opened Lollapalooza III in Philadelphia by walking onstage naked with duct tape over their mouths and one letter of "PMRC" written on each of the chests of the four band members. They then stood motionless in front of the audience for their entire set amidst the sound of guitar and bass feedback.

The synthesis of metal and rap during the early 1990s not only illustrates a further connection between the two genres, but largely laid the foundation for a metal subgenre that has been extremely popular since the late 1990s, nü metal. This subgenre grew out of the synthesis of rap vocal articulation and the musical structure of metal. Apart from the collaborations that characterize the *Judgment Night* soundtrack, rappers began appearing more frequently on songs by metal bands. For instance, rapper Ice Cube, who was a member of NWA on *Straight Outta Compton,* appeared on the Korn song "Children of the Korn," from *Follow the Leader* (1998). The album also featured rappers Fred Durst of Limp Bizkit and Tre Hardson of Pharcyde on three of the thirteen songs. From 1998 to 2007, this synthesis style of metal and rap increased in popularity, and nü metal bands like Korn, Limp Bizkit, and Linkin Park released albums that reached #1 on the U.S. Billboard and UK Album charts. Today, however, the nü metal classification has broadened to include bands like Godsmack, Staind, and Taproot, which do not incorporate rap elements in the drums or vocals as strongly.[25]

Another common thread linking metal and rap is the public reception of these genres and the feelings of unity among fans. From my personal experience, it seems reasonable to assert that metal and rap elicit some of the strongest responses, either positive or negative, among music consumers. Ronald Botelho's comment that "hard rock has a very limited and dedicated clientele" summarizes the position of the genre within popular music, and the same can be said for gangsta rap.[26] Very few people have lukewarm reactions to this music and I have yet to meet someone who is ambivalent about Slayer or NWA. Although metal is strongly fragmented into subgenres and gangsta rap frequently witnesses feuds among artists (Dr. Dre and Eazy-E; Tupac Shakur and Biggie Smalls) or even between record companies (Bad Boy Records and Death Row Records), the negative reaction from those who dislike the music in general often strengthens the bonds and feelings of unification among fans. Writing about metal, Bettina Roccor suggests, "In spite of all their differences, what contributes considerably to the 'we feeling' of the scene is the negative perception among outsiders of the heavy metal subculture."[27] Even fans who take sides in the classic East Coast versus West Coast rivalry of gangsta rap appear united in their stance against those who criticize or dislike the genre. The negative reception of metal and gangsta rap frequently serves as an important factor in forging connections among fans, even if these fans oppose one another within the internal conflicts of the subculture. As it relates to soldiers' musical practices, this factor may indirectly impact the sense of bonding among soldiers in their pre-mission listening; the metal and rap communities generally tend to be more strongly unified in opposition to those who dislike their music than fan bases of other genres. The feelings of community within metal and rap subcultures may subtly operate in soldiers' pre-combat listening rituals.

Gender, race, and social class also operate in important ways within metal and rap. As metal scholars have shown, the genre is deeply rooted in lower/lower-middle class, white, male youth culture. In his study of the northeastern Ohio metal scene, Harris Berger demonstrates that metal in this region is strongly connected to deindustrialization and working-class disenfrachisement.[28] These issues, however, can be manifest in different ways across metal subgenres. Speaking about gender, Walser proposes, "Heavy metal as a genre includes a great variety of gender constructions, contradictory negotiations with dominant ideologies of gender that are invisible if one is persuaded by metal's critics that the whole enterprise is a monolithic symptom of adolescent maladjustment."[29] A consideration of gender in glam and thrash metal provides a good example of Walser's point. Glam metal bands, like Mötley Crüe and Poison, seem to project aspects of gender in contradictory ways. While members of these groups frequently dress in spandex or fishnet stockings, use copious quantities of hair spray, and even wear makeup, some of their song lyrics have been criticized for objectifying women in sexually explicit ways (the PMRC's "porn rock"). The feminine aspects of their image seem at odds with the sexually aggressive or even exploitative content of some lyrics. On the other hand, the lyrics of thrash metal bands, like Metallica or Slayer, rarely engage topics of love, romance, or sexual conquest, and the genre is largely characterized by a "jeans and black T-shirt" image, even among the smaller percentage of female performers and fans. Although the sociocultural fan base of metal primarily consists of lower/lower-middle class white males, the genre as a whole cannot be summarized by a single gender position or outlook.

Likewise, rap exhibits diversified attitudes about gender, race, and social class. The genre is primarily produced by young African American men, but is also consumed by a large white audience, mostly men. While "party rap" and gangsta rap are predominantly created by male artists, these subgenres express varying attitudes about women and social class. Gangsta rap can be unapologetically misogynistic and positions itself from a lower-class, ghetto point of view. Meanwhile, "party rap" typically views women as objects of romance and sexual desire, and while the subgenre maintains certain "street" roots, artists typically boast of their acquired wealth and do not position their class status within the poverty and violence of lower-class ghetto life.

The discussions that follow engage the varying ways that gender, race, and social class operate in the specific contexts of soldiers' listening and how these topics are factors in soldiers' choices of particular metal and rap songs. I examine how aspects of metal and rap ideologies operate within the music of military recruiting, as well as music as an inspiration for combat, as a psychological tactic, and as a form of soldier expression.

METAL AND MILITARY RECRUITING

The U.S. military's recent inclusion of metal songs in commercials and videos represents a significant change in the music of recruiting efforts. While the use of metal suggests a new way to musically depict the familiar recruiting strategy of action, adventure, and excitement, this dramatic shift invites an examination from the perspective of metal ideology. One of the first issues to address is why metal was chosen over other popular music genres to represent aspects of military service. In the past, military advertising employed songs by Johnny Cash, such as "Won't Back Down," and techno/electronica-influenced music, as in the air force's "No One Comes Close" commercial; however, the use of metal appears to be more widespread now, perhaps due to its associations with the concept of power. Scholars identify power as one of the most important aesthetic expressions of metal music, and the power connected to the metal sound in recruitment advertisements reflects the power of the military. Military groups are, by their nature, manifestations of power. Within most societies, military organizations attempt to display their power to self-defend and defeat an enemy, their strength to protect civilians and intimidate opposition through violence. Metal, then, "adds value" (after Chion) to the videos by signifying the overall strength of the military as an institution through metal's projection of power.

Metal music can also be interpreted as an appeal to the power of the individual. Gross mentions that "individuals who belong to the 'cult of heavy metal' are either seeking some form of power, or believe that they have found it in the music and trappings of heavy metal."[30] The connection of this music to scenes of individual soldiers in advertising videos suggests that military service enhances the power of the individual. By associating metal with military images, including guns and combat training, the music inscribes the ideological component of power to characteristics of military service, and thus seeks to attract recruits by appealing to their sense of personal empowerment.

The relationship between metal music and military recruiting may extend more deeply than these observations suggest. The power element of metal can also be understood as a reflection of the power relationships within the military itself. The power of command, obedience, and subordination is perhaps nowhere manifested more intensely than in military institutions. The hierarchical structure of military rank and superiority is largely based on power relationships of one individual over another. As Atkinson mentioned, one of the purposes of Basic Combat Training is to "very much refocus you into doing everything the way the Army wants you to."[31] Metal, then, could be seen as metaphorically signifying the power structure inherent in the hierarchy of military command, and individuals can aspire to such power by ascending the ranks of the military.

The metal music employed in advertisements fits within the military recruiting strategy of action, adventure, and excitement. As illustrated in chapter 1, metal now has strong associations with these features in television, film, MTV, video games, and sports television. Commercials and videos depicting soldiers' training exercises with a metal soundtrack display military service as an experience of action, adventure, and excitement similar to the scenes that metal often accompanies in these media. In video games and sports television, for example, metal is frequently used for the purposes of invoking an adrenaline rush. Certainly, elements of power emerge in these contexts, like the power to defeat a sports rival or a video game enemy, but the music is also intended to increase the experience of excitement for the viewer. In the majority of television and film, metal is not only associated with action, adventure, excitement, and violence, but there is also a subtle relationship between these types of scenes and aspects of heroism. Action sequences involving metal in television and film frequently present a scenario in which a protagonist triumphs over an adversary. Sometimes battered and bruised, but rarely killed, a hero almost always defeats an enemy, either through capture or death. These culturally conditioned associations may be operating at certain levels within the metal music of military recruiting. Through the metal reference, soldiers might be comparably interpreted as indestructible heroes. While I am not claiming that the military is consciously making this type or degree of reference, metal music portrayals of action and violence typically suggest a good-versus-evil conflict resulting in the defeat of an evil adversary and the survival of the protagonist. We cannot rule out that this type of connection, whether consciously made or not, could shape a viewer's interpretation of the sounds and images.

The music of military recruiting also reflects the popularity of metal subgenres. Metal encompasses vastly differing subgenres, not only in terms of sociocultural activity, but with respect to musical structure as well. A distinguishing feature of the metal music I described in the first chapter is that it mostly falls into the subgenre of nü metal. While the metal music of military recruiting adopts the less rap-influenced style, it displays many characteristics of nü metal (heavily distorted, detuned guitars and syncopated, riff-based music), as illustrated by the Godsmack songs in the navy's "Accelerate Your Life" commercials. The narrow focus on nü metal should not be surprising considering the subgenre's popularity. Since the late 1990s, nü metal has been the most popular of all metal subgenres, largely consumed by young, white men from lower-middle and middle socioeconomic levels. This demographic is also the primary target group of military recruiting.

The original texts of nü metal songs, however, are most often absent from military advertisements. Lyrics are rarely sung in soundtracks to military commercials, and in the instance of "The Creed," the words are derived from slogans and texts about army service. When the lyrical themes of the subgenre are omitted from these advertisements, the music becomes the sole means of inscribing power to the message of action, adventure, and excitement. In television and film depictions of these types of scenes, metal operates in much the same way. For the most part, lyrics are included in these soundtracks only if the words relate directly to the scene or characters in some way. In fact, musical excerpts may be used even when the original song lyrics conflict with the message of the scene. Mötley Crüe's "Live Wire," for instance, accompanies the opening action sequence to the movie *Charlie's Angels*, but a verse of the song expresses a sexually violent attitude toward women: "I'll either break her face or take down her legs. Get my ways at will, go for the throat. Never let loose, going in for the kill. Take my fist, break down walls, I'm on top tonight." This is strongly paradoxical. While the "angels" are highly sexualized and based on cinematic female stereotypes, they function as the action heroines of the movie who fight and ultimately defeat numerous male aggressors. It is puzzling why a song with lyrics about violence against women would be used in a film where women are the main action heroines. Although these lyrics are not heard in the song excerpt from the film, the example underscores the idea that the music, not text, is the most important communicator of meaning for metal music's depictions of action, adventure, and excitement.

One question I am often asked regarding music in military recruiting is why the military selected metal for recruiting efforts and not rap. This is not an easy question to answer. As outlined above, certain aspects of metal and rap ideologies overlap, and in the present popular music market, rap is no longer consumed primarily by an African American audience. Young white males purchase a significant amount of rap, particularly gangsta rap, which suggests that the genre also appeals to the military's primary recruiting pool. Considering that metal has a limited following among African American music audiences, rap might have a wider musical appeal than metal within the total framework of military recruiting. All this presents a compelling case for at least the inclusion of rap in soundtracks to military propaganda.

Yet because rap does not appear in these advertisements, I would like to explore some reasons for its exclusion. First, the concept of power functions differently in rap ideology than it does in metal. Power is the single unifying aesthetic element of all metal subgenres. While rap expresses power, it does so mainly through its lyrical themes and vocal delivery. Since military commercials typically use the music, not the texts or song lyrics, any element of power is conveyed more immediately through the sound of metal as opposed to the music of rap, which is more text-dependent. Second, metal has been employed in mainstream media depictions of action, adventure, excitement, and violence over the last twenty-five years. This distinguishes metal among popular music genres as having these associations, but also overlaps with one of the two primary recruiting strategies of military recruiting, namely, that military service is a source of action, adventure, and excitement. Rap does not convey these references as clearly as metal.

Finally, I suspect that the absence of rap from military recruiting soundtracks also involves racial perceptions of the military in U.S. culture. The use of rap in military recruiting would most likely be seen as a direct appeal to young African American males. Throughout its recent history, the military has been sharply criticized by civil rights leaders and groups for unfairly targeting African Americans and placing them in military jobs with greater risks. These criticisms were well grounded at the beginning of the Vietnam War. In 1965 and 1966, African Americans constituted 11 percent of the U.S. population, but they represented 20 percent of war casualties. The rates fell to 11.5 percent by 1969 and, overall, approximately 12.5 percent of all Vietnam War casualties were African Americans. More support for such criticisms came in the late 1970s when African American soldiers were disproportionately represented in the military. In 1979, African Americans constituted 36.7 percent of the military, more than triple their percentage of the national population.[32] Today, African Americans remain the highest represented minority ethnic group in the U.S. military, approximately 16.3 percent (compared to 11.3 percent of the population); 9.5 percent of casualties in Iraq as of March 2008 have been African American. The use of rap in military commercials and videos would likely generate significant criticism because it would be interpreted as an effort to target a minority group that has been historically overrepresented in the military.

INSPIRATION AS TRANSFORMATION

Most of the American soldiers I interviewed for this project commented that they listened to metal and rap music before going out on patrols or missions to prepare for the possibility of combat. As presented in chapter 2, soldiers frequently listen to metal or rap songs, either individually or in a group, as an inspiration for combat: Colby Buzzell said that he listened to Slayer, which "got me in the mood for it, it just gets you pumped up"; Jennifer Atkinson explained that her husband's unit would call this "getting crunked" and listened to Lil' John's "I Don't Give a Fuck" as a group before missions; C. J. Grisham and his tank mates listened to Metallica and Mudvayne, and during their assignment to Fallujah played "Go To Sleep" by DMX, featuring Eminem and Obie Trice, as a pre-mission anthem. What is it that links metal and rap music to the process of "getting crunked" before missions? How do these musical genres operate within the psychological context of combat preparation?

The discussion of musical meaning in chapter 1 provides a suitable framework for engaging these questions and understanding soldiers' reception of metal and rap. Musical meaning is constructed in highly varying ways for different listeners, and factors like age, gender, sexuality, and socioeconomic and cultural background play important roles in how listeners may interpret meaning within music. Steven Feld's work emphasizes that musical communication is a process of listener experience, whereby music exists through social construction and creates meaning through social interpretation.[33] As it relates to soldiers, their combat environment seems to largely influence how they interpret meaning in metal and rap. The songs chosen as an inspiration for combat appear to lend themselves, through timbre, performance, text, or some musical feature, to an understanding of meaning that relates to the experience of combat or violence. Tia DeNora mentions that "musical affect is contingent upon the circumstances of music's appropriation; it is, as I wish to argue, the product of 'human-music interaction,' by which I mean that musical affect is constituted reflexively, in and through the practice of articulating or connecting music with other things."[34] In this way, some soldiers connect the music to aspects of their surrounding environment, which involves combat. The social interpretation of metal and rap is constructed such that aspects of these genres "articulate" or reinforce soldiers' feelings and experiences of combat and violence. As I show, soldiers may interpret meaning in metal or rap songs in different ways than the artists themselves have intended.

Almost all the metal songs selected by soldiers as an inspiration for combat involve themes of chaos. A favorite song among soldiers is Metallica's "One," about a fictional World War I soldier, Joe Bonham, who is injured in an attack and loses his arms, legs, and the ability to see, hear, smell, and taste. "One" was popular not only among American soldiers, but as Ziv Shalev indicated, among some Israeli soldiers as well. Soldiers appear to relate to these lyrical themes of death, war, and violence as reflections of their own combat experiences. They also tend to reinterpret lyrical meanings or phrases within metal songs to suit their specific circumstances of combat inspiration. For example, the repeated refrain "Let the bodies hit the floor" to Drowning Pool's "Bodies" has adopted different meanings for soldiers than the original intent of the lyrics. The band claims that the refrain refers to the audience "hitting the floor" in the mosh pit at a concert, not bodies falling to the ground from acts of violence, which is how many soldiers reinterpret the meaning. Another example is "Angel of Death" from Slayer's *Reign in Blood* (1986). This album is credited as one of if not the seminal album of the death metal subgenre. The lyrics below were written by guitarist Jeff Hanneman to describe the experimental atrocities committed by Josef Mengele, a Nazi physician, on people at the Auschwitz concentration camp. Soldiers appear to recontextualize the song's themes of violence and death within phrases of these lyrics to apply to combat preparation.

"ANGEL OF DEATH"

Auschwitz, the meaning of pain
The way that I want you to die
Slow death, immense decay
Showers that cleanse you of your life
Forced in, like cattle you run
Stripped of your life's worth
Human mice, for the angel of death
Four hundred thousand more to die.

Angel of death
Monarch to the kingdom of the dead.

Sadistic, surgeon of demise
Sadist of the noblest blood
Destroying, without mercy
To benefit the Aryan race
Surgery, with no anesthesia
Felt the knife pierce you intensely
Inferior, no use to mankind
Strapped down screaming out to die.

Angel of death
Monarch to the kingdom of the dead
Infamous butcher
Angel of death.

Pumped with fluid, inside your brain
Pressure in your skull begins pushing through your eyes
Burning flesh, drips away
Test of heat burns your skin, your mind starts to boil
Frigid cold, cracks your limbs
How long can you last in this frozen water burial?
Sewn together, joining heads
Just a matter of time 'til you rip yourselves apart
Millions laid out their crowded tombs
Sickening ways to achieve the holocaust.

Seas of blood, bury life
Smell your death as it burns deep inside of you
Abacinate, eyes that bleed
Praying for the end of your wide awake nightmare
Wings of pain, reach out for you
His face of death staring down, your blood running cold
Injecting cells, dying eyes
Feeding on the screams of mutants he's creating
Pathetic harmless victims, left to die
Rancid angel of death, flying free.

Perhaps more important than chaotic textual themes, the notions of power inscribed in the metal sound provide a highly influential tool for soldiers as they prepare for combat. Any discussion of "sound" and "timbre" is a difficult endeavor because, as Krims points out, Western musicology has struggled to develop a method for analyzing the cultural resonances of timbre.[35] I share this concern and understanding of the theoretical limitations inherent within discussions of timbre. My approach to timbre, then, is based on analyses by David Brackett, Susan Fast, Allan Moore, and others, who have discussed timbre as a fundamental component of popular music in their works.[36] Like these scholars, I find timbre too important not to be addressed, even if the methodological grounds are still a bit uncertain.

Just as metal timbres served as the principal musical communicators of meaning in military advertisements, the sound of metal seems particularly conducive to combat inspiration, resulting from the timbres, performance style, and musical structure of specific songs. Mark Miner claims that he did not listen to metal before deploying to Iraq, but the music somehow fit his experience of war, and Buzzell mentions that he hears a direct, almost "surreal" connection between combat and Slayer's music.[37] The first issue I consider is the possible parallelism between aspects of metal music and soldiers' experiences of combat. Many metal songs that operate effectively for soldier motivation demonstrate rapid double-pedal bass drum parts and tremolo-style guitar picking.[38] "Angel of Death" provides a good example. While Slayer never made a music video for this song, video example 28 shows the band performing it live at a 1996 Ozzfest concert. Many of the guitar riffs are played at circa 210 beats per minute and involve extremely fast, tremolo guitar picking. Quite often, the double-pedal bass drum mimics the guitar tremolo, creating a sonic barrage of unyielding rhythm. Example 6.1 presents a transcription of the introductory and main riff of "Angel of Death"; the guitar rhythm is doubled at some points in the song by the double-pedal bass drum. The correlation between this music and combat, which is felt by many soldiers, derives from how the music re-creates the sense of gunfire and shooting an automatic weapon. The relentless, unsyncopated rhythm of "Angel of Death" sounds considerably like the consistent discharge of bullets fired from an automatic gun. The rhythm of the music mimics the rhythm of gunfire and the sonic experience of combat; the rapid guitar tremolos emulate the firing patterns of automatic weapons. Harrell, in fact, draws the analogy explicitly, noting that "the double bass drums create a 'machine gun' rhythm that corresponds to the overall tone of the music."[39] The element of inspiration may be created through the sense of power a soldier feels when firing an automatic weapon. The violent expression of power associated with firing a gun becomes sonically replicated in the rhythms of the music. Because these rhythms are articulated in ways that resemble gunfire, soldiers may feel empowered by the music that, for them, evokes the sounds of combat.

EXAMPLE 6.1. "Angel of Death," introductory and main guitar riff

Another important factor for conveying power in metal is guitar timbre. Most of the metal songs employed as an inspiration for combat use high levels of guitar distortion. Greater degrees of distortion within the overall guitar sound tend to operate as timbral signifiers of harshness, aggression, and sonic dissonance.[40] The general characterizations of metal as angry or assertive arise, in part, from the nature of the distorted guitar timbre. Sheila Whiteley, for instance, claims that the acoustic properties of guitar distortion "produce an 'aggressive' quality through the introduction of many high frequency harmonics."[41] The heavy guitar distortion characteristic of metal songs "pumps up" soldiers by timbrally conveying feelings of intensity and aggression. The distortion psychologically empowers soldiers by communicating an energized aggressor's mindset. In this context, power is manifested as feelings of violent superiority over an adversary through the guitar timbre.

Guitar distortion and performance style are not the only factors involved in metal inspiring soldiers for combat. Aspects of musical structure play significant roles as well. For instance, the basic unit of pitch in metal, the power chord (root and fifth), helps create an aggressive quality by reinforcing the fundamental tones of metal riffs. Power chords musically add strength or "power" to the sound, which is particularly effective with a distorted guitar timbre. Also, the primarily Phrygian/Locrian-based modality of many metal songs may evoke feelings of anger and assertion; recall that Plato believed the Phrygian mode could incite aggressive behavior. The idea that a mode can evoke different emotions may be difficult to verify empirically, but many times such meanings are culturally produced and the note structure of metal tends to emphasize dissonant relationships among pitches, particularly the half step and tritone.[42]

Finally, the vocal articulation in the metal songs soldiers listen to as an inspiration for combat typically ranges from pitched yelling to gutteral growls.[43] The yelling articulation profoundly emphasizes the sonic expression of anger, aggression, and power. Ultimately, I believe that all these factors make metal especially conducive for combat inspiration. The timbres, performance, and musical structure of metal communicate feelings of power and aggression, which operate in highly impacting ways for soldiers as they prepare for combat.

The influence of gangsta rap seems to derive more frequently from the lyrical themes rather than from timbre. While the "hardness" of gangsta rap sounds and the aggressive vocal delivery style may operate to some degree, soldiers appear to relate more strongly to the texts as an inspiration for combat. The songs chosen by soldiers tend to be the most violent within the lyrical themes of the subgenre. Grisham, for instance, said that the lyrics of "Go To Sleep" would pump them up for "the forthcoming hell of being ambushed" while stationed in Fallujah.[44] The first verse and refrain of "Go To Sleep," which he and other soldiers sang and shouted before missions, follow:

"Go To Sleep," *Cradle 2 The Grave* soundtrack (2003), DMX, featuring Eminem and Obie Trice, first verse and refrain

Eminem:
I ain't gonna eat, I ain't gonna sleep
Ain't gonna breathe, 'til I see what I wanna see
And what I wanna see, is you go to sleep, in the dirt
Permanently, you just being hurt, this ain't gonna work
For me, it just wouldn't be, sufficient enough.
'Cause we, are just gonna be, enemies
As long as we breathe, I don't ever see, either of us
Coming to terms, where we can agree
There ain't gonna be, no reasoning, speakin' with me
You speak on my seed, then me, no speak-a Ingles (English)
So we gonna beef, and keep on beefin', unless
You're gonna agree, to meet with me in the flesh
And settle this face to face, and you're gonna see
A demon unleashed in me, that you've never seen
And you're gonna see, this gangster beat on himself
I see you D-12 [a rapper], and thanks, but me need no help
Me do this one all by my lonely, I don't need fifteen of my homies
When I see you, I'm seeing you, me and you only
We never met, but best believe you gonna know me
When I'm this close, to see you exposed as phony
Come on, bitch, show me, pick me up, throw me
Lift me up, hold me, just like you told me
You was gonna do, that's what I thought, you're pitiful
I'm rid of you, all of you, Yah, you'll get it too.

Refrain:
So go to sleep bitch
Die, motherfucker die
Uh, time's up bitch, close your eyes
Go to sleep, bitch (what?)
Why are you still alive?
How many times I gotta say, close your eyes?

Go to sleep bitch (what?)
Die, motherfucker die, bye, bye motherfucker, bye, bye
Go to sleep, bitch (what?)
Why are you still alive?
Why? Die motherfucker, ha ha ha..

By listening to gangsta rap, soldiers appear to identify with the lyrical themes of violence and the survival of the fittest. The opposing forces in Iraq replace the gangsta rap "other" and become the targets of aggression and violent acts. Another example is Lil' John's "I Don't Give a Fuck," which Atkinson's husband and his fellow soldiers shouted together as an inspiration for combat. The last verse and refrain of the song further demonstrate the urban, survival-of-the-fittest attitude expressed through references to violence, guns, and a detached worldview to which the soldiers related.

"I Don't Give a Fuck," Kings of Crunk (2002), Lil' John & the Eastside Boyz, final verse and refrain

Rapper Krayzie Bone:
Y'all niggas ain't ready for this
Motherfuckers ain't steady for this
'Cause y'all still ain't learn
Nigga got a 44 [handgun] cocked and a flow so hot, make a motherfucker feel
    that burn
Niggas ain't workin' with an urn
You stay up off my dick, don't back talk, my nigga finna' [finally] get up in 'em
Back up off my dick, if you don't wanna get fucked up, then shut up the talkin'
Barkin', better block 'em off, the nigga talkin', sparkin'
Better watch and dodge, and never mind me, call it
Where the thugs at, up in this bitch?
Fuck a nigga up, y'all represent
Gimme some gin, gimme some hen [Hennessy]
No, just gimme both and I'll mix it all in
Who wanna take a lil' sip of this sin?
Let me get you twisted, man
Niggas on fire
Don't stop droppin' them, that's a lie
We just won't die
We come back flyer than ever, higher than ever this time
We feelin' this rhyme
So any nigga wanna get involved, what?
You think you can fuck with my dogs [friends]?

Nigga you thinkin' you rubbin' us while we're thuggin' this?
Did you think you can fuck with us? Bone, bone, bone, bone, bone
You ready to do this? The hell with the song
We ain't got to tell you it's on
You know it's poppin', the glock [handgun] to put a stop to the whole shit
Y'all still can't fuck with us and never will because
We too fuckin' bold, too fuckin' cold,
With too many soul-jahs [soldiers] ready to roll with the god damn bones.

Refrain:
You ride up to the club nigga, I don't give a fuck
Shakin' your ass in the club bitch, I don't give a fuck
Drinkin' Cris [Cristal champagne] in the V.I.(P.), I don't give a fuck
Talkin' shit about me bitch, I don't give a fuck
You got a pocket full of money nigga, I don't give a fuck
You drinkin' off with them ho's bitch, I don't give a fuck
In the club with your pussy clique, I don't give a fuck
Security on my dick bitch, I don't give a fuck.

The idea of power in gangsta rap lyrics is manifested through the ability to commit violent acts against an enemy, and soldiers appear to use these notions of empowerment in combat preparation.

Expressions of violence in gangsta rap are typically cast within urban environments, where handguns and small arms are the instruments of fighting an enemy. Rivals engage one another among local populations, in civilian residences, businesses, or other urban locations, like the "club" in "I Don't Give a Fuck." A prevalent method of attack is the drive-by shooting, in which one group attempts to catch another off guard by surprising them with gunfire from a moving or momentarily stopped vehicle, and then driving from the scene.[45] To a certain degree, these features of gangsta rap lyrics exhibit a correlation to the context of some soldiers' combat experiences. On 1 May 2003, President George W. Bush announced the end of major combat operations in Iraq, approximately six weeks after the war began on 19 March. During this time, the war was fought according to relatively traditional models of warfare in which (mostly) uniformed armies fought on a large scale for the control of the country. After the defeat of the Iraqi military, smaller movements began fighting on local and neighborhood levels, principally in Baghdad and other major cities. The resistance groups embedded and disguised themselves within civilian communities, using guerilla tactics such as IEDs, car bombs, and small arms ambushes to battle American forces. In many cases, soldiers operated against these movements by using small-scale weaponry, like rifles, machine guns, and vehicle-born firearms. This type of warfare has characterized much of the fighting in Iraq for many years.

In these ways, gangsta rap may be particularly well suited as an inspiration for combat because its lyrical themes parallel some of the contexts in which soldiers engage in war. To be sure, there are significant differences between the conflicts depicted in gangsta rap and soldiers' fighting in Iraq, like the references to money, alcohol, "the club," drugs, sex, and many others (what we might consider to be gangsta rap's dionysian themes), and I am not claiming that American street violence and the war in Iraq are closely related. However, certain features of the violence articulated within the lyrical chaotic themes of gangsta rap overlap with how soldiers conduct combat operations—ambush-style attacks are fought among urban, civilian populations with small-scale firearms. Gangsta rap can operate effectively as a musical inspiration for combat because soldiers can directly relate to certain aspects of its texts.[46]

While soldiers frequently reinterpret textual meanings in metal songs to suit their specific circumstances, soldiers' interpretations of gangsta rap lyrics appear to be more literal. Some rap scholars, like Robin D. G. Kelley, have proposed that much of the violence glorified in gangsta rap should be understood as a deeper commentary on the reality of poor, urban existence.[47] She believes that those who disapprove of the genre as irresponsibly glamorizing gang life tend to overlook its cultural criticism, in which violence expresses a rebellion against larger social and racial oppression.[48] Despite this understanding of gangsta rap violence, most soldiers are not concerned with the possible social or racial commentary underlying the music they use for combat inspiration; rather, they relate directly to the lyrics. Their involvement with gangsta rap lyrics tends to unfold primarily on the immediate, surface level of listener identity, and many times, in the context of combat inspiration, they prefer the more explicitly violent and nihilistic songs over those with lyrics of social and racial criticism or texts expressing sexual exploitations of women or misogyny.

But there is a paradox here in that, as Cheryl L. Keyes and many others observe, not all gangsta rap is based on the reality of day-to-day, street life experiences. As gangsta rap has become more popular, many rappers have attempted to assert superiority over other rap artists by writing lyrics that are more explicitly violent. While issues of authenticity and street credibility are important within the genre, some rappers have admitted that their lyrics are not based on real occurrences, but on imagined violence meant to shock an audience. Eminem's song "Stan," for instance, addresses a fan who misinterprets his violent, misogynist lyrics as truth. He raps, "I say that shit, just clownin' dogg, Come on, how fucked up is you? You got some issues, Stan, I think you need some counseling, to help your ass from bouncing off the walls when you get down some. . . . I really think you and your girlfriend need each other or maybe you just need to treat her better."

It appears, however, that some of the exaggerated violence in gangsta rap correlates with soldiers' experiences. In the director's commentary to *Soundtrack to War*, George Gittoes comments, "This is a generation that has been brought up on rap, gangsta rap—the idea of being a tough guy in the street. Here they were, actually fighting professional soldiers to this gangsta rap music by rappers who'd never seen anything like the action they'd been through."[49] In this situation, the process of listener identity may work in reverse. Gangsta rap typically portrays violence as an aspect of urban reality, and the ability to relate to this street life is an important component of listener identity. Nonetheless, the more extreme violence of gangsta rap lyrics is sometimes the product of exaggerated fantasy. The thematic content is an embellishment of violence, but the soldiers are able to relate to the lyrical themes as a direct reflection of their own experiences. The process of identifying with the reality of gangsta rap becomes juxtaposed in that the listener is able to relate to the lyrics as an accurate reflection of their personal experience, but the original lyrical content is based on exaggeration.

Gender, race, and social class also emerge as relevant to metal and rap. Interestingly, however, the majority of soldiers seemed somewhat puzzled when I asked them whether these issues ever factored into their listening experiences; William Thompson was typical in this regard when he replied, "I'm having a hard time thinking of how these things played in. I didn't think about it until you asked."[50] In all, issues of gender, race, and class arose in my interviews only sporadically. This posed a challenge from a research perspective because even though soldiers did not highlight these issues as strongly involved in their listening experiences, many studies of metal and rap have in fact found gender, race, and class to be fundamental to the genres. Here again, the limitation of not being able to pursue onsite research was problematic. Many metal and rap scholars find onsite research invaluable when examining gender, race, and class. Their conclusions have even suggested relationships that in some ways contradict the perspectives of fans and practitioners. Such was the case in Berger's analysis of deindustrialization and working-class disenfranchisement in the metal scene of northeastern Ohio.[51] His primary research participant, Dann Saladin, at first resisted Berger's notion that this subculture is connected to larger social contexts in which working-class youths have been denied genuine economic opportunities. Saladin placed a far greater emphasis on personal responsibility as a component of social mobility. Clearly, Berger would not have been able to form his conclusions about class had he relied solely on Saladin's remarks and not been able to actively observe the metal scene. In my case, I was unable to notice subtle issues concerning gender, race, and class that the soldiers themselves did not point out; my research was limited by what I was told and by what I observed or experienced. Considering that many soldiers did not find these issues directly relevant to their musical practices when I asked, it became even more difficult to explore. This does not imply that gender, race, and class are not involved in the contexts of soldiers' listening that I am examining, rather, these issues did not appear immediately apparent to many soldiers. Onsite fieldwork would have dramatically improved my ability to engage these important topics.

Notwithstanding these limitations, my research leads to several significant points. As mentioned, metal and rap are largely consumed by male audiences, including soldiers in Iraq. This music is predominantly made by men, and scholars like Walser, Keyes, and others identify these genres as mostly male expressions of power.[52] Generally speaking, metal and rap can be characterized as musical genres primarily produced and consumed by men as musical styles that frequently exhibit masculine expressions of strength and survival. With regard to combat preparation, soldiers' song choices typically contain lyrical themes of male-against-male power struggles and aggression. Rarely if ever did topics of sexuality or gender (i.e., "porn rock" or gangsta rap's sexual exploitation or misogyny) appear in these contexts of soldiers' listening.

In addition to the fact that metal and rap are male-dominated genres within popular culture, a major factor for the gender specificity in using this music as an inspiration for combat lies in the gender policies of the military. I learned from Atkinson that women are not officially permitted to serve in direct ground combat, which excludes them from most Military Occupational Specialties in combat units. As a result, women rarely go on patrols or missions that regularly encounter ground combat to the same degrees as infantry or armored units, so they do not usually participate in pre-combat rituals. This exclusion, she says, is not based on gender discrimination, but on the reasoning that tasks involved in ground combat, which include the operation of heavy artillery, are too physically demanding for most women. Atkinson explains, "Women aren't allowed to have those jobs. Sometimes they are just too physically demanding. Like I can't be a tank crewman, I'm just not physically strong enough. Those shells weigh 100 pounds, I think, and you have to be able to shove them, you know, be able to pick them up, lift them to your chest, and put them in a tube. I can't do that. I'm not a small woman by any means, but I can't do that."[53] Women are not involved in the war in the same ways as men, particularly as it relates to their participation in combat, and these differences are reflected by casualty statistics. As of March 2008, 2.4 percent of American casualties in Iraq were women. Overall, one in seven U.S. soldiers (14.3 percent) in Iraq is a woman, and this correlates with the general percentage of women in the military (15 percent).[54] For these reasons, this study of musical practices is largely focused on men.

In terms of race, soldiers' interaction with metal and gangsta rap mostly reflects the ways in which different ethnic groups consume music within the American civilian population. As one might expect, metal is popular among white soldiers, and attracts limited interest from African American or Hispanic soldiers.[55] While gangsta rap is still primarily produced by African Americans, the genre's fan base does not seem as racially lopsided; it is now a mainstream musical genre, consumed by white as well as African American audiences. Within American culture, though, white audiences have received a degree of backlash for their interest in this music. Particularly among suburban white youths, those listening to gangsta rap are sometimes characterized as poseurs who pretend to associate with the urban violence of gangsta rap or adopt a voyeuristic fantasy about ghetto life, when in fact they have never experienced life "in the hood."[56] Ironically, while gangsta rap songs sometimes express attitudes of distrust, anger, and violence toward white society in general, white audiences still purchase this music in considerable quantities. For white soldiers in Iraq, however, listening to this music within a combat zone does not appear to attract this type of disapproval. Even if they come from suburban or rural backgrounds, the reality of their violent surroundings in the war seems to transcend such criticisms (often based on race) that accompany listening to gangsta rap. Joshua Revak, for instance, took part in freestyle rap sessions where he was the only white rapper. The racial tensions that would likely have accompanied such a situation in U.S. society were not present in this circumstance. Additionally, military units are more integrated than they have been in the past, and music sometimes facilitates connections among members of different ethnic groups. As Buzzell mentioned, music was a means for establishing cliques in the military, and Grisham (a white soldier) said, "If soldiers were listening to rap music, the main group would be black but I never felt excluded."[57]

On the other hand, musical preference in some settings has been shown to intensify divisions among racial groups. For instance, in a recent Armed Forces Vietnam Network forum discussion, a Vietnam veteran, "Forrest," recounted how music was a source of racial tension during his deployment: "Toward the end of my tour music became a contentious issue in the base camps. Units coming in from the field had serious race problems over soul and C&W [country and western] music. One battalion I know of came in for a five day stand down and ended up being sent back out the same day they arrived because they tore the EM club apart over this very issue."[58]

Social class seems to operate on a number of levels in the military. Most soldiers did not find the primary source of tension in their military experiences to arise from gender, race, or socioeconomic background, but rank. The class hierarchy of the military is based on the division between officers and enlisted soldiers. Thompson mentioned that some enlisted-rank soldiers view officers as privileged leaders who are not exposed to danger as frequently because they are more valued within the military hierarchy.[59] This creates a degree of animosity among enlisted soldiers analogous to a social class division. On a deeper level, though, the structure of the officer and enlisted ranks is largely a product of soldiers' socioeconomic backgrounds. The requirement that officers must have college degrees largely favors those from more affluent backgrounds who tend to have greater educational opportunities. The majority of enlisted rank soldiers come from working-class backgrounds, and while they may earn money for college education by serving in the military, their initial position is limited to the enlisted rank without a college degree. Moreover, officer rankings tend to correlate to the number of years of service; hence higher-ranking officers are usually older. Garry Trudeau's *Doonesbury* comic, shown in figure I.2, satirizes how the divisions of rank and age seem to correlate to soldiers' listening preferences. Because most enlisted-rank soldiers come from working-class backgrounds, metal and rap appear far more frequently among these younger soldiers. Grisham, in his mid-thirties, observed that even at his rank of noncommissioned officer, "I think it's more of an age thing than a race thing. When people hear me listening to Static-X [a metal band] or DMX, they're surprised. My soldiers thought it was funny that the First Sergeant was cranking rap music in his office!! We're supposed to be listening to Perry Como or Barry Manilow or something."[60] The choices of metal and rap music, which largely fall out according to rank, can also be understood as reflections of socioeconomic status. Metal and rap are enjoyed predominantly by enlisted-rank soldiers, but the majority of these soldiers come from working-class backgrounds without the education required for promotion to officer.

While musical genres whose primary elements involve empowerment and the thematic content of death, war, and violence seem appropriate for soldiers preparing for combat, the roles of metal and gangsta rap may be more complex than what is first apparent. The majority of soldiers say that listening to metal or rap pumps them up for missions, but some also claim that the music exercises a psychological power that transforms them beyond their normal selves. Obtaining data on such intimate, personal experiences presents many challenges. In general, members of the military have not been known to speak openly about their emotions. Soldier life tends to emphasize toughness, typically framed within a masculine sensibility where expressions of emotions or feelings signify femininity or weakness.[61] When soldiers told me about the music they would listen to during combat preparation, I often followed up with the question, "Did you feel that music affected you in any way?" Many times, soldiers would initially respond in the negative, but would then proceed to outline how they related to the music. In many cases, their first response may have resulted from the question's reference to feelings or emotions. It certainly appears that the metal and rap used as an inspiration for combat had a significant impact on the psychological state of some soldiers.

Soldiers' descriptions of pre-combat listening experiences suggested that music can, to varying degrees, artificially alter their state of mind so that they are able to handle the reality of their involvement in the war. Saunders, for instance, believes that "war is people having to step outside of themselves. It is you having to become what I consider to be a monster."[62] "American Soldier" wrote that music "would provide motivation to get in the 'zone' before a very dangerous mission. It was part of my experience and I can still recall certain songs that would get me where I needed to be."[63] Other soldiers said that metal and rap music had similar effects on their experiences as an inspiration for combat. David Schultz noted that Drowning Pool's "Bodies" "did put you in a little different state of mind. . . . I think definitely that that hard rock type music is more indicative of the feelings that are being stirred up before you know you are fixing to go outside the wire and probably be targeted—you know, someone trying to kill you."[64] Speaking about metal and gangsta rap music before missions, Revak said, "I am a firm believer that music speaks to the soul, any music. . . . I don't think it's to the point where if you listen to Eminem that you are going to go kill your girlfriend, or your wife, or whatever. But I think that it definitely speaks to the soul. Music—it does, it affects the kind of person that you are. I really believe that it affects who you are in some way or another."[65]

The idea of individuals, as Saunders believes, stepping "outside of themselves" resonates with certain aspects of metal and rap ideologies. In *Running with the Devil,* Walser claims that "metal energizes the body, transforming space and social relations," and Weinstein quotes a fan as saying that "the whole point of heavy metal music is to get out of your mind."[66] In the scene from *Occupation: Dreamland* in which soldiers watch a video of Slayer's "Bloodline" before going on patrol, a soldier says, "Yes, Slayer. I hear and obey." This is followed by a brief chorus of laughter, but the soldiers' silence and intense staring into the television as they watch the video imply the seriousness of their approach to combat preparation. The comment also suggests that the soldier jokingly viewed himself as being brainwashed by the music. In one way, the robotic tone of his delivery poked fun at himself for watching the video with such intensity, but it acknowledged that the music could have the power to transform a person's state of mind.

Similarly, in *Rap Music and Street Consciousness,* Keyes claims that "gangsta rap artists argue that the tales from the hoods range from truthful accounts to exaggerated fantasies."[67] Much of the fantasy element within these songs involves violence or physical gratification—thematic content similar to the chaotic or dionysian themes identified by Weinstein in metal music. In *Soundtrack to War,* Gittoes finds that gangsta rap music can have a transformative impact on soldiers. He points out that a quiet, mild-mannered soldier undergoes a radical transformation into an explicitly graphic porno rapper when he participates in freestyle rap sessions: "He goes through a personality change when he's not performing, he's very quiet, almost intellectual. . . . He's a very mild-mannered person, but something comes out, there's this transformation."[68] For other soldiers, the fantasy element is more about stepping outside of themselves to be able to handle the realities of war (destruction, combat, death) than to enter a world of pleasurable fantasy. Talking about "Go To Sleep," Grisham says, "It's a very negative song, and I'm almost even embarrassed to say it was our theme song. But hey, that's what happens in war. You've got to become inhuman to do inhuman things. And by that I just mean, shooting a weapon in the direction of a living person. . . . The worst part is that I didn't used to use profanity, but at some point I snapped. Now that I've returned to normal, I can't listen to this song."[69] Grisham identifies with the song in the process of becoming "inhuman" and psychologically "snapping." In the process of transformation or fantasy, soldiers place themselves in the position of the gang criminal and adopt the perspective toward violence and death articulated in the lyrical themes of the gangsta rap song. Some soldiers move into a state of mind outside of their "normal" selves as they prepare for combat in order to come to terms with their violent surroundings, and certain aspects of gangsta rap ideology, like survival and violence, operate as important catalysts in this process.

Grisham also emphasizes that music can function as a way of becoming "inhuman" in relation to soldiers' experiences of war:

War is so ugly and disgusting, and it's very inhuman. It's an inhuman thing. It's unnatural for people to kill people. It's something that no one should ever have to do, unfortunately, someone does. And we happen to be that someone sometimes. And so listening to music would artificially make you aggressive when you needed to be aggressive. If you knew you were going out and you were going to get shot at, you didn't want to go out there thinking everything was hunky-dory, and you had to go out there with an aggressive mindset, hoping you wouldn't have to use that aggression. And so how it affected me is that it was really able to keep me alert. It made me—when I needed to get aggressive, I'd put some aggressive music on.[70]

Grisham highlights the music's power to keep soldiers in a state of heightened awareness, but also to make them capable of committing inhuman acts. Psychologists Robert W. Rieber and Robert J. Kelly observe that the circumstances of war can cause combatants to develop inhuman or dehumanizing views: "Self and object-directed dehumanization are inevitably heightened in situations where the threat of combat is present."[71] In these instances, the music could be said to have a transformative power that removes the humanity element from human identity. Music becomes a means of dehumanizing an adversary or oneself.

The ways in which the Iraq War has been fought may contribute to the process of dehumanization as well. On the Vietnam War, Robert J. Lifton says that intense feelings of enmification and dehumanization arose because of the circumstances related to the fighting: "Thrust into this alien revolution in an alien culture, assigned an elusive enemy who is everyone and no one, sent into dangerous nonbattles in a war lacking the most elementary rules and structures of meaning, what do we expect him [a soldier] to do? He in fact finds himself in exactly the situation Jean-Paul Sartre has described as inevitably genocidal—troops from an advanced industrial nation engaged in a counterinsurgency action in an underdeveloped area, against guerillas who merge with the people."[72] While there are many differences between the Vietnam and Iraq Wars, Lifton's description parallels aspects of the military conflict in Iraq. He believes that this type of warfare tends to induce strong feelings of dehumanization against an enemy or even the "inevitably genocidal" attitude proposed by Sartre. Because U.S. soldiers in Iraq are fighting in similar situations, there may be a greater tendency to psychologically reduce an enemy to an inhuman status. Given this predisposition, the metal and rap music could be even more strongly influential as an inspiration for combat. Not only does this music pump soldiers up, but in some cases it assists in a process of psychological transformation where soldiers develop attitudes of dehumanization toward their adversaries, resulting from the music and specific circumstances of the fighting.

I do not suggest that the transformative possibilities of metal and rap music, or the specific circumstances of the Iraq War, affect all soldiers in the same way or somehow relieve soldiers of responsibility for their actions. Rather, music seems to influence soldiers to varying degrees. For some, the music does nothing more than pump them up and provide an adrenaline rush, but for others it may trigger some form of mental transformation. Judith Becker's research on trance and "deep listening" provides an insightful framework for understanding this latter group. "Deep listeners," a term Becker adapts from composer Pauline Oliveros, describes a person with an intense emotional interaction with music, resembling a secular trance.[73] Trance is usually associated with non-Western religious ceremonies in which persons experience an altered spiritual consciousness induced, at least in part, by music. The ways in which Becker describes deep listening, trance, and music's potential impact on the human psyche provide an avenue for understanding how some soldiers experience metal and rap music as an inspiration for combat.

Becker's account of Balinese *bebuten* trancing, in fact, reveals a degree of parallelism with the transformative event of deep listening for some soldiers:

> The Rangda/Barong ritual in Bali, Indonesia, is an event invoked to restore balance between the people and the "other" world of the deities, spirits, and demons. If some misfortune befalls a village, such as a crop failure, pestilence, or frequent cases of mental illness, or the ritual calendar prescribes it, the village will stage an encounter opposing the great witch Rangda and her followers against the mythic beast Barong and his followers. Before the ceremony begins, all the participants are put into a trance at the temple to the accompaniment of long lines of classical poetry sung slowly, in unison, by a chorus of women from the village. . . . These men confront the witch and with the help of the Barong ultimately neutralize her power.[74]

Unlike many rituals, *bebuten* trance is not joyful or ecstatic; rather, the trancers feel intense fury, "a homicidal rage" against Rangda, in order to restore balance to the community.[75] The musically induced trance gives the villagers the power and context psychologically to kill an enemy. Some soldiers' use of metal and rap as an inspiration for combat resembles this form of trance. The music communicates intense feelings of power, aggression, and violence, and puts soldiers in an altered state of mind to the point of creating a dehumanizing, homicidal perspective. In the cases where the soldiers yell or scream the lyrics, their interaction with music provides a stronger internalization of this process.

Becker's theory of trance consciousness suggests that some trancers experience a loss of the autobiographical self during trance, which we might consider analogous to soldiers "stepping outside of themselves."[76] Through timbre and lyrical themes, metal and rap can create a deep listening experience for some soldiers in which they adopt attitudes about violence and dehumanization not typically associated with their autobiographical self. Music in this circumstance induces an aggressive mindset and operates as a pretext for the possibility of violent action. One important difference, though, is that soldiers remain within their existing state of consciousness. Clearly, they must maintain a heightened awareness of their immediate surroundings given the life or death consequences of combat. We might say that the depth of their listening is limited to a fully conscious, aware experience. Another difference is that the *bebuten* trancers ultimately direct the focus of their rage back upon themselves. They act out the fight against Rangda through self-inflicted violent acts with knives and daggers, whereas the soldiers direct their aggressive attitudes toward others.

At the end of chapter 3, I drew a number of comparisons between the ways in which music functions as an inspiration for combat for both U.S. soldiers and anti-American and anti-Israel movements. Thompson's account of the nasheeds played from the mosques during the Sunni/Shi'a battles demonstrated one way that music, or sacred recitation, motivated Muslim fighters. While it is difficult to fully assess to what degree, if any, the nasheeds may have had a transformative influence, I believe that there could be some elements of psychological transformation for Muslim fighters. Walid Shoebat suggests that suicide bombers perform their attacks in states of altered consciousness: "The suicidal act often involves a variety of disassociative processes, such as narrowing of vision, altered states of attention, absorption in the act, detachment from feelings of the body, semi-hypnotic ecstasy, and the self-surrendering sense of merging with a transcendental power. I know this to be true, since it is exactly what I experienced during my bomb operation. I was disconnected from reality."[77] Many psychological studies of suicide, like those conducted by Israel Orbach and Edwin Schneidman, have proposed high levels of dissociative mental states when committing this act.[78] Speaking about the "Allahu Akbar" chanting before and during combat, Thompson also stated, "It's almost like they are praying that they can do what they need to do."[79]

Although music and chanting play a role in this possible change of mind-set, I suspect that religious beliefs are more influential in the transformative process. Many Muslim suicide bombers and insurgents have been indoctrinated to believe that suicide and death in defense of Islam grants salvation in the afterlife. Thompson noted, "They see fighting as they're going to die, and they're going to go to heaven if they die in combat"; likewise, Shoebat claims, "The perception of death as an alternative and a more attractive state-of-being is the main attraction promoted by religious and educational groups, which act as the facilitators of the Jihad agenda."[80] More so than music, these types of religious beliefs operate as the transformative catalysts for Muslim fighters. Their belief in the promise of religious salvation if they die in defense of Islam seems to be the primary source of psychological alteration. To a certain degree, the religious component of this mental state resembles a non-music-inspired trance. While acts of violence against others are rarely involved in religious trancing, a similarity emerges through the religiously derived alteration of consciousness, involving ecstasy and union with a higher spiritual power. Notice how Shoebat explains some of his feelings when he performed a bombing attack with the words "semi-hypnotic ecstasy, and the self-surrendering sense of merging with a transcendental power." These features parallel many of the emotional states of trancing communities described by Becker. Like the U.S. soldiers, however, the Muslim fighter's "trance" is not an enveloping alternate state of consciousness; they are still aware of their surroundings to the point of being able to commit suicide or wage violence. Although they would not qualify as "deep listeners" because music is not used to emote a psychological change, the Muslim fighters seem to experience some degree of mental transformation, akin to trance, derived from religious beliefs and the desire to create a union with a higher spiritual power.

One might be skeptical about whether Muslim fighters' psychological states constitute a form of trance, or whether soldiers' musical interactions have anything in common with *bebuten* trancing or deep listening. As we have seen, the soldiers themselves were often hesitant to talk about any effect of the music on their psyche beyond pumping them up. Becker, however, points out that American culture is not particularly accepting of trance, and this should not discourage us from proposing a level of connection. Given soldiers' comments about "becoming inhuman," "having to become what I consider to be a monster," "affect[ing] the kind of person that you are," and Shoebat's comments about "ecstasy" and "merging with a transcendental power," we should not immediately reject that similar or related phenomena are taking place. Many people within Western cultures have experienced an intense emotional response involving music. Whether it be chills, tears, or laughter, the ability of music to operate as an intense emotional trigger seems common. As such, the idea of a psychological transformation resulting from music should not be foreign to most people's experiences; it may only be a matter of the degree to which music is influential.

The idea of the transformative influence of music or religious beliefs among combatants in the Iraq War may be paradoxically encouraging. The self-transformation of combatants suggests that both sides of the conflict must take steps, in some way, to alter their psychological state such that they are capable of killing. Many soldiers viewed the condition of war as unnatural. Indeed, this points to the idea that people of radically different societies and beliefs, like American soldiers and Muslim insurgents, often take measures for self-transformation in order to be capable of committing extremely violent acts. This process suggests that the fundamental psychological condition, regardless of cultural background and perceived enemy, may be one of nonviolence. As Thompson remarked, "It goes against any human nature to kill people."[81]

THE BATTLEFIELD PSYCHOLOGY OF TIMBRE

The power of music to inspire can be counterbalanced by its equally intense potential to frustrate and irritate. In psychological tactics, the U.S. military sometimes employs music, typically through loudspeakers, in attempts to impair insurgents' ability to fight, or to break their will if they refuse to answer questions in interrogation. Music plays a role as part of a sonic arsenal that includes any frustrating or irritating sound, like Grisham's tape of babies crying, but metal appears to be used in these situations due to a number of important factors. First, the loudness of the sound, particularly in the enclosed setting of interrogation, contributes to the feelings of irritation. Of course, any sound a person finds frustrating gains potency when played at a higher volume. Most soldiers' accounts of metal in interrogation reveal that the music is, in fact, played at a high volume, but the decibel level does not appear to be the principal source of antagonism. If sheer volume had this impact, the military would most likely have begun utilizing loud music during interrogations in earlier conflicts. Certainly, the audio technology available during the Vietnam and Korean Wars and World War II was able to deliver high-intensity sound, so it is unlikely that the overall loudness of the sounds or music, while a factor, is the main influence. Additionally, Grisham stated that interrogators were required to be present in the room and subjected to the same conditions as a detainee, which would seem to rule out playing the music at levels that could cause physical damage to the ear, although it is certainly possible that interrogators did not always follow this guideline.[82]

Another possibility may be that metal and other genres are considered culturally offensive to insurgents. In *Soundtrack to War*, Gittoes interviews members of an Iraqi metal band, Acrassicrauda, who believe that metal music is viewed as "satanic" and "anti-God" by some Iraqis.[83] Similarly, Grisham believes that some detainees reacted adversely to metal because they viewed it as "satanic." Thus detainees might consider rap, children's songs, and even music by pop artists like Britney Spears or Christina Aguilera to be the music of the "infidels," since Western popular music is considered culturally offensive and a source of irritation.

Nevertheless, such cultural and religious differences do not appear to be the only reason detainees are affected by Western or American music. Grisham remarks that other pop artists, like Michael Jackson, are very popular in Iraq, and he could not have used his music because it would have been ineffective against insurgents.[84] Even though the genres selected for interrogation may be culturally offensive to detainees in some instances, the power of music to irritate or frustrate seems to stem from more a mix of complex factors rather than from cultural symbolism. While Western mainstream pop, rap, and children's songs have been employed in these circumstances, metal seems to be the most frequently used genre. If the musical representation of Western culture were the principal source of antagonism, one would expect a greater degree of musical diversity in the music used during interrogation.

The reaction of detainees to metal, as described by interrogators, suggests that the source of irritation derives to a large degree from the timbres of the music. Since most detainees are not sufficiently fluent in English to decipher the lyrics, the text of any song has little impact, negating the potential effects of even extremely chaotic or violent lyrics. On the other hand, many of the musical features of the genre described by Walser, like vocal timbre, mode and rhythm, melody, guitar solos, and the distorted guitar power chord, contribute to the music's ability to break the will of a detainee.[85] More than any one of these elements in isolation, the distorted guitar sound and vocal articulation appear to be the most significant in causing the reaction of frustration and irritation. The majority of songs employed in interrogation and loudspeaker tactics contain high levels of guitar distortion, and Whiteley's analysis of this timbre, with its high frequency harmonics, provides insight as to why it might be particularly effective: "Naturally produced sound waves have only a few harmonics, but these (distorted) 'clipped' waves have many, especially at a high level and this is what gives off the piercingly painful effect. Natural guitar sounds at loud volume are not so nearly painful to listen to, and hence far less aggressive."[86] Whiteley's assessment of guitar distortion suggests that the "painful" aspect of the sound is not due to the volume at which the music is usually played, but stems from the nature of multiple, high-frequency harmonics in the guitar distortion. The combination of the guitar distortion effect and the vocal articulation of metal songs, which consist of pitched screaming or guttural, unpitched yelling, may have a powerful effect on certain listeners.

The imposed irritation does not seem to be culturally specific to Iraqis or persons from the Middle East. The rough, distorted timbres are also largely the reason that metal generates such a strong negative reaction among some Western popular music audiences. James Hetfield, lead singer and guitarist of Metallica, offers an interesting perspective on notions of power in metal and why his band's music may be useful in sensory deprivation: "We've been punishing our parents, wives, and loved ones with this music forever, why should the Iraqis or whoever it is be any different? [laughter]. But I really know the reason. It's the relentlessness of the music. It's completely relentless to break their will. If I listened to a death metal band for twelve hours in a row, I'd go insane, too. I'd tell you anything you wanted to know."[87] Fast tempo songs demonstrating rapid guitar riffs and "machine gun" double pedal bass drum passages lend the music its unyielding affect and enhance the effectiveness of this sonic harassment technique. However, we have seen that it is precisely the musical manifestations of power within metal, such as timbre and performance, that appeal to soldiers as an inspiration for combat. On one hand, soldiers find the music empowering as they prepare for missions and patrols; on the other, the power element within the metal sound frustrates and irritates insurgents. In this case, the concept of power in metal operates in a context-dependent, multi-faceted, but diametrically opposed way.

Music is selected for psychological tactics according to its ability to induce frustration and irritation. Metal songs, like "Bodies" by Drowning Pool, are employed in interrogation, and we have seen how this song has an intricate relationship with the Iraq War. After reaching great popularity in the summer of 2001, "Bodies" was taken off popular radio immediately after 11 September 2001, and then made a resurgence among American soldiers as an inspiration for combat, including the first Grouchy Media music video. In addition, "Bodies" was used during the interrogation of noncompliant detainees as form of irritation and frustration tactics. The use of the song for interrogation seems to have been foreshadowed in the video for the song (video example 29), released in the spring of 2001, which displays scenes implying an interrogation scenario. The video opens with singer Dave Williams whispering the phrase, "Let the bodies hit the floor" into the ear of an older man who sits calmly in a chair. On the fourth repetition, Williams screams, "Floor," and the man cringes as the song begins. Numerous scenes in the video present the man sitting in an armless chair and Williams standing over him, singing and yelling the lyrics at a close distance. While the video implies the setting of a psychiatric hospital, the frightened expression on the man's face and the aggressive postures that Williams assumes as he towers over him give the impression that he is trying to psychologically break down the older man in some way. The man mouths the words "nothing wrong with me" as Williams repeats, "Something's got to give." There certainly appears to be a parallel between the scene depicted in the video and the act of interrogation. This may only be a coincidence, but it adds a further layer to the relationship between "Bodies" and the Iraq War.

While metal appears to be the genre most frequently used in interrogation due to its timbral power and relentlessness, rap, pop, and children's songs have also been employed in psychological tactics. Interrogators believe that some timbres in these songs are especially irritating to listeners who find the sounds unfamiliar. More than rap and pop, children's songs demonstrate a high degree of relentlessness, which probably explains their prevalence over the other two genres. The relentless aspect of children's songs does not derive as much from timbral "painfulness" or aggressive sounds, even though some people may find the vocal and musical timbres in children's songs annoying, but from sheer repetition—aside from how many times interrogators may play the same song again and again.

One of the children's songs used by interrogators is "I Love You," from the television program and videos of Barney, the purple dinosaur. The minute-long song consists of two approximately equal sections differentiated by a key change. The melody is sung after a short instrumental introduction and repeats with a slight textual variation up a half step in the second section. In addition to the repeated statements of the entire melody, there are smaller-scale, repeated patterns within the melody itself. The motion G-E-G, sung to the words, "I love you," repeats for the second line of the song, "You love me." Including the instrumental introduction, which plays the G-E-G melody twice, this melodic fragment is heard six times in one minute, four as G-E-G and twice as G♯-E♯-G♯ in the raised half-step section. If "I Love You" were played repeatedly for an hour, the complete melody would be heard 120 times and the main melodic motive would be heard 360 times. Adding to the repetition, the singing style of the children, presumably Barney's target audience of preschoolers or young children, seems unnaturally uniform and calm. It is hard to imagine a group of four- to six-year-olds singing with such precision, clarity, and restraint, and for me, the vocal performance is unnervingly artificial. The repetitive timbres of music intended for children make for a powerful source of antagonism—one might recall that these factors caused Buzzell to "cringe" when he remembered listening repeatedly to the Chipmunks Christmas CD in his vehicle. Moreover, one can see the obvious textual contradiction of using "I Love You" in interrogation. Although the detainees may not fully understand the lyrics, playing a song about loving one another, being a family, and giving hugs and kisses is highly ironic within the framework of interrogation.

The type of children's music used in psychological tactics sometimes elicits a humorous reaction in American society. In November 2004, for instance, *St. Petersburg Times* reporter Lane DeGregory remarked that the army has been slow to recognize the irritation potential of children's songs:

> It shouldn't have taken the Army this long to discover it. Anyone who's had a preschooler knows the pain: sing-songy, cotton-colored puppets crooning over and over again about happy, joyful things. Dancing, smiling puppets. So pleased you tuned in. You can't tune them out. Then your little one joins in, even during commercials. Incessant. Mind-numbing. An agonizing infliction of unbearable assault. Reruns were bad enough. Now with videos, the rewinds never stop. Once Barney gets going, there is no escape.[88]

As mentioned, Hetfield initially expressed amusement about metal and his own music: "We've been punishing our parents, wives, and loved ones with this music forever, why should the Iraqis or whoever it is be any different?" Similarly, referring to the famous scene from *One, Two, Three*, Dan Kuehl noted, "I would confess to being a member of al-Qaeda if someone did that for an hour [made him listen to 'Itsy Bitsy Teeny Weeny Yellow Polka-Dot Bikini']. After ten hours of that, I'd confess to being Osama bin Laden."[89] I encountered a similar reaction when I presented a paper for an audience of about sixty to seventy people in California and played "I Love You" on repeat for 75 seconds. As the repetition of the song began, a chorus of groans and laughter erupted from the audience.

Why do people tend to react this way? The use of children's songs or other irritating music as an interrogation technique tends to evoke a humorous response in American society because many people can immediately relate to the situation of having to listen to music they do not like. Suzanne Cusick documents a variety of blogosphere exchanges in which people adopt a humorous stance on music in interrogation by relating it to personal experiences.[90] While interrogation is clearly a different context, most people have occasionally found themselves forced to listen to music they intensely disliked. Whether it was loud party or techno music blasting from a house at 3 AM, the muzak of a doctor or dentist's office, or a heavy metal guitarist practicing for hours in an adjacent apartment, the shared response to being annoyed by music often involves laughter. DeGregory goes so far as to suggest that having to listen to music one finds "unbearable" is an expected component of parenthood. The commonality of such an experience, though, does not fully explain the joking reaction. Just because a large group of people can relate to a particular event does not mean that they will adopt a humorous attitude about it.

One of the underlying sources of humor may be the opposite emotional reactions people have to music. In the cases of metal and rap—two of the most polarized popular music genres—those who love it are often among the most avid fans of any popular music style, and those who hate it can barely tolerate a few minutes of it. The same could be said for children's songs, like "I Love You." Young children seem to thoroughly enjoy the songs. When I was a nanny for my nieces, they would sing songs like "I Wanna Be a Dog" or "I Know a Song That Gets on Everybody's Nerves" for what seemed like hours. DeGregory's comments accurately summarize how I felt at the time. The humor arises from the contradiction that one person's musical pleasure is another's intense pain—one listener greatly enjoys the source of another listener's sonic anguish. Because most people have found themselves on the anguished side of listening, unable to stop the music, they seem to respond in a humorous way.

These pleasure/pain reactions highlight the more serious issue of the highly subjective experience of listening to music. As a part of battlefield psychological tactics, timbre has a powerful influence on listeners, so much so that it has been used in interrogation and even considered to constitute torture. The pleasure/pain dichotomy of musical reception is still largely a mystery within musicology and the cognitive sciences; who can say why someone enjoys a particular genre, song, or sound? Most of us recall grade school teachers scratching their nails across a blackboard to silence a rowdy class. The noise was probably no louder than what a person experiences on a typical day, so why was it disturbing? The fields of cognitive science and psychology do not appear to have examined this type of issue. Most scientific or psychological studies of sound-based irritation still use the subjective method of asking individuals to rate levels of annoyance, on a scale of 1–10, for example. In trying to understand the causes of musical annoyance, Sally Jo Cunningham, J. Stephen Downie, and David Bainbridge propose that "the songs that we dislike depend as much upon ourselves as upon characteristics of the songs."[91] While the scientific "why" of these questions may be difficult to answer because of the subjective nature of musical experience, the consequences of our responses seem much clearer. Sound can have such a strong impact on people that it can psychologically break their will. Music can irritate and frustrate to the point that one's resistance to answer questions is shattered. These issues raise complicated ethical questions about different uses of music. Can music be an instrument of violence? Where is the line between annoyance and true psychological stress? Can timbre be torture? If so, who decides and how? What rights do artists have regarding the uses of the music they write? While these questions begin to be debated, music in psychological tactics shows the extent to which sound can affect the human psyche and behavior. Soldiers' experiences have shown the transformative effect of music in combat preparation, and timbre has the power to bolster confidence and motivate listeners outside of themselves. But paradoxically, the same sounds can irritate, frustrate, and psychologically break people down. It appears that metal, and to a slightly lesser degree rap, have the dubious distinction of being capable of both psychological effects.

The psychological power of music is not always employed in ways that appear harmful or divisive; in fact, there have been propaganda efforts in the Iraq War in which the United States has used music as a cultural "bridge builder."[92] Radio Sawa ("together" or "togetherness"), which the U.S. government created in March 2002, broadcasts news and popular music, both Western and indigenous, throughout the Middle East, including Jordan and the West Bank, the Persian Gulf, Iraq, Egypt, and Morocco. Its target audience is 15- to 29-year-olds. According to Kuehl, the purpose of Radio

Sawa is "to try to create a base psychological perspective that brings sides of the population together because they listen to the same music. Kids who listen to the same music, then maybe twenty years from now, when the twenty-year-old is a forty-year-old policy maker, it will start paying off some dividends and building some bridges between us."[93] Certainly, as we saw in World War II, the effectiveness of radio propaganda is always debatable. Botelho points out that most Iraqis are distrustful of media efforts involving the United States: "Part of the problem is that we still write the material and Iraqis are distrustful of that. So if we have a hand in it, then they are distrustful. And if someone has distrust about something, then you can't really win them over."[94] While it remains to be seen how well Radio Sawa may bridge cultural gaps, the station appears to be very popular. According to a document released by the U.S. General Accounting Office in April 2004, *US International Broadcasting,* Radio Sawa is the top international broadcaster in six Middle Eastern countries, and attracts approximately 38 percent of the general population and 49 percent of its intended audience.[95]

4TH25 AND (ANTI-) GANGSTA RAP

Chapter 5 outlined the diversity of music soldiers write and record in Iraq. From acoustic guitar-based folk songs to gore metal, this music reveals a wide variety of styles and lyrical themes. The unifying thread within the great range of soldiers' creativity is that the music represents a form of soldier expression about their wartime experiences. Describing the songs of soldiers in the Vietnam War, Lydia Fish writes, "These songs served as a strategy for survival, as a means of unit bonding and definition, as entertainment, and as a way of expressing emotion," and the same can be said for most soldiers in Iraq.[96] The music operates as an expressive outlet for their feelings about war. While soldiers write original music in many different styles, much of my research has focused on 4th25 and the album *Live from Iraq.* Keeping with my analysis of metal and rap in this section, I examine the aesthetic position of 4th25, and specifically the ideas of the group's leader, Neal Saunders, in relation to gangsta rap ideology.

As a form of soldier expression, rap may appear to be a recent phenomenon, but it fits naturally within the history of soldier-produced art. The emphasis on texts that lies at the heart of the rap genre creates a link to earlier forms of soldier writing. Many rap scholars view the lyrics as a style of African American urban poetry, and this poetic aspect forges a connection with much of the poetry written by soldiers in earlier conflicts. World War I, for example, was well known for trench poetry written by soldiers. According to Stuart Lee, "The First World War provides one of the seminal moments of the twentieth-century in which literate soldiers, plunged into inhuman conditions, reacted to their surrounding in poems reflecting Wordsworth's 'spontaneous overflow of powerful feeling.'"[97] In many of these poems, soldiers describe their life in the trench warfare of World War I.

Rap is well suited to continue this tradition. In addition to being a genre driven by texts, rap parallels trench poetry in its affinity for rhymed verse and reality-based lyrical themes. The reality rap subgenre focuses on the difficult aspects of human existence, often within violent surroundings. This topical focus is analogous to the rhetorical position of much trench poetry, in which World War I soldiers describe the frequently violent reality of life in the trenches. In its freestyle form, rap becomes even more rooted in texts through the absence of musical instruments. In these ways, *Live from Iraq* could be considered part of the trench poetry tradition. While set to music, the lyrics address a variety of experiences related to the reality of soldier life at war.

Within the rap genre, *Live from Iraq* would most likely fall into the category of reality rap. The album is framed as a poetic narrative in which the soldiers of 4th25 address the violence and painful consequences of their surroundings, as well as their frustrations with the Iraqi people and commanding officers. Given the violence and feelings of aggravation at forces beyond their control that emerge throughout the album, *Live from Iraq* demonstrates a link to the gangsta rap subgenre. Many aspects of gangsta rap ideology, such as the survival of the fittest attitude, in which death and violence are portrayed as essential components of survival and attitudes of rebellion against oppressive forces, are recontextualized in the album to depict the experience of combat violence and life/death situations in the lives of soldiers in Iraq. For example, in "Behind the Screens," Saunders expresses intense animosity toward his commanding officers who prohibit soldiers from exercising full force when their lives are threatened. He feels that officers have the luxury of controlling soldiers this way—such as restricting the rules of engagement so that car bombs and IEDs can more easily target soliders—because they are not the ones fighting and dying. The expression of anger against an oppressive force with life or death circumstances similarly characterizes components of gangsta rap. Additionally, while "I Ride" is a song dedicated to the memory of soldiers who were killed in combat, it adopts the gangsta rap perspective of revenge as a way to honor the dead. The text commemorates soldiers by threatening violent retaliation against those who were responsible for their deaths, a common gangsta rap outlook.

As the main composer and lyricist, Saunders not only addresses the topics of war and violence in his texts, but also attempts to timbrally represent these feelings in the music. The song "Lace Your Boots," for example, describes the experience of combat. To help convey the sense of confusion in a gunfight, Saunders uses a technique of reversing the sound wave on selected keyboard parts, so that these sounds shift unpredictably forward and backward. In addition, he sonically portrays the slowing down of time during combat by altering the pitch of the vocals so that the voice seems to move at an unnaturally slow tempo. Although the album evokes certain aspects of the gangsta rap subgenre by portraying reality as a violent condition of survival, Saunders's perspectives directly contest many of gangsta rap's defining features. He considers the album and the system of beliefs expressed within it to oppose many of the ideological elements of gangsta rap. In fact, he claims that gangsta rap does not express "reality" at all.

For Saunders, gangsta rappers are motivated by the possibilities of lucrative album sales, and they exaggerate stories about "being hard" or the violence of street life. He asserts that the preferred corporate image of gangsta rappers as violent criminals corrupts the genre and removes any reality from it. Rappers act hard because it sells, but they have never experienced the reality of life that he has experienced in war. As such, Saunders feels a responsibility to describe his life in war and express how, by way of comparison, the violence of gangsta rap glorifies a criminal lifestyle that could never be as hard as his life as a soldier in Iraq.

There is no gangsta rapper that's going to have the same—you know, it's not as real as a cat who's been to war and told the story. So I don't think they [the major record companies] want to touch it [his album] for that reason, because then you can't have all these fuckers acting hard, because they're not. Because as soon as one soldier makes it, he just made it harder for everybody else, you know, to tell the same story—the same I sell drugs on the corner shit, and I shoot people with my 45, and that crap. Majors [the record companies] have a lot of money invested in that. . . . I wanted people to understand what war really was, or what combat really was. And it's not smiles, it's not anything where people can be happy, and it's not something you laugh about. And it's not something we'll all just joke about some day.[98]

Saunders's assessment accurately characterizes the tendency of some gangsta rap lyrics to inflate violent content. While the gangsta rap genre may have emerged by exposing the violence and racial and social oppression within urban environments from a mostly African American, male perspective, many contemporary gangsta rappers—and even those who were among the first performers of the subgenre—acknowledge a "fantasy" element or exaggerated degree of violence and misogyny in the lyrics. When Saunders began to work on the album, many soldiers expressed interest in joining the group, but he refused them because of their desire to perpetuate the often-exaggerated themes of gangsta rap and ignorance of the reality of their surroundings: "Everybody else wanted to talk about rims, and cars, and girls, and then they want to talk about gunplay and carrying guns and how they were so hard. And I'm like, 'I know you. I knew you last year. I never saw you with a pistol in your lap or tucked under your jeans. And for the first time ever, here you are really carrying a gun and really shooting at people and you don't have nothing to fucking say. You'd rather make it all up.'"[99]

Likewise, Saunders criticizes other soldier rap groups for trying to blend their experience of war with elements of popular culture and allowing themselves to be exploited by small record companies that assemble and produce the groups in the United States:

It happened there. It's not like I waited, cheated, and came back home and did it. It's not like some guy had to tell me, "Hey, Neal. Here is what you need to do, now go do it." And that's what's happening now is, none of these soldiers are doing this on their own because they feel that way about it or the music is so important to them. They are doing it because they are trying to make a dollar off of that shit, not because they care. And that is totally bad. And I feel like, I definitely feel like that's not why I did it . . . and I listened to it and I just wanted to fucking throw up because a dude is talking about "he can't wait to come home" or something like that, which you can do a good song about that. But then he is talking about "he can't wait to get home and ride on chrome." And I was like no, no you didn't. The rest of these people are taking something that, man, I just put so much emotion in and they are just fucking me.[100]

Saunders recalls that, in many cases, he was first approached by record companies whose producers wanted to control his public image and marketing in order to increase sales. He felt that his musical voice was too "sacred" to allow others to manipulate it for the sake of profit or for the media's glamorization of the war.

The rivalry Saunders creates with gangsta rappers and other soldier rap groups recalls the typical enmity associated with gangsta rap. For as much as he claims to be different, gangsta rap is about claiming to be different and questioning the authenticity of other rappers.[101] In this sense, Saunders seems to be acting within the framework of gangsta rap—a genre that he claims to oppose. However, gangsta rap rivalries are usually waged in terms of power, through threatened violence, strength, and the possession of money, alcohol, drugs, and women. Gangsta rappers claim superiority by asserting that they are more violent, wealthier, and more able to obtain physical gratification. On one hand, from the perspective of violence and power, Saunders engages in this type of rivalry. He challenges the legitimacy of gangsta rap's frequently exaggerated texts by comparing them to the violence of his life as a soldier in Iraq, and casts doubts upon the authenticity of other soldier rap groups. On the other hand, he refuses to compromise his image or inflate the levels of violence he experienced in order to personally profit from lucrative record contracts, and this refusal runs counter to the practices of most gangsta rappers.

Additionally, Saunders opposes many elements that define gangsta rap. The rhetorical position most often expressed in gangsta rap involves mostly African American, male youths lashing out against a society that has oppressed them through poverty, racism, and the conditions of street life into adopting a nihilistic perspective. Some members of the African American community e-mail Saunders, calling him a murderer and saying that he is naïve for not recognizing the ways he is being used by the government and white society in the Iraq War. They claim Saunders has been a pawn in white society's war for oil in Iraq.[102] However, Saunders, himself an African American, believes that their depiction of his victimization results from an unwillingness to accept personal accountability for one's actions and situation: "Black people really piss me off more than anybody. Because, oh my goodness, I think they have a huge history of never taking responsibility for themselves what-so-fucking ever. If you're black, nothing is your fucking fault. So when they e-mail me, I get all kinds of propaganda-type shit from them. They talk about how the government is using you and 'the man' got you over there fighting for some oil that you'll never see money from. It's all just a bunch of crazy shit."[103]

Concerning the portrayals of life in gangsta rap, Saunders feels that it is easier to claim to be the victim of a racist society than to initiate a positive social change. For example, he confronts the popular gangsta rap topic of police profiling, in which rappers express hostile and violent attitudes about being unfairly targeted by the police due to their African American ethnicity. Saunders argues that police profiling has less to do with race than with breaking the law:

You can do what you want, but whose fault is it when bad shit happens to you? People are just like, "It's not my fault." Like a little kid that wants to ride spinners and drive, and be like 17 or 18 and smoke weed like Snoop Dogg. And act like he's a fuckin' gangsta and shit. But as soon as the police pull him over man, he's talkin' about profiling. Whether the police profiled your punk ass or not, if they pull you over and they find something, shit, maybe there is something to profiling. Maybe it fuckin' works. And maybe people just need to become a whole lot smarter. It's like I never knew a gangster from back in the day, the gangster era, that was just tellin' everybody he's a gangster—this is all the dirt that I do—because that stuff attracts attention man. And just nowadays that is what they [rappers] seem to be doin'. They want everybody to know what they have and how they get it—we break the law. And when they get caught up for it, it's like "Oh, got me because I'm black."[104]

Saunders believes that the claims of gangsta rappers and those who emulate the gangsta rapper image regarding this form of racism are hypocritical. While they position themselves as victims of racial profiling, the glorification of violence and criminal behavior characteristic of gangsta rap draws attention to these illegal acts. For Saunders, if they are being true to the reality they articulate in their lyrics or in the image of that lifestyle by breaking the law, then they deserve the measures taken against them. Saunders views such cases as issues of personal responsibility, rather than racism, because they have knowingly and publicly glamorized a criminal lifestyle. He interprets claims of racism as ways to avoid responsibility, even when gangsta rappers call attention to the fact that they may be breaking the law.

Another way in which Saunders stands ideologically opposed to gangsta rap is through his emphasis on moral values like honesty, integrity, and personal responsibility; he consistently stresses the importance of assuming responsibility for one's actions. "Integrity is a big thing to me and understanding the truth and being able to decipher that from all the bullshit that gets passed along. . . . And just tell people basically, man, empower themselves. And stop waiting on somebody else to do something for you because they are going to do absolutely nothing for you especially if you won't even attempt to do anything for yourself."[105] Saunders expresses his belief in personal integrity by openly criticizing his superior officer in the 4th25 song "Pussy." The song recalls a day in combat when a rocket-propelled grenade attack left numerous soldiers injured and the staff sergeant did not leave the Humvee to fight or apply first aid to the wounded soldiers. Upon arriving back at the base, the staff sergeant went to the aid station with minor scrapes and was later awarded a purple heart. Saunders objects to the fact that the staff sergeant received the same award as other soldiers who lost limbs in the attack and killed ten insurgents. As a result, Saunders refused to attend the ceremony in which these purple hearts were awarded. Below is an excerpt from "Pussy."

> Now how the fuck did y'all get that
> Cause you ain't do shit
> Look I was there when Marion went down
> And you ain't get hit
> And if I recall you ain't bleed at all
> He almost lost a limb
> Now how the fuck do you deserve
> The same purple heart as him
> And when they presented you with it
> You accepted it proudly
> And if I ever see you wearing it
> Oh it's coming the fuck off don't doubt me.

These beliefs in integrity and personal responsibility, which motivate much of Saunders's criticism of his superior officers and gangsta rappers, oppose many of the ideas professed in gangsta rap. Whereas gangsta rap represents life as a violent, nihilistic pursuit, many of the songs on *Live from Iraq* and Saunders's personal beliefs emphasize moral values of honesty, integrity, and personal accountability. For Saunders, the violence of street and gang life depicted in gangsta rap is socially irresponsible because it glorifies a criminal lifestyle and is motivated by record sales, where greater violence translates to better sales.

Through the music of 4th25, he undermines many of the fundamental ideologies of gangsta rap and challenges the authenticity of gangsta rap's reality by comparing it to the life of a soldier in Iraq. Many of the textual themes explored in *Live from Iraq* resemble those of gangsta rap, such as the establishment of rivalries, hostility against oppressive forces, violence, and survival of the fittest. Unlike the factors of gang life and social and racial oppression that typically motivate gangsta rap, however, the album's themes are often driven by values like integrity and responsibility. Saunders adopts the rhetorical framework of gangsta rap to attack many of the ideological beliefs on which the genre is based. In this way, Saunders employs a trope of the genre to challenge it, and his oppositions to gangsta rap are expressed through the gangsta rap genre itself.

BEYOND METAL AND RAP

This study represents one of the first examinations of the complex relationship between music and American soldiers in Iraq. Clearly, music plays a significant role in the lives of many American soldiers. I have focused primarily on metal and rap music within the contexts of military recruiting, soldier inspiration, psychological tactics, and soldier expression, but my research represents only one perspective on a variety of ways in which these topics might be pursued. In this final section, I propose a few areas for further analysis, among many, that emerged during my research period but did not fit within the scope of the book.

Within the context of soldier life in Iraq, music often provided soldiers with a vehicle for expressing personal nostalgia. Svetlana Boym points out that nostalgia has historical roots in the longing of soldiers for home.[106] In *The Future of Nostalgia,* she traces the term nostalgia to the Swiss doctor Johannes Hofer, who used it in his 1688 medical dissertation to describe a condition among Swiss soldiers involving a sad longing for one's homeland.[107] While nostalgia was thought to be a treatable and even curable disease, music was identified as a profound trigger for nostalgia among soldiers. Boym explains, "Supposedly the sounds of 'a certain rustic cantilena' that accompanied shepherds in their driving of the herds to pasture immediately provoked an epidemic of nostalgia among Swiss soldiers serving in France. Similarly, Scots, particularly Highlanders, were known to succumb to incapacitating nostalgia when hearing the sound of bagpipes—so much so, in fact, that their military superiors had to prohibit them from playing, singing or even whistling native tunes in a suggestive manner."[108] For many soldiers in Iraq, music operates nostalgically as a psychological escape from their surroundings, especially as they listen to music associated with happy memories or loved ones. As Johnson recalled, "Sometimes a song would come on that was a big hit in my high school days and that would take me back to that time and it would make me feel better for a few minutes."[109] Atkinson was separated from her husband for close to thirty months and listened to "Here Without You" by Three Doors Down, a song she describes as their theme song; it was a way to "lose yourself in a little bit of home."[110]

She also recalled that another soldier, "Dave," who is a "big, Blackhawk crew chief," would listen to children's songs and nursery rhymes to remind him of his young son.[111] Dave made recordings of himself reading Dr. Seuss stories to his son and stored them on his iPod. Erik Holtan listened to pop singer Jessica Simpson as a way to create an emotional connection with his wife, but also to regain his sensitivity to romance and love within the context of war.

> Jessica Simpson probably impacted me the most because I missed my wife and a lot of those songs were love songs. And those were the songs that impacted me the most as far as just having the void of my wife not being there. You know what I mean? And a way to kind of feel like I had still maybe that—I wasn't all macho in me. You go over there, you know, everything's a hard shell. You're a hard shell and you're hard to crack, and you don't have a lot of people to talk to about the sensitive side. . . . Maybe you don't know how to explain it to anybody, but having you listen to the song is a way to cope.[112]

Holtan would occasionally listen to songs that his children enjoyed as well, even if he was not particularly fond of the music.

DeNora's work on musical memory provides a useful interpretive context for understanding these types of relationships. She proposes that music can be more than a source of psychological "priming," in which moods or emotions are connected with music; music can "serve as a container for the temporal structure of past circumstances. . . . Musical structures may provide a grid or grammar for the temporal structures of emotional and embodied patterns as they were originally experienced."[113] By listening to music associated with past events, these events are more than simply recalled; they can be reexperienced. Just as music can have a transformative influence on the mindset of soldiers, so too can it transport soldiers to a different, imagined time or space, away from their surroundings. The music leads them back into the experiential framework of memories usually associated with loved ones or happy experiences. While not all soldiers experience this interaction with music and memory, music seems to have a strong impact in this way for many. One soldier interviewed, "Major Pain," effectively speaks to this power: "Music can help you escape the terror and terrible things you may see. Make you think and see things back home or bring smells of a Christmas morning from home to you in a hellhole. Music can take you through a time warp and even though for a second, can make forget the hell around you."[114]

The transportive influence of music can also work in the opposite way, returning soldiers to their deployment to Iraq. Miner said, "I hear songs that we played in our Humvee and it takes me right back to Baghdad."[115] Similarly, Grisham said that specific metal and rap songs return him to the psychological state he experienced in Iraq, and he cannot listen to these songs because of these associations.[116] Buzzell also felt transported back to Iraq when he awoke one morning in his wife's home in Brooklyn, to the sacred recitations being broadcast from a nearby mosque:

It's just one of the noises that I heard out there that I'll never forget. And the weird thing is, my wife was living in New York and I got out of the Army. I moved into her place in Brooklyn. She has to go to work and she leaves for work and I'm sleepin'. All of a sudden, I hear this, "buh, buh, buh." I wake up and I'm like, "What the fuck?" I distinctly hear it and I go outside, take a look around, and she lives right around a mosque—there was like a little mosque right there and they did that too out there. I was all excited to leave Iraq, hoping to never hear that sound and then I move to New York and there is a mosque right around the corner. I was like, "Jesus Christ!" They would blast it several times a day. It's like background music to a lot of people, but for me, whenever I hear it, I'm just like, "Bam!" I'm instantly reminded of Iraq.[117]

For some soldiers, music also contributes to physical or psychological recovery from the experience of war. Revak stated that working on *In the Hours of Darkness* was a vital factor during his time on convalescent leave after being wounded. The emerging field of music therapy shows promising work regarding music in response to trauma and Post Traumatic Stress Disorder (PTSD). For example, the American Music Therapy Association, largely funded by The Recording Academy, ran the New York City Music Therapy Relief Project aimed at providing music therapy services for children, victims' families, and others, to help them cope with the 11 September 2001 attacks. Preliminary evidence shows that these programs were highly successful. Similar music therapy could prove effective for soldiers recovering from physical and psychological trauma. In my own fieldwork, however, I found it problematic if not impossible to gain access to major military medical recovery facilities and wards, like Ward 57, the amputee wing of the Walter Reed Medical Center. As such, research on music and soldier recovery may be difficult to pursue from a nonmedical perspective.

There are seemingly innumerable ways to examine music and the Iraq War. As I have shown, soldiers' interactions with music vary considerably depending on factors like personal preference, ethnicity, geographic background, Military Occupational Specialty, rank, among others. Issues ranging from gender, sexuality, race, and religion to soldiers' acoustic guitar music, military bands, and the impact of USO-sponsored concerts would benefit greatly from further investigation. Over the last few years, the scholarly academic community has begun addressing these and other important issues surrounding the more general topic of music and conflict. Conference themes, such as the 2007 meeting of the Society for Ethnomusicology, "Music, War, and Reconciliation"; the 2008 Experience Music Project (EMP) conference, "Shake, Rattle: Music, Conflict, and Change"; and Stonehill College's 2008 "The Music of War: An Interdisciplinary Conference," have brought many scholars together to present recent work on music and war. Much of what has been presented, such as Lisa Gilman's "An American Soldier's iPod: Layers of Identity and Situated Listening in Iraq," J. Martin Daughtry's "'A Symphony of Bullets': Towards a Sonic Ethnography of Contemporary Baghdad," and many others, seems very promising for future research, and I eagerly anticipate the great variety of forthcoming scholarship.[118] My hope is that this book will provide a platform from which others might engage their own areas of interest and will contribute to the growing literature on music and war.

Postscript

As mentioned in the introduction, this book raises more questions than it answers. Many of the ideas proposed in this study suggest that the influence of music may be more potent in the context of war than in daily life. Songs expressing power, violence, death, patriotism, home, the memory of loved ones, and more operate in intensely influential ways for soldiers, but there are still many questions about music in soldier life that could be addressed. Can we understand soldiers' interactions with music as less intense ways of listening when compared to our own? Or do they represent fundamentally different listening experiences? Many athletes, for instance, listen to music before competitions, and in some sports, like football, players are frequently seen leaving buses plugged in to mp3 players or iPods. During the 2004 Summer Olympics, NBC broadcast American swimmer Michael Phelps's pre-competition iTunes playlist and invited viewers to listen along as Phelps listened to his iPod in preparation for races. Is this similar in some way to the process of soldiers inspiring themselves through music for the possibility of combat? To be sure, no one would argue that the contexts of sports are similar to combat, but clearly sports uses much of the descriptive language of war. In football, for example, we analogize to war when discussing "the battle in the trenches" of linemen, the "field general" quarterback, and even the "blitz" (derived from the German "blitzkrieg"). There has been a backlash in some cases, however, as when ESPN aired and later removed a commercial describing college football games as "Saturday soldiers fighting for every touchdown." Music is often used as an inspiration by athletes; how, then, does it compare to soldiers' preparations, particularly in instances where much of the rhetoric surrounding the game draws analogies to war?

Another interesting issue that emerges from this work is how music is used to indoctrinate listeners with certain ideological views. In chapter 3, I proposed that much of the anti-American and anti-Israel music was employed as a recruiting tool and an inspiration for combat, but it was also a way to indoctrinate listeners with aspects of fundamentalist Islam. Clearly, these movements are not the first to utilize music in this way. For example, Romanian Communists used songs to attempt to insert themselves into the cultural legacy of Romania in order to legitimize their regime, and certain Evangelical Christian churches use music to instill religious doctrine in children. From this follows an important question: Are American soldiers similarly indoctrinated through music? Running and marching cadences, while helpful in building camaraderie and assisting on long physical training exercises, are also a way of instilling values in soldiers. Although they are a component of the process of soldierization—transforming civilians into soldiers—certain cadences, like "Somebody, Anybody Start a War," which includes the line "I'm gonna go to Vietnam and be a mercenary, gonna even that battle, gonna even that score, gonna kill me a Commie," seem to express more than the nationalist/patriotic sentiments one might expect in these circumstances. How much do these cadences play a role in reinforcing or changing certain attitudes held by recruits? Are American soldiers, in their own way, indoctrinated through music as well?

The discussion of music in interrogation might spark the most passionate reactions given the high-profile and politically sensitive status of such a topic. My intention was not to answer the question of whether music in these situations is or is not torture, but to shed light on the subject from the perspective of soldiers' training and practices. Research on such subjects is always problematic because the corroboration of information is extremely difficult, and it is critical to acknowledge the limitations placed on any research on this subject and the conclusions that can be drawn from it. At the same time, this is an important question to ask and discuss from any number of perspectives—ethical, legal, moral, and others.

The purpose of posing these questions (and many more could be asked) at the conclusion of the book is not to provide answers, but to introduce some of the important issues that emerge from my study that we may want to consider more closely. Before engaging such questions, however, I believe that the first step is to understand the distinct cultures that compose the U.S. military. I use the plural "cultures" to underscore the idea that different branches, divisions, unit, and platoons may adopt distinct practices, making these groups worth considering apart from others in the military. Jennifer Atkinson noted that after spending four months with an Infantry unit, "I could not construct a sentence without the word—I'm going to get a little vulgar here—was unable to construct a sentence without the word 'fuck' in it. It was a verb, it was an adjective, it was a noun. When I got back to the transportation company my sergeant pulled me aside, I think he pulled all of us aside, and said, 'I just want to let you know that you kind of need to watch your language,' and I looked at him and said, 'I don't know what the f[uck] you're talking about.'"[1]

It is easy to think that because these men and women are Americans listening to the music of popular culture, we already have a degree of understanding concerning the larger cultural contexts that surround and influence them and their musical practices. This can be a problematic assumption. I began to illustrate in chapter 5 the challenges of interpreting the lyrics to "Mortaritaville," which some readers may have found offensive. As I probed further, I found that "Mortaritaville" was not only part of a tradition of barracks humor that extended back through numerous wars, but that dark or black humor in general was common in enlisted soldier life. Colby Buzzell mentioned that members of his unit gathered before going to Iraq to have a "We're All Going to Die" party, and he ironically included songs like Louis Armstrong's "What a Wonderful World" and John Lennon's "Give Peace a Chance" on his iPod playlist during deployment.[2] After talking to soldiers about this type of humor, it appears to be much more of a coping mechanism that pokes funs at their surroundings and aspects of military life than an expression of genuine attitudes about opposing forces or whatever happens to be the topic of a song or joke. An attitude of black humor exists among many enlisted soldiers that makes fun of the enemy and of themselves. "Mortaritaville" jokingly mocks the Iraqis, but David Schultz also mocks himself for volunteering to be in the army, which ultimately led him to Iraq: "I'd like to kick my recruiter straight square in the teeth, but I know, it's my own damn fault." This type of joking attitude, especially concerning recruiters, even exists in officially sanctioned running cadences. The cadence "My Recruiter" opens with, "My recruiter he told me a lie, he said 'Join the Rangers and learn to fly.' Oh I signed my name on the dotted line, all I'm doing is double time. Hey all the way, running every day." This may be what *New York Times* writer Joseph Treaster meant when he wrote about American soldiers' songs in Vietnam, that "the songs reflect the wartime Yank's ability to laugh at himself in a difficult situation."[3] Of course, my explanation does not provide an excuse for what some may find insensitive or even prejudiced sentiments, and indeed, some soldiers may genuinely feel as a song or joke states. But I think that such reactions would have to consider the cultural context in which this music or ideas are being expressed. If one were not to understand the tradition and practices of barracks humor, and the history of the U.S. military as a collection of cultures, one would overlook a significant framework for the production of this music. Answering many of the questions that were asked earlier seems to begin with understanding the U.S. military as a set of cultures; and particularly when the circumstances of military life involve deployment to a combat zone, the idea of engaging musical practices as distinct cultures or subcultures appears even more important.

Ultimately, *Sound Targets* represents an introductory examination of the relationship between metal and rap music, and American soldiers in Iraq within specific contexts of military service. I believe, however, that these issues are too interesting and relevant to remain unexplored, even if we are still scratching the surface. Much more should and I hope will be said about these and other topics related to music and war. Through this study, I have come to a greater appreciation of music's ability to influence the human condition.

SOLDIER E-MAIL AND SAMPLE QUESTIONS FROM SOLDIER INTERVIEWS

Dear (name),

Hi, my name is Jon Pieslak and I am a professor of music at The City College of New York. I am working on a study that explores how music plays a role in the war in Iraq and came across your e-mail/blog/web site as I was doing my research. As part of my work, I am very interested in getting the opinions and perspectives of soldiers, and I was wondering if you might be interested in being a part of my study. Basically, I want to e-mail you a few questions about music and your time in Iraq—like, "Could you describe the roles of music, if any, in your life in Iraq" and questions like that. It wouldn't take up too much of your time and I will respect your anonymity if you wish. If possible, I'd love to speak to you over the phone, but I understand that you may be busy and e-mail may be preferable.

I want to present the viewpoints of soldiers in an uncensored form and allow their voices to be heard without editorializing. There is no ambition to profit from your experiences or to express political views through this scholarship. It would be great to have you as part of this study, so please let me know if you might be interested. Even if you are not, I would like to wish you a safe and healthy future.

Best wishes, Jon.

The following questions served as a general outline for my personal and e-mail interviews with soldiers. I did not always strictly adhere to this sequence of questions, but followed the natural course of conversation as it related to each individual soldier.

Background

1. Could you tell me a little about yourself, your background, and history in the military? For instance, where were you born? What was it like growing up? Did music factor into your life as a child? How did you become involved with the military?

2. When and where were you deployed? In what capacities did you serve in Iraq? Could you describe your duties while in Iraq? What did you do all day?

3. Prior to going to Iraq, did you enjoy particular kinds of music? If so, in what circumstances? How frequently did you listen, daily, weekly, rarely? Music in Iraq

4. While in Iraq, did you listen to music? If so, what kinds of music? Describe your musical environment while there. Did your musical preferences change while in Iraq?

5. How did music fit into a typical day in Iraq, if at all? Did you have specific kinds of music for certain activities, such as music for hanging out?

6. Was there combat around your area or when you went into the field? Did you ever listen to music before going into the field? If so, what kinds of music? Describe this experience.

7. Did you feel that music affected you in any way? If so, could you describe how? How did you relate to the music you listened to, if at all? If you felt music had an impact on you, was it the lyrics, the sounds, or both?

8. Are you familiar with any uses of music in PSYOPS or interrogation? If so, how was music employed in these situations?

9. Did you write music while in Iraq? If so, could you tell me about the music you wrote and what you were trying to express? Did you record music? If so, could you describe how you recorded it?

10. Please feel free to say anything else about the role music played in your life in Iraq.

GLOSSARY OF MILITARY RANKS

Most of the soldiers interviewed for this book are, or have been, members of the U.S. Army or Marine Corps. The ranks and hierarchy of these two military branches are presented below. All major branches of the military are divided into two larger categories, Officers and Enlisted. Officers are commissioned in the name of the President of the United States and command enlisted soldiers and Marines. Noncommissioned Officers (NCOs), at ranks of corporal (in the Marine Corps), sergeant (in the army), or higher, are those within the enlisted rank who are granted lesser degrees of authority than officers. They typically function as liaisons between enlisted soldiers and officers. Rankings are listed in descending chain of command.

ARMY, ENLISTED

CSM, Command Sergeant Major
SGM, Sergeant Major
1SG, First Sergeant
MSG, Master Sergeant
SFC, Sergeant First Class
SSG, Staff Sergeant
SGT, Sergeant
CPL, Corporal
SPC, Specialist
PFC, Private First Class

ARMY, OFFICER

GEN, General
LTG, Lieutenant General
MG, Major General
BG, Brigadier General
COL, Colonel
LTC, Lieutenant Colonel
MAJ, Major
CPT, Captain
1LT, First Lieutenant
2LT, Second Lieutenant

MARINE CORPS, ENLISTED

SGTMAJ, Sergeant Major
MGYSGT, Master Gunnery Sergeant
1st SGT, First Sergeant
MSGT, Master Sergeant
GYSGT, Gunnery Sergeant
SSGT, Staff Sergeant
SGT, Sergeant
CPL, Corporal
LCPL, Lance Corporal
PFC, Private First Class

MARINE CORPS, OFFICER

GEN, General
LTGEN, Lieutenant General
MAJGEN, Major General
BRIGGEN, Brigadier General
COL, Colonel
LTCOL, Lieutenant Colonel
MAJ, Major
CAPT, Captain
1st LT, First Lieutenant
2nd LT, Second Lieutenant

NOTES

INTRODUCTION

1. While "soldier" tends to designate members of the enlisted rank of the army, including noncommissioned officers (NCO), I use the term in a more inclusive way to refer to all members of a country's military.

2. http://www.slayerized.com/band/didyouknow.html, accessed 8 January 2004.

3. Michael Sager, "Fact: Five Out of Five Kids Who Kill Love Slayer," *Esquire* (February 1992): 82–85.

4. "American Soldier," e-mail communication, 17 April 2006.

5. C. J. Grisham, interview by the author, tape recording, New York, 1 May 2006. Each soldier's military rank was their rank as of the date of correspondence with the author.

6. Colby Buzzell, interview by the author, tape recording, New York, 27 April 2006.

7. Erik Holtan, interview by the author, tape recording, New York, 18 April 2006.

8. Buzzell, interview.

9. Ronald Botelho, interview by the author, tape recording, New York, 8 June 2007.

10. Ibid.

11. See Colby Buzzell, *My War: Killing Time in Iraq* (New York: Putnam Adult, 2005), and John Crawford, *The Last True Story I'll Ever Tell: An Accidental Soldier's Account of the War in Iraq* (New York: Riverhead, 2005).

12. Bruno Nettl, "The Institutionalisation of Musicology: Perspectives of a North American Musicologist," in *Rethinking Music*, ed. Nicholas Cook and Mark Everist (New York: Oxford University Press, 1999), 289.

13. Daniel L. Schachter, *Searching for Memory: The Brain, the Mind, and the Past* (New York: Basic Books, 1996), 5–6.

14. Kay Kaufman Shelemay, *Let Jasmine Rain Down: Song and Remembrance among Syrian Jews* (Chicago: University of Chicago Press, 1998), 8.

15. George Devereux, *From Anxiety to Method in the Behavioral Sciences* (Paris: École Pratique des Hautes Études, 1967).

16. See Michael H. Agar, *The Professional Stranger: An Informal Introduction to Ethnography* (New York: Academic Press, 1996); Charles L. Briggs, *Learning How to Ask: A Sociolinguistic Appraisal of the Role of the Interview in Social Science Research* (New York: Cambridge University Press, 1986); Clifford Geertz, *Work and Lives: The Anthropologist as Author* (Stanford, Calif.: Stanford University Press, 1988).

17. Philip V. Bolman, "Musicology as a Political Act," *Journal of Musicology* 11, no. 4 (1993): 436.

18. Bruno Latour and Steve Woolgar, *Laboratory Life: The Social Construction of Scientific Facts* (London: Sage, 1979).

19. Ruth Behar, *The Vulnerable Observer: Anthropology That Breaks Your Heart* (Boston: Beacon, 1996); Harris Berger, *Metal, Rock, and Jazz: Perception and the Phenomenology of Musical Experience* (Hanover, N.H.: Wesleyan University Press, 1999).

20. Neal Saunders, interview by the author, tape recording, New York, 18 April 2006.

21. Anonymous, former army interrogator, e-mail communication, 11 July 2007.

1. MUSIC AND CONTEMPORARY MILITARY RECRUITING

1. Thomas W. Evans, "The All-Volunteer Army after Twenty Years: Recruiting in the Modern Era," *Army History: The Professional Bulletin of Army History* 27 (1993), http://www.shsu.edu/~his_ncp/VolArm.html.

2. Jennifer Harper, "'Army Strong' to be New Recruiting Slogan," *Washington Times,* 10 October 2006.

3. Evans, "The All-Volunteer Army."

4. Ibid.

5. Counter-recruiting activism has been common on high school and college campuses. Initiatives like http://www.counter-recruitment.org protest the distribution of students' contact information to the military under the No Child Left Behind Act, and question the ethical practices of recruiters. Over the last six years, the practices of military recruiters have come under harsh scrutiny. The mainstream news media has broadcast and printed numerous stories about recruits who claim they were incessantly harassed by telephone calls or even lied to by recruiters. The military seems to have responded to these claims through television advertisements and a web site, www.todaysmilitary.com, which encourages parents and potential recruits to inform themselves about military service.

6. U.S. Congressional Budget Office, *Recruiting, Retention, and Future Levels of Military Personnel,* October 2006, 9.

7. Ibid. Also see James N. Dertouzos, *Is Military Advertising Effective? An Estimation Methodology and Applications to Recruiting in the 1980s and 90s* (Arlington, Va.: Rand, 2003), 87.

8. Propaganda videos include DVDs shown at recruiting/information sessions. They tend to be longer than the typical thirty-second television advertisement, but do not differ in other significant ways.

9. Carrie McLaren, "Salesnoise: The Convergence of Music and Advertising," http://www.stayfreemagazine.org/archives/15/salesnoise.html, accessed 27 November 2006.

10. Ibid.

11. Ann E. Kaplan, *Rocking around the Clock: Music Television, Postmodernism, and Consumer Culture* (New York: Methuen, 1987), 12.

12. Kelly Askew, "Introduction," in *The Anthropology of Media: A Reader,* ed. Kelly Askew and Richard R. Wilk (Oxford: Blackwell, 2002), 2.

13. Roger Hillman, "Narrative, Sound, and Film: Fassbinder's *The Marriage of Maria Braun,"* in *Fields of Vision: Essays in Film Studies, Visual Anthropology, and Photography,* ed. Leslie Decereaux and Roger Hillman (Berkeley: University of California Press, 1995), 182.

14. Michel Chion, *Audio-Vision: Sound on Screen,* ed. and trans. Claudia Gorbman (New York: Columbia University Press, 1994), 9.

15. Ibid., 5.

16. Ibid., 216.

17. Ibid., xxvi.

18. Many of the video examples are linked to www.youtube.com and are governed by YouTube's laws of fair use and copyright. In other instances, the laws of fair use and copyright are adhered to according to the respective web sites.

19. See Leonard Meyer, *Emotion and Meaning in Music* (Chicago: University of

Chicago Press, 1956); Jean Molino, "Fait musicale et sémiologie de la musique," *Musique en jeu* 17, 37–62; Jean-Jacques Nattiez, *Fondements d'une sémiologie de la musique* (Paris: Union Générale des Éditions, 1975), and *Music and Discourse: Towards a Semiology of Music,* trans. Carolyn Abbate (Princeton, N.J.: Princeton University Press, 1990).

20. Meyer, *Emotion and Meaning in Music.*

21. Robert Walser, *Running with the Devil: Power, Gender, and Madness in Heavy Metal Music* (Hanover, N.H.: University Press of New England, 1993), 31.

22. See, for example, Steven Feld, "Communication, Music, and Speech about Music," in *Music Grooves,* ed. Charles Keil and Steven Feld (Chicago: University of Chicago Press, 1991), 77–95.

23. Thomas Turino, "Signs of Imagination, Identity, and Experience: A Peircian Semiotic Theory for Music," *Ethnomusicology* 43, no. 2 (1999): 221–55.

24. Thomas Turino, *Nationalists, Cosmopolitanists, and Popular Music in Zimbabwe* (Chicago: University of Chicago Press, 2000), 174–75.

25. Charles Keil and Steven Feld, *Music Grooves* (Chicago: University of Chicago Press, 1991), 151–94.

26. Nicholas Cook, "Music and Meaning in the Commercials," *Popular Music* 13, no. 1 (1994): 39.

27. Claudia Gorbman, *Unheard Melodies* (Bloomington: Indiana University Press, 1987), 3.

28. David Huron, "Music in Advertising: An Analytic Paradigm," *Musical Quarterly* 73, no. 4 (1989): 560.

29. The Coast Guard, which has used campaign slogans like "Be Part of the Action," is not included in my study because of the limited exposure the Coast Guard has in television commercials. In "Recognition of Military Advertising Slogans Among American Youth," Wayne Hintze and Jerry Lehnus show that recognition of Coast Guard slogans is significantly lower than the other branches of the military—most likely due to budget limitations. See Wayne Hintze and Jerry Lehnus, "Recognition of Military Advertising Slogans Among American Youth," paper presented at the International Military Testing Association (IMTA) Conference, 1996. Available online, http://www.ijoa.org/imta96/paper19.html.

30. Genre and subgenre distinction in popular music can be a difficult, complicated task. In my work on the music of metal bands like Meshuggah and Korn, I point out that distorted guitar timbres and/or power chords are frequently the sole determinant used by scholars to qualify music as metal or exhibiting a metal influence. Power chords are a pitch unit made up of root and fifth, usually associated with distorted amplification. The term "heavy metal" is typically used interchangeably with "metal" to describe these musical features. See Jonathan Pieslak, "Re-casting Metal: Rhythm and Meter in the Music of Meshuggah," *Music Theory Spectrum,* 29, no. 2 (2007): 219–45.

31. Nü metal is a subgenre that emerged in late 1990s and "can be characterized by aggressive, rap-influenced, angst-ridden and pitched yelling vocals, hip-hop style beats or drum samples, and heavily distorted, detuned guitars playing largely syncopated, riff-based music with a distinct absence of solos and overt displays of instrumental virtuosity." Jonathan Pieslak, "Text, Sound and Identity in Korn's 'Hey Daddy,'" *Popular Music* 28, no. 1 (2008): 38. Godsmack is a very popular nü metal band; their album *Faceless,* which followed *Awake,* debuted at #1 on the Billboard charts in 2003.

32. The music was written by Section 8 Studio founder, Garrett Flynn.

33. Chion, *Audio-Vision,* 167.

34. Pieslak, "Rhythm and Meter in the Music of Meshuggah," 243.

35. Walser, *Running with the Devil,* 44–51.

36. Of course, I am not claiming that all depictions of action, adventure, and violence in television during this time made metal allusions. Rather, some shows began incorporating this music into its sound tracks.

37. David Ehrenstein and Bill Reed, *Rock on Film* (New York: Delilah, 1982).

38. Ibid., 110.

39. Walser, *Running with the Devil*, 5.

40. Gorbman, *Unheard Melodies*, 163.

41. My thanks to Dan Cavicchi for bringing the *Iron Eagle* movies to my attention.

42. Stephen Totilo, "EA Offers Up Snoop, Peas Tracks; Exec Talks Future of Video Game Music." http://www.mtv.com/games/video_games/news/story.jhtml?id=1553668, accessed 1 March 2007.

43. Ibid.

44. "Song 2" also accompanied the television trailer to the 1997 action/adventure movie, *Starship Troopers*.

45. http://en.wikipedia.org/wiki/Song_2.

46. Andrew Goodwin, *Dancing in the Distraction Factory: Music Television and Popular Culture* (Minneapolis: University of Minnesota Press, 1992), 135. Also, see Jack Banks, *Monopoly Television: MTV's Quest to Control the Music* (Boulder, Colo.: Westview Press, 1996), 124.

47. Stacy L. Smith and Aaron R. Boyson, "Violence in Music Videos: Examining the Prevalence and Context of Physical Aggression," *Journal of Communication* 52, no. 1 (2002): 79.

48. Ibid. Smith and Boyson's study is consistent with earlier studies of violence in music videos. See R. H. DuRant, M. Rich, S. J. Emans, E. S. Rome, E. Allred, and E. R. Woods, "Violence and Weapon Carrying in Music Videos: A Content Analysis," *Archives of Pediatric and Adolescent Medicine* 151 (2002): 443–48; J. Tapper, E. Thorson, and D. Black, "Variations in Music Videos as a Function of Their Musical Genre," *Journal of Broadcasting and Electronic Media* 38 (1994): 103–13.

49. The film is an adaptation of the 1939 novel by Dalton Trumbo.

50. My observations regarding music and imagery in military recruiting are reinforced in an episode of *The Simpsons*. In episode 1805 (aired 11 November 2006), two Army recruiters show a propaganda video to an auditorium of elementary school students. The video begins with heroic music and shows soldiers in a helicopter shooting missiles at Nazi soldiers, a man dressed as an Arab (possibly meant to be Osama bin Laden), a man holding a knife in a hockey mask, and a cloud with the script "deadly hurricane" on it. The helicopter lands in a stadium full of people and the soldiers jump out with guitars, playing a distorted guitar riff from "Communication Breakdown" by Led Zeppelin. The video ends with a narrator saying, "The Army, it's everything you like." While clearly satirical, the video references the military's recruiting strategies of portraying military service as an honorable duty and a source of action, adventure, and excitement. Additionally, the ending scene references rock music and implies that being in the military is somehow like being at a rock concert. The fact that the satire in the video revolves around heroic acts, action/excitement, honorable duty music, and rock music suggests that these are common components of military recruiting propaganda.

51. McLaren, "Salernoise."

52. Buzzell, interview.

53. http://groups.google.com/group/grouchymedia/browse_thread/thread/d5183ca6f2f56cc2#7f89139224fade04.

54. Drowning Pool's "Bodies" has a fascinating history in relation to the Iraq war. This song, from the 2001 album *Sinner*, was enormously popular on commercial radio during

the summer of 2001 but was immediately pulled from most radio broadcasts after 11 September 2001 due to its repeated chorus lyrics, "Let the bodies hit the floor." The song is now popular among soldiers in Iraq and used in the first video on Grouchy Media. Drowning Pool's popularity in the military seems to have influenced the band. In 2007, they released a song, "Soldiers," dedicated to American soldiers.

55. John H. Farris, "The Impact of Basic Combat Training: The Role of the Drill Sergeant," in *The Social Psychology of Military Service,* ed. Nancy L. Goldman and David R. Segal (Beverly Hills: Sage, 1976), 13–24.

56. Jennifer Atkinson, interview by the author, tape recording, New York, 3 May 2006.

57. *Run to Cadence: Special Forces Green Berets* (Documentary Recordings, 460CD, 1996).

2. MUSIC AS AN INSPIRATION FOR COMBAT

1. C. A. Malcolm, *The Piper in Peace and War* (London: John Murray, 1927) (reprint, London: Hardwick Press, 1993), 24. It has been proposed that bagpipes motivated soldiers in combat preparation long before their documented use by Scottish clans; see the Westminster Kind Productions television series "Bagpipes: Instrument of War, Part 1" (1998).

2. The fife is a cross flute or transverse flute.

3. George Washington, The Writings of *George Washington from the Original Manuscript Sources, 1745–1799, 8* (Washington, D.C.: U.S. Government Printing Office, 1931), 181–82.

4. Charles D. Page, *History of the Fourteenth Regiment Connecticut Volunteer Infantry* (Meriden, Conn.: Horton, 1906), 120–21. Also, see similar descriptions in Kenneth E. Olson, *Music and Musket: Bands and Bandsmen of the American Civil War* (Westport, Conn.: Greenwood, 1980).

5. Bell Irvin Wiley, *The Life of Billy Yank* (Indianapolis: Bobbs-Merrill, 1952), 157, and Eric A. Campbell, "Civil War Music and the Common Soldier: The Experiences of Charles Wellington Reed," in *Bugle Resounding: Music and Musicians of the Civil War Era,* ed. Bruce C. Kelley and Mark A. Snell (Columbia: University of Missouri Press, 2004), 202–28.

6. Albert Marple, "Wireless Music for Wounded Soldiers," *The Wireless Age,* April 1918, 590, 593.

7. Guy Sajer, *The Forgotten Soldier* (Dulles, Va.: Brassey, 1990), 418.

8. Bruce Brown, personal communication, Plainfield, N.J., 12 September 2006.

9. Ibid.

10. http://afrts.dodmedia.osd.mil.

11. BBC Propaganda Broadcasts, "Glenn Miller and His AEF Orchestra," November 1994.

12. http://uso.org.

13. http://groups.yahoo.com/group/afvn/, accessed July 2007. My thanks to Christopher Sabis for initiating the discussion on this forum. Sabis's senior thesis, "Through the Soldiers' Ears: What Americans Fighting in Vietnam Heard and Its Effects," from the University of Rochester, provides an insightful examination of soldiers' interaction with music in Vietnam. See http://www.geocities.com/afvn3/historymenu.html.

14. http://phpbb2.desert-storm.com/viewtopic.php?t=1683&postdays=0&postorder =asc&start=0, accessed 20 July 2007.

15. http://groups.yahoo.com/group/afvn/, accessed July 2007.

16. Ibid., accessed 7 February 2007 and 8 July 2007.

17. Ibid., accessed 14 June 2007.

18. Ibid.

19. Holtan, interview.

20. Grisham, interview.

21. Buzzell, interview; Saunders, interview.

22. Atkinson, interview.

23. Buzzell, interview.

24. Grisham, interview.

25. Joshua Revak, interview by the author, tape recording, New York, 4 April 2007.

26. William Thompson, interview by the author, tape recording, New York, 22 June 2007.

27. David "JR" Schultz, interview by the author, tape recording, New York, 22 June 2007.

28. Michael Tucker, *Gunner Palace* (Palm Pictures, 2004); Ian Olds and Garrett Scott, *Occupation: Dreamland* (Greenhouse Pictures, 2005); George Gittoes, *Soundtrack to War* (Melee Entertainment, 2006).

29. Bing West, *No True Glory: A Frontline Account of the Battle for Fallujah* (New York: Bantam, 2005), 176.

30. Ronald Botelho, interview by the author, tape recording, New York, 8 June 2007.

31. Ibid.

32. Gittoes, *Soundtrack to War.*

33. Mark Miner, e-mail communication, 29 April 2006.

34. Anonymous, personal communication, 25 May 2007.

35. Buzzell, interview.

36. Tia DeNora, *Music in Everyday Life* (New York: Cambridge University Press, 2000), 111.

37. Buzzell, interview.

38. Grisham, interview.

39. DeNora, *Music in Everyday Life,* 60–61.

40. Saunders, interview.

41. Buzzell, interview.

42. Grisham, interview.

3. LOOKING AT THE OPPOSING FORCES

1. For example, see http://www.pmw.org.il/car/Animals/c208646.html.

2. Hadith are sacred texts of words and deeds attributed to Muhammad.

3. Hizbullah (Hezbollah) Press Office, 20 March 1998. Hezbollah is a Shi'a political and military movement located in Lebanon.

4. Margaret Sarkissian, "'Religion Never Had It So Good': Contemporary Nasyid and the Growth of Islamic Popular Music in Malaysia," *Yearbook for Traditional Music* 37 (2005): 124.

5. When appropriate, I include the different spellings that might appear for Arabic words. Words like "nasheed" or "haraam" (forbidden) have multiple spellings, depending upon the cultural background of the writer.

6. Regula Qureshi, "Islam and Music," in *Sacred Sound: Experiencing Music in the World Religions,* ed. Guy L. Beck (Waterloo, Ont.: Winfrid Laurier University Press,

2006), 91–92.

7. Amnon Shiloah, *Music in the World of Islam: A Socio-Cultural Study* (Detroit: Wayne State University Press, 1995), 4–5.

8. Thompson, interview.

9. Sarkissian, "'Religion Never Had It So Good.'"

10. Ibid., 147.

11. See

http://www.islamonline.net/livedialogue/english/Browse.asp?hGuestID=74hx7c.

12. For example,

http://talk.islamicnetwork.com/showthread.php?t=1389&page=7&pp=10,

http://www.ummah.com/forum/showthread.php?t=69225&page=3,

http://forum.bodybuilding.com/showthread.php?t=757284,

http://www.ummah.com/forum/showthread.php?p=690300#post690300.

Postings on these online discussion forums occasionally resemble the type of fan admiration characteristic of Western popular music artists. Participants discuss which traditional nasheed songs and artists they like over others. In one forum, a woman talked about how a Muslim warrior, Umar Ibn Al Khattab, who gave up his fortune to fight for Allah in jihad, is, "from a sister's perspective, one of the most handsome men I've ever laid eyes on." Another woman responded, "Alhamdulillah [Thank God] sis, I agree. That's the type of husband I dream of 2. And many other sisters too I'm sure. Inshallah [God willing] this dua [promise or pledge] will be fulfilled. Marriage to a mujihad [freedom fighter]—**allahuakbar!!** (God is greatest)." See http://www.ummah.com/forum/showthread.php?p=690300#post690300, accessed 7 July 2005.

13. Ibid., accessed 7 March 2006.

14. Ibid., accessed 10 March 2006.

15. Qom is the name of a holy city in Iran, but it is not explicitly related to the lyrics of the nasheed.

16. Translation by http://www.Inflovlad.net.

17. http://clearinghouse.infovlad.net/archive/index.php?t-7254.html, accessed 1 June 2007.

18. "Qom" is very popular with fans of this music. In a recent discussion thread on www.ummah.com, many discussants included "Qom" in their favorite twenty war/jihad nasheed; see http://www.ummah.net/forum/showthread.php?t=117818.

19. Translation by www.at-taifahstudios.com, http://www.youtube.com/watch?v=gwrTvHvIlfs.

20. Thompson, interview.

21. Additional ISI videos can be viewed at www.liveleak.com.

22. Translation of "Sanakhudu Ma'arikana Ma'ahoum" by http://clearinghouse.infovlad.net/archive/index.php?t-7254.html, accessed 1 June 2007, and http://www.lyricsandsongs.com/song/707296.html. Translation of "Asad al-Fallujah" by al-Akh Abul-Fadl al-Shaamee, http://www.ummah.com/forum/showthread.php?t=48435. In an interesting twist, Marine Corps major Douglas A. Zembiec was given the nickname "Lion of Fallujah" in April 2004 when he told reporters that his Marines "fought like lions" in a battle for Fallujah. Zembiec was killed in action on 10 May 2007.

23. A brief clip from a Fatah parade is curiously inserted in the middle of the video. This footage is accompanied by a nasheed with percussion and drums.

24. Walid Shoebat, *Why We Want to Kill You* (Newton, Pa.: Top Executive Media, 2007), 73–74.

25. Ibid., 74.

26. Ibid., 73–74.

27. For example, see http://www.sallawat.com.

28. Hugh Rimintin, http://www.cnn.com/2007/world/meast/05/22/iraq.children/index.html, accessed 22 May 2007.

29. A similar version of this song was sung by a Palestinian girl on Palestinian Authority TV, 26 February 2006: "Daddy gave me a present, a machine gun and a rifle. When I am big, I will join the Liberation Army. The liberation army has taught us how to defend our homeland." http://pmw.org.il/tv%20part3.html.

30. Founded in 1987, Hamas ("Islamic Resistance Movement") is the ruling party in the Palestinian-controlled Gaza Strip.

31. "Farfour" translates as "mouse." He was "martyred" in a 29 June 2007 episode, portrayed as having been killed by Israeli security forces. He was replaced on the program by Nahoul the Bee on 13 July 2007.

32. http://www.memri.org, the organization responsible for the translations in "Tomorrow's Pioneers," has come under criticism for exaggerating the tone and degree of violence in dialogue from the series. Of particular controversy is the translation of a young girl's remarks in an April 2007 episode. Memri translated her statement as, "We will annihilate the Jews," while other Arabic speakers consulted by CNN translated the comment as "The Jews are killing us," or "The Jews will shoot us." The Arabic translations appearing in *Sound Targets* were independently verified by Amber Ferenz, an Arabic linguist. She claims that the Memri translations to the songs of video example 23, while not the most elegant English, accurately reflect the words, tone, and intent of the comments. Amber Ferenz, Arabic translation, 21 June 2007.

33. The development of propaganda aimed at children is not unique to Hamas or Islamic movements in the Middle East, and has numerous precedents. In recent history, many former Soviet bloc countries had formal programs that taught songs to children in an effort to mold them into dedicated Communists. Romanian dictator Nicolae Ceausescu, for example, developed programs for children called "The Falcons" (for kindergarten-age students) and "The Pioneers" (for elementary school children), and songs were an important part of this program, exposing children to Communist doctrine. While there may not be a conscious borrowing, it is interesting that the Hamas television show and Ceausescu's program have similar goals and titles, "Pioneers."

34. Thompson, interview.

35. Jason Sagebiel, interview by the author, tape recording, New York, 19 August 2007.

36. Svanibor Pettan, "Music and Music Research in the Context of Political Changes and War in Croatia during the 1990s," *Muzika 5*, no. 1 (2001): 31.

37. This translation of the Hamas Covenant 1988 is provided by the Avalon Project at the Yale University Law School, http://www.yale.edu/lawweb/avalon/mideast/hamas.htm.

38. The National Research Council Committee on the Youth Population and Military Recruitment, *Evaluating Military Advertising and Recruiting: Theory and Methodology*, ed. Paul R. Sackett and Anne S. Maver (Washington, D.C.: National Academies Press, 2004), 4.

4. MUSIC AS A PSYCHOLOGICAL TACTIC

1. Sun Tzu, *The Art of War* (Boston: Shambhala Publications, 1983), 104.

2. For an examination of the history of psychological weapons, see Leo Braudy, *From Chivalry to Terrorism: War and the Changing Nature of Masculinity* (New York:

Knopf, 2003); John Keegan, *A History of Warfare* (New York: Vintage, 1993); David Miller, *Conflict Iraq: Weapons and Tactics of the U.S. and Iraqi Forces* (St. Paul: MBI, 2003). Another excellent source of information on the history of psychological weapons is www.psywarrior.com. This web site was created by retired Army major Ed Rouse, a military specialist in psychological operations (PSYOPS) and psychological warfare (PSYWAR), and contains numerous articles by Rouse and retired sergeant major Herbert A. Friedman, the American representative to the International Psychological Warfare Society.

3. Dan Kuehl, interview by the author, tape recording, New York, 2 May 2006.

4. Ed Rouse, e-mail communication, 26 April 2006.

5. Kuehl, interview.

6. Similar radio efforts can be seen in almost every conflict since World War II, such as "Hanoi Hannah" in the Vietnam War and "Baghdad Betty" during Operation Desert Storm.

7. http://www.psywarrior.com/psyhist.html.

8. Ibid.

9. Mark Lloyd, *The Art of Military Deception* (London: Leo Cooper, 1997), 146.

10. Ibid.

11. Herbert A. Friedman, "The Wandering Soul PSYOP Tape of Vietnam," http://www.psywarrior.com/wanderingsoul. Also, see Lloyd, *The Art of Military Deception*, 165.

12. Ibid.

13. Botelho, interview.

14. Philip Taylor, e-mail communication, 3 May 2006. Philip Taylor is a professor at the Institute of Communication Studies at the University of Leeds. His web site is a useful resource for information concerning psychological warfare, international communications, "strategic" communications, and information operations. See http://ics.leeds.ac.uk/papers/index.cfm?outfit=pmt.

15. Kuehl, interview.

16. Ben Abel, as quoted in Lane DeGregory, "Soldiers Take on Insurgents with a Musical Vengeance, Cranking up the Volume to Distress the Enemy," *St. Petersburg Times*, 21 November 2004.

17. Buzzell, interview.

18. Schultz, interview.

19. Grisham, interview.

20. Botelho, interview.

21. Grisham, interview.

22. DeGregory, "Soldiers Take on Insurgents."

23. Abel, quoted in DeGregory. Again, the television series *The Simpsons* references this psychological tactic in a satirical way. In episode 172 (aired 6 April 1997), two characters (Edna Krabappel and Seymour Skinner) lock themselves in the local elementary school to protest their recent job dismissals because they have pursued a personal relationship, involving rumors that exaggerate the nature of their physical intimacy. The police attempt to force them out by playing music through loudspeakers and shining bright lights at the school. In typical *Simpsons* humor, the police play "Embraceable You," sung by Frank Sinatra, which has the opposite impact of irritation and frustration. The music sets a romantic mood and the two characters dance with each other.

24. West, *No True Glory*, 176. West's spelling of "Lallapalooza" is incorrect. The name of the summer festival is "Lollapalooza."

25. Botelho suggested that music was probably played through helicopter speakers in

Vietnam, but locating evidence is difficult as much of the detailed information regarding PSYOPS is classified.

26. Grisham, interview.

27. Ibid.

28. "Major Pain," e-mail communication, 20 June 2007.

29. Svanibor Pettan, "Music, Politics, and War in Croatia in the 1990s: An Introduction" in *Music, Politics, and War: Views from Croatia,* ed. Svanibor Pettan (Zagreb: Institute of Ethnology and Folklore Research, 1998): 17.

30. Adam Piore, "Psyop: The Love's Not Mutual," *Newsweek,* 26 May 2003, 13.

31. Ibid.

32. Kuehl, interview.

33. Suzanne Cusick, "Music as Torture, Music as Weapon," *Revista Transcultural de Música (Transcultural Music Review)* 10 (2006), http://www.sibetrans.com/trans/trans10/cusick_eng.htm, and Suzanne Cusick, "'You are in a place that is out of the world . . .': Music in the Detention Camps of the 'Global War on Terror'," *Journal of the Society for American Music* 2, no. 1 (2008): 3.

34. Alfred W. McCoy, *A Question of Torture: CIA Interrogation, from the Cold War to the War on Terror* (New York: Metropolitan Books, 2006), 32–39, 52.

35. Ibid., 21–29. Russia, China, and North Korea were suspected of administering hypnosis techniques and mind-alteration drugs on American POWs in the Korean War; the so-called "Manchurian Candidate" experiments.

36. Plenary Court Judgment of the European Court of Human Rights, Case of Ireland vs. The United Kingdom (Application no. 5310/71), Strasbourg, France, 18 January 1978, 24.

37. Ibid. The other techniques included "wall-standing," "hooding," "deprivation of sleep," and "deprivation of food and drink."

38. See, for instance, Donald Vance's account in Cusick, "Music in the Detention Camps," 19–23.

39. Grisham, interview.

40. Ibid. Much of Grisham's explanation originally appeared in Jonathan Pieslak, "Sound Targets: Music and the War in Iraq," *Journal of Musicological Research* 26, nos. 2–3 (2007): 128–33, 143–45.

41. Cusick claims, "If one reads the press and human rights organization accounts of 'no touch torture' carefully, these incidents can all be traced not to uniformed servicemen, but to occasions when multiple-agency teams—that is, teams that include CIA operatives, and Behavioral Science Consultants—administer the interrogation." Cusick, "Music as Torture." As demonstrated by the circumstances of Grisham's military service, Army personnel frequently conduct such interrogations.

42. BBC Radio 4 Today, 20 May 2003, http://news.bbc.co.uk/1/hi/world/middle_east/3042907.stm. Hoffman also stated that music in interrogation was "rather new."

43. http://webdb.iu.edu/sem/scripts/aboutus/aboutsem/positionstatements/position_statement_torture.cfm, accessed February 18, 2007.

44. Ibid. Other professional academic societies have followed SEM in creating position statements on music and torture. The International Association for the Study of Popular Music-US Branch (IASPM-US) proposed a similar statement to SEM in April 2007; see http://www.iaspm-us.net/publications/index.php, Summer/Fall 2007 newsletter.

45. European Court of Human Rights, Case of Ireland vs. The United Kingdom (Application no. 5310/71), 24.

46. Ibid., 39–40.

47. The Convention against Torture and Other Cruel, Inhuman or Degrading Treatment or Punishment, 1990 Senate Resolution, adopted by unanimous agreement of the United Nations General Assembly on 10 December 1984, and signed by the United States on 18 April 1988.

48. FM 34–52, Intelligence Interrogation, Headquarters, Department of the Army, Washington, D.C., 28 September 1992, 1-7-1-9.

49. Borchelt et al., *Break Them Down: Systematic Use of Psychological Torture by US Forces* (Cambridge, Mass.: Physicians for Human Rights, 2005).

50. Gretchen Borchelt, personal communication, 12 June 2007.

51. Ibid.

52. Grisham, interview.

53. Thompson, interview.

54. Ibid.

55. It is not my intention to debate the more controversial aspects of the Military Commissions Act of 2006, such as the new "unlawful enemy combatant" category created for al Qaeda and Taliban insurgents.

56. FM 2-22.3 (FM 34-52), Human Intelligence Collector Operations, Headquarters, Department of the Army, Washington, D.C., 6 September 2006, Article 5-75, 5-21.

57. *The Economist,* 12–18 May 2007, 32, and http://www.armytimes.com. The other two possible choices in the survey were "No, torture is never acceptable" and "Don't know/No opinion." Readers of the Army Times web site were polled, and 49 percent agreed that "Yes, it should be used to gather vital information,"—a far greater percentage than among members of the military.

58. http://www.soldiersperspective.us, accessed 10 May 2007.

59. Ibid.

60. See also McCoy, *A Question of Torture,* 190–206.

61. Botelho, interview.

62. http://www.cnn.com, accessed 21 July 2007. I am struck by the many differences between the interrogator's accounts Cusick cites, such as Tony Lagouranis, and the one provided by Grisham (see Cusick, "Music in the Detention Camps," 9–11). There appear to be major differences in the interpretation of interrogation guidelines, interrogator's training, who administers these techniques, and how they are administered. Perhaps these inconsistencies are due to the varying practices among detainee facilities and the diverse guidelines established for different government agencies that I suggest. Cusick points out that much of the evidence we, as scholars, have access to amounts to a "trickle" of information, and my hope is that our work will collectively begin to shed light on what remains a very difficult topic to examine due to the classified status of many documents and the sometimes impossible task of corroborating accounts (ibid., 5). Her work provides an important counterpart to my ethnographic engagement with soldiers as she focuses more on covert interrogation practices and detainee perspectives. See Cusick, "Music in the Detention Camps."

63. Thompson, interview.

5. MUSIC AS A FORM OF SOLDIER EXPRESSION

1. Les Cleveland, *Dark Laughter: War in Song and Popular Culture* (Westport, Conn.: Praeger, 1994), 29.

2. Annie J. Randall, "A Censorship of Forgetting: Origins and Origin Myths of 'Battle Hymn of the Republic,'" in *Music, Power, and Politics,* ed. Annie J. Randall (New York:

Routledge, 2005), 9.

3. See ibid. for an in-depth examination of the historical background to "Battle Hymn of the Republic." Randall (17) also points out that different scholars have traced "Say Brothers Will You Meet Us" to African American spirituals or a pre-1700 Swedish drinking song.

4. Joseph B. Treaster, "G.I. View of Vietnam," *New York Times Magazine,* 30 October 1966, 106, quoted in Lydia Fish, "Songs of Americans in the Vietnam War," http://faculty .buffalostate.edu/fishlm/folksongs/americansongs.htm.

5. Cleveland, *Dark Laughter,* 29.

6. "D-Day Dodgers" originated as a parody sung by British soldiers, but it soon became popular among soldiers of all Allied forces.

7. Keith and Rusty McNeil, *Colonial and Revolution Songbook* (Riverside, Calif.: Wem Records, 1996), http://www.mcneilmusic.com/rev.html.

8. Bruce Brown, personal communication, New York, 20 July 2007.

9. http://www.loc.gov/folklife/guides/WorldWarII.html. Also, see Les Cleveland, "Soldiers' Songs: The Folklore of the Powerless," *New York Folklore* 11, no. 1 (1985): 79–98.

10. Sabis, "Through the Soldiers' Ears," http://www.geocities.com/afvn3/ historymenu.html.

11. Fish, "Songs of Americans in the Vietnam War."

12. http://phpbb2.desert-storm.com/viewtopic.php?t=1683&postdays=0&postorder =asc&start=0, accessed 8 July 2007.

13. George Gittoes, *Soundtrack to War.*

14. Ibid.

15. Ibid.

16. Ibid.

17. Post Exchange (PX) stores are typically located on military bases and offer retail merchandise at a discount to military personnel.

18. Holtan, interview.

19. Holtan, e-mail communication, 17 April 2006.

20. Atkinson, interview.

21. Revak, interview.

22. A recording of this and other songs mentioned in the chapter can be heard on Revak's web site, http://www.crutchhiker.com.

23. http://www.myspace.com/americantanker.

24. http://soldiersmind.com, accessed 21 July 2007.

25. Gittoes, *Soundtrack to War.*

26. Monica Davey, "Fighting Words: Soldiers Rap about Frustrations of Iraq War," 20 February 2005, http://www.nytimes.com/2005/02/20/arts/music/20dave.html?ex=12666 42000&en=9a4f611a5c26bd77&ei=5090&partner=rssuserland.

27. Ibid.

28. Gittoes, *Soundtrack to War.*

29. Additionally, in 2006, a private, military-only record company was founded, To The Fallen Records. Their first release was an entirely hip-hop/rap CD of music written by American soldiers.

30. Sagebiel, interview.

31. Ibid.

32. Schultz, interview.

33. http://www.iraq-songs.com.

34. Ibid.

35. Ibid.

36. Cleveland, *Dark Laughter*, 85.

37. Ibid., 132. "Dink" is a derogatory term referring to combatants in the North Vietnamese Army.

38. David "JR" Schultz, e-mail communication, 23 January 2008.

39. Thompson, interview.

40. Ibid.

41. Saunders, interview.

42. Ibid.

43. Ibid.

44. Ibid.

45. Ibid.

46. Ibid.

47. Davey, "Fighting Words."

48. Revak, interview.

49. Schultz, interview.

6. METAL AND RAP IDEOLOGIES IN THE IRAQ WAR

1. It is important to reiterate that not all soldiers' musical experiences involve metal or rap. Some soldiers do not regularly leave the "Green Zone" in Baghdad or military bases during their deployment and are not involved in combat-related specialties. Their musical practices are significantly different from many of the soldiers considered here because my focus is primarily on combat-related listening contexts.

2. Karl Marx and Frederick Engels, *The German Ideology Part One, with Selections from Parts Two and Three, Together with Marx's "Introduction to a Critique of Political Economy"* (New York: International Publishers, 2001), 47.

3. Louis Althusser, for example, revises Marx's definition to include aspects of Jacques Lacan's "the real," while Fredric Jameson, largely influenced by Althusser, distinguishes among the ideologies in a historical epoch, not just dominant ones. See Louis Althusser, *Lenin and Philosophy, and Other Essays,* trans. Ben Brewster (New York: Monthly Review Press, 2001), 108; Fredric Jameson, *Postmodernism, or, the Cultural Logic of Late Capitalism* (Durham: Duke University Press, 1991), 6.

4. Mostafa Rejai, "Ideology," in *Dictionary of the History of Ideas*, ed. P. P. Weiner (New York: Scribner, 1973), 558.

5. Kay Dreyfus and Joel Crotty, "Editorial: 'Music and Ideologies,'" *Journal of Musicological Research* 26, nos. 2–3 (2007): 86. This definition is largely based on the work of Marcello Source Keller.

6. Bruce Friesen and Jonathon Epstein, "Rock 'n' Roll Ain't Noise Pollution: Artistic Conventions and Tensions in the Major Subgenres of Heavy Metal Music," *Popular Music and Society* 18, no. 3 (1994): 13; Pieslak, "Re-Casting Metal," 243.

7. Adam Krims, *Rap Music and the Poetics of Identity* (New York: Cambridge University Press, 2000), 46–92.

8. Robert Walser, *Running with the Devil: Power, Gender, and Madness in Heavy Metal Music* (Hanover, N.H.: University Press of New England, 1993), 2. The term "heavy metal" is typically used interchangeably with "metal" to describe the musical features of the genre. According to Walser, this includes songs based on a single tonal center, in the Dorian/Aeolian or Phrygian/Locrian modes, the loud, distorted power chord as the fundamental unit of pitch, and repeated, power chord-driven riffs in 4/4 time. The vocal

articulation in metal ranges from a quasi-operatic, vibrato-laden style to unpitched yelling or screaming. As mentioned in the first chapter, the use of a distorted guitar timbre and/or power chords is frequently the sole determinant used by scholars to qualify the music as metal or as exhibiting a metal influence. See Walser, *Running with the Devil,* 44–51, and Pieslak, "Re-Casting Metal," 243.

9. Deena Weinstein, *Heavy Metal: A Cultural Sociology* (New York: Macmillan, 1991), 23.

10. See Jack Harrell, "The Poetics of Destruction: Death Metal Rock," *Journal of Popular Music and Society* 18, no. 1 (1994): 91–103; Robert L. Gross, "Heavy Metal Music: A New Subculture in American Society," *Journal of Popular Culture* 24, no. 1 (1990): 119–30; Robert Pielke, *You Say You Want a Revolution: Rock Music in American Culture* (Chicago: Nelson-Hall, 1986).

11. The following discussion is based on Pieslak, "Re-Casting Metal," 243–44.

12. Walser, *Running with the Devil,* 44–51.

13. Pielke, *You Say You Want a Revolution,* 202; Harrell, "The Poetics of Destruction," 93.

14. Krims, *Rap Music,* 55.

15. Ibid., 56–57, 70–80.

16. Tricia Rose, *Black Noise: Rap Music and Black Culture in Contemporary America* (Middletown, Conn.: Wesleyan University Press, 1994), 2.

17. Krims, *Rap Music,* 70. Also see Cheryl Keyes, *Rap Music and Street Consciousness* (Urbana: University of Illinois Press, 2002), 90 and 166.

18. Michael Eric Dyson, *Between God and Gangsta Rap: Bearing Witness to Black Culture* (New York: Oxford University Press, 1996), 179.

19. Cornel West, *Race Matters* (New York: Vintage Press, 1994), 23.

20. Robert Walser, "Rhythm, Rhyme, and Rhetoric in the Music of Public Enemy," *Ethnomusicology* 39, no. 2 (1995): 193–217.

21. U.S. Congress, Senate, *Record Labeling (Senate Hearing 99–529),* 3.

22. Walser, *Running with the Devil,* 137–39, and Weinstein, Heavy Metal, 249–54.

23. Keyes, *Rap Music,* 4. Also see Dyson, *Between God and Gangsta Rap,* 182–84.

24. U.S. Senate, Committee on Governmental Affairs, Subcommittee on Oversight of Government Management, Restructuring, and the District of Columbia, "Music Violence: How Does it Affect Our Children: Hearing Before the Subcommittee on Oversight of Government Management, Restructuring, and the District of Columbia of the Committee on Governmental Affairs, Unites States Senate, One Hundred Fifth Congress, first session, 6 November 1997," 105–395.

25. Pieslak, "Sound, Text, and Identity," 3.

26. Botelho, interview.

27. Bettina Roccor, "Heavy Metal: Forces of Unification and Fragmentation within a Musical Subculture," *The World of Music,* 42, no. 1 (2000): 90.

28. Harris Berger, *Metal, Rock, and Jazz: Perception and the Phenomenology of Musical Experience* (Hanover, N.H.: Wesleyan University Press, 1999), 251–94.

29. Walser, *Running with the Devil,* 135.

30. Gross, "Heavy Metal Music," 124.

31. Atkinson, interview.

32. Thomas W. Evans, "The All-Volunteer Army After Twenty Years," *Army History: The Professional Bulletin of Army History* 27 (1993).

33. Steven Feld, "Communication, Music, and Speech about Music," 83–85.

34. Tia DeNora, *Music in Everyday Life* (New York: Cambridge University Press, 2000), 33.

35. Krims notices the lack of "culturally relevant information" offered by scientific examinations of timbre, like spectrographs. Krims, *Rap Music*, 53–54.

36. See David Brackett, *Interpreting Popular Music* (Berkeley: University of California Press, 2000); Susan Fast, "Politics and Musical Expression: Music Contexts and Meaning in U2," in *Expression in Pop-Rock Music: A Collection of Critical and Analytical Essays*, ed. Walter Everett (New York: Routledge, 2000), 33–58; Allan Moore, Rock: *The Primary Text* (Burlington: Ashgate, 2001).

37. Miner, interview; Buzzell, interview.

38. A double-pedal bass drum has two pedals, operated by the feet. This allows the drummer to perform bass drum parts of greater rhythmic speed.

39. Harrell, "The Poetics of Destruction," 93.

40. Benjamin Harbert's work on the nature of guitar distortion may suggest future frameworks for interpreting this timbre. See Benjamin Harbert, "Until Our Ears All Bleed: Poetics of the Grotesque in International Extreme Metal," paper presented at the fifty-second annual meeting of the Society for Ethnomusicology, 25 October 2007, Columbus, Ohio.

41. Sheila Whiteley, "Progressive Rock and Psychedelic Coding in the Work of Jimi Hendrix," in *Reading Pop: Approaches to Textual Analysis in Popular Music*, ed. Richard Middleton (New York: Oxford University Press, 2000), 260.

42. See Charles Keil, *Tiv Song: The Sociology of Art in a Classless Society* (Chicago: University of Chicago Press, 1979), 45–46.

43. Pieslak, "Text, Sound, and Identity," 3.

44. Grisham, interview.

45. Popular gangsta rappers Tupac Shakur and Biggie Smalls were both killed in drive-by shootings in 1996 and 1997, respectively.

46. The violence of gangsta rap is also based on the control of territory or local "turf." Threats to a gangsta rapper's "hood" (neighborhood), street, or block can often serve as a motive for violence. Here as well, there might a similarity to soldiers' experiences. The urban battleground of city streets in Iraq may be viewed as parallel with the gangsta rap "hood." The fight for control of small urban territories pervades both gangsta rap and soldier combat.

47. Robin D. G. Kelley, *Race Rebels: Culture, Politics, and the Black Working Class* (New York: Free Press, 1994), 183–227.

48. Ibid.

49. Gittoes, *Soundtrack to War*.

50. William Thompson, telephone conversation, 3 February 2008.

51. Berger, *Metal, Rock, and Jazz*, 282–94.

52. See Walser, *Running with the Devil*, 114–17; Keyes, *Rap Music*, 186–89.

53. Atkinson, interview.

54. Atkinson's interview also presents some of her general thoughts and experiences of being a woman in the military.

55. C. J. Grisham, e-mail communication, 22 January 2008. Country music is also very popular among white soldiers, especially those from southern states, but not to a significant degree within the context of combat preparation.

56. Keyes, *Rap Music*, 5 and 220.

57. Grisham, e-mail.

58. http://groups.yahoo.com/group/afvn/, accessed 24 July 2007.

59. Thompson, telephone conversation.

60. Grisham, e-mail.

61. Sagebiel believes that Western gender stereotypes are reversed in Iraqi society:

"One of my observations about the local people in Iraq is that they sort of switch stereotypes. In America and even in Europe, we think of men as the strong, stoic types and women are the more fickle and outwardly emotional types. I found the opposite to be true in Iraq. It was the men who were outwardly emotional and expressive and the women were the strong, silent types, which was quite an interesting thought especially since we always hear about all this Islamic oppression of women." Sagebiel, interview.

62. Saunders, interview.

63. "American Soldier," e-mail.

64. Schultz, interview.

65. Revak, interview.

66. Walser, *Running with the Devil*, 2; Weinstein, *Heavy Metal*, 122.

67. Keyes, *Rap Music*, 4.

68. Gittoes, *Soundtrack to War*.

69. Grisham, interview.

70. Ibid.

71. Robert W. Rieber and Robert J. Kelly, "Substance and Shadow: Images of the Enemy," in *The Psychology of War and Peace: The Image of the Enemy*, Robert W. Rieber ed. (New York: Plenum, 1991), 17.

72. Robert J. Lifton, "Existential Evil," in *Sanctions for Evil: Sources of Social Destruction*, ed. Nevitt Sanford and Craig Comstock (San Francisco: Jossey-Bass, 1971), 40–41.

73. Judith Becker, *Deep Listeners: Music, Emotion, and Trancing* (Bloomington: Indiana University Press, 2004), 2.

74. Ibid., 82–83.

75. Ibid., 83.

76. Ibid., 144–47.

77. Walid Shoebat, *Why We Want to Kill You* (Newton, Pa.: Top Executive Media, 2007), 29 and 140.

78. Israel Orbach, "Dissociation, Physical Pain, and Suicide: A Hypothesis," *Suicide and Life-Threatening Behavior* 24, no. 1 (1994): 68–79; Edwin Schneider, *Suicide as Psychache: A Clinical Approach to Self-Destructive Behavior* (Northvale, N.J.: Jason Aronson, 1993).

79. Thompson, interview.

80. Ibid., and Shoebat, *Why We Want to Kill You*, 29.

81. Thompson, interview.

82. See Cusick, "Music in the Detention Camps."

83. Gittoes, *Soundtrack to War*.

84. Grisham, interview.

85. Walser, *Running with the Devil*, 44–51.

86. Whiteley, "Progressive Rock," 260.

87. James Hetfield, "Fresh Air," National Public Radio, 29 November 2004.

88. DeGregory, "Soldiers Take on Insurgents."

89. Kuehl, interview.

90. Cusick, "Music as Torture."

91. Sally Jo Cunningham, J. Stephen Downie, and David Bainbridge, "'The Pain, the Pain': Modeling Music Information Behavior and the Songs We Hate," *Proceedings of the 2005 International Conference on Music Information Retrieval*, 477.

92. Kuehl, interview.

93. Ibid.

94. Botelho, interview.

95. U.S. General Accounting Office, *US International Broadcasting: Challenges*

Facing the Broadcasting Board of Governors, Testimony Before the Subcommittee on International Operations and Terrorism, Committee on Foreign Relations, U.S. Senate, 29 April 2004, 9–10, http://www.gao.gov/new.items/d04711t.pdf.

96. Lydia Fish, "The Vietnam Veterans Oral History and Folklore Project," Voices 30 (2004), http://www.nyfolklore.org/pubs/voic30-3-4/vietvets.html.

97. http://www.oucs.ox.ac.uk/ltg/projects/jtap/tutorials/intro/intro.html.

98. Saunders, interview.

99. Ibid.

100. Ibid.

101. The theme of individualism that Saunders seems to be expressing creates a link with aspects of metal ideology. In his analysis of death metal, Berger shows that this ideology emphasizes the notion of the individual apart from the social, and in his opposition to the ideological commitments of gangsta rap, Saunders positions himself apart from other rappers in ways that resemble individualism in metal. See Berger, *Metal, Rock, and Jazz,* 264–69.

102. Saunders, interview.

103. Ibid.

104. Ibid.

105. Ibid.

106. Svetlana Boym, *The Future of Nostalgia* (New York: Basic Books, 2001), 3–18.

107. Ibid., 3.

108. Ibid., 4.

109. Stephen Johnson, e-mail communication, 21 July 2007.

110. Jennifer Atkinson, e-mail communication, 30 April 2006.

111. Atkinson, interview.

112. Holtan, interview.

113. DeNora, *Music in Everyday Life,* 65 and 67–68.

114. "Major Pain," e-mail.

115. Miner, e-mail communication, 29 April 2006.

116. Grisham, interview.

117. Buzzell, interview.

118. Lisa Gilman, "An American Soldier's iPod: Layers of Identity and Situated Listening in Iraq," paper presented at the fifty-second annual meeting of the Society for Ethnomusicology, 25 October 2007, Columbus, Ohio; J. Martin Daughtry, "'A Symphony of Bullets': Towards a Sonic Ethnography of Contemporary Baghdad," paper presented at the fifty-second annual meeting of the Society for Ethnomusicology, 25 October 2007, Columbus, Ohio.

POSTSCRIPT

1. Atkinson, interview.

2. Buzzell, interview.

3. Treaster, "G.I View of Vietnam."

BIBLIOGRAPHY

INTERVIEWS AND CORRESPONDENCE WITH SOLDIERS

"American Soldier." E-mail communication. 17 April 2006.
Anonymous. Former Army Interrogator. E-mail communication. 11 July 2007.
Atkinson, Jennifer. E-mail communication. 30 April 2006.
———. Interview by the author, tape recording. New York, N.Y. 3 May 2006.
Botelho, Ronald. Interview by the author, tape recording. New York, N.Y. 8 June 2007.
Brown, Bruce. Personal communication. Plainfield, N.J. 12 September 2006.
———. Personal communication. New York, N.Y. 20 July 2007.
Buzzell, Colby. Interview by the author, tape recording. New York, N.Y. 27 April 2006.
Grisham, C. J. Interview by the author, tape recording. New York, N.Y. 1 May 2006.
———. E-mail communication. 22 January 2008.
Holtan, Erik. E-mail communication. 17 April 2006.
———. Interview by the author, tape recording. New York, N.Y. 18 April 2006.
Kuehl, Dan. Interview by the author, tape recording. New York, N.Y. 2 May 2006.
Johnson, Stephen. E-mail communication. 21 July 2007.
"Major Pain." E-mail communication. 20 June 2007.
Miner, Mark. E-mail communication. 29 April 2006 and 8 May 2006.
Revak, Joshua. Interview by the author, tape recording. New York, N.Y. 4 April 2007.
Rouse, Ed. E-mail communication. 26 April 2006.
Sagebiel, Jason. Interview by the author, tape recording. New York, N.Y. 19 August 2007.
Saunders, Neal. Interview by the author, tape recording. New York, N.Y. 18 April 2006.
Schultz, David "JR." Interview by the author, tape recording. New York, N.Y. 22 June 2007.
———. E-mail communication. 23 January 2008.
Shalev, Ziv. Interview by the author, tape recording. New York, N.Y. 17 April 2007.
Thompson, William. Interview by the author, tape recording. New York, N.Y. 22 June 2007.
———. Telephone conversation. 3 February 2008.

OTHER SOURCES

Agar, Michael H. *The Professional Stranger: An Informal Introduction to Ethnography.* New York: Academic Press, 1996.
Althusser, Louis. *Lenin and Philosophy, and Other Essays.* Trans. Ben Brewster. New York: Monthly Review Press, 2001.
Anonymous. Personal communication. 25 May 2007.
Askew, Kelly. "Introduction." In *The Anthropology of Media: A Reader,* ed. Kelly Askew and Richard R. Wilk, 1–14. Oxford: Blackwell, 2002.
Banks, Jack. *Monopoly Television: MTV's Quest to Control the Music.* Boulder, Colo.: Westview Press, 1996.
Becker, Judith. *Deep Listeners: Music, Emotion, and Trancing.* Bloomington: Indiana

University Press, 2004.

Behar, Ruth. *The Vulnerable Observer: Anthropology That Breaks Your Heart.* Boston: Beacon, 1996.

Berger, Harris. *Metal, Rock, and Jazz: Perception and the Phenomenology of Musical Experience.* Hanover, N.H.: Wesleyan University Press, 1999.

Bolman, Philip V. "Musicology as a Political Act." *Journal of Musicology* 11, no. 4 (1993): 411–36.

Borchelt, Gretchen. Personal communication. 12 June 2007.

Borchelt, Gretchen et al. *Break Them Down: Systematic Use of Psychological Torture by US Forces.* Cambridge, Mass.: Physicians for Human Rights, 2005.

Boym, Svetlana. *The Future of Nostalgia.* New York: Basic Books, 2001.

Brackett, David. *Interpreting Popular Music.* Berkeley: University of California Press, 2000.

Braudy, Leo. *From Chivalry to Terrorism: War and the Changing Nature of Masculinity.* New York: Knopf, 2003.

Briggs, Charles L. *Learning How to Ask: A Sociolinguistic Appraisal of the Role of the Interview in Social Science Research.* New York: Cambridge University Press, 1986.

Buzzell, Colby. *My War: Killing Time in Iraq.* New York: Putnam Adult, 2005.

Campbell, Eric A. "Civil War Music and the Common Soldier: The Experiences of Charles Wellington Reed." In *Bugle Resounding: Music and Musicians of the Civil War Era,* ed. Bruce C. Kelley and Mark A. Snell, 202–228. Columbia: University of Missouri Press, 2004.

Chion, Michel. *Audio-Vision: Sound on Screen.* Ed. and trans. Claudia Gorbman. New York: Columbia University Press, 1994.

Cleveland, Les. *Dark Laughter: War in Song and Popular Culture.* Westport, Conn.: Praeger, 1994.

———. "Soldiers' Songs: The Folklore of the Powerless." *New York Folklore* 11, no. 1 (1985): 79–98.

Cook, Nicholas. "Music and Meaning in the Commercials." *Popular Music* 13, no. 1 (1994): 27–40.

Crawford, John. *The Last True Story I'll Ever Tell: An Accidental Soldier's Account of the War in Iraq.* New York: Riverhead, 2005.

Cunningham, Sally Jo, J. Stephen Downie, and David Bainbridge. "'The Pain, the Pain': Modeling Music Information Behavior and the Songs We Hate." *Proceedings of the 2005 International Conference on Music Information Retrieval,* 474–77.

Cusick, Suzanne. "Music as Torture, Music as Weapon." *Revista Transcultural de Música (Transcultural Music Review)* 10 (2006). http://www.sibetrans.com/trans/trans10/cusick_eng.htm.

———. "'You are in a place that is out of the world...': Music in the Detention Camps of the 'Global War on Terror.'" *Journal of the Society for American Music* 2, no. 1 (2008): 1–26.

Daughtry, J. Martin. "'A Symphony of Bullets': Towards a Sonic Ethnography of Contemporary Baghdad." Paper presented at the fifty-second annual meeting of the Society for Ethnomusicology, 25 October 2007, Columbus, Ohio.

Davey, Monica. "Fighting Words: Soldiers Rap about Frustrations of Iraq War." Accessed 20 February 2005. http://www.nytimes.com/2005/02/20/arts/music/20dave.html?ex=1266642000&en=9a4f611a5c26bd77&ei=5090&partner=rssuserland.

DeGregory, Lane. "Soldiers Take on Insurgents with a Musical Vengeance, Cranking up the Volume to Distress the Enemy." *St. Petersburg Times,* 21 November 2004.

DeNora, Tia. *Music in Everyday Life*. New York: Cambridge University Press, 2000.

Dertouzos, James N. Is *Military Advertising Effective? An Estimation Methodology and Applications to Recruiting in the 1980s and 90s*. Arlington, Va.: Rand, 2003.

Devereux, George. *From Anxiety to Method in the Behavioral Sciences*. Paris: École Pratique des Hautes Études, 1967.

Dreyfus, Kay, and Joel Crotty. "Editorial: 'Music and Ideologies.'" *Journal of Musicological Research* 26, nos. 2–3 (2007): 85–90.

DuRant, R. H., M. Rich, S. J. Emans, E. S. Rome, E. Allred, and E. R. Woods. "Violence and Weapon Carrying in Music Videos: A Content Analysis." *Archives of Pediatric and Adolescent Medicine* 151 (2002): 443–48.

Dyson, Michael Eric. *Between God and Gangsta Rap: Bearing Witness to Black Culture*. New York: Oxford University Press, 1996.

Ehrenstein, David, and Bill Reed. *Rock on Film*. New York: Delilah, 1982.

Evans, Thomas W. "The All-Volunteer Army after Twenty Years: Recruiting in the Modern Era." *Army History: The Professional Bulletin of Army History* 27 (1993). http://www.shsu.edu/~his_ncp/VolArm.html. Accessed 17 March 2005.

Farris, John H. "The Impact of Basic Combat Training: The Role of the Drill Sergeant." In *The Social Psychology of Military Service*, ed. Nancy L. Goldman and David R. Segal, 13–24. Beverly Hills: Sage, 1976.

Fast, Susan. "Politics and Musical Expression: Music Contexts and Meaning in U2." In *Expression in Pop-Rock Music: A Collection of Critical and Analytical Essays*, ed. Walter Everett, 33–58. New York: Routledge, 2000.

Feld, Steven. "Communication, Music, and Speech about Music." In *Music Grooves*, ed. Charles Keil and Steven Feld, 77–95. Chicago: University of Chicago Press, 1991.

Fish, Lydia. "The Vietnam Veterans Oral History and Folklore Project." Voices 30 (2004). http://www.nyfolklore.org/pubs/voic30-3-4/vietvets.html. Accessed 10 January 2005.

FM 34-52, Intelligence Interrogation. Headquarters, Department of the Army. Washington, D.C. 28 September 1992.

FM 2-22.3 (FM 34-52), Human Intelligence Collector Operations. Headquarters, Department of the Army. Washington, D.C. 6 September 2006.

Friedman, Herbert A. "The Wandering Soul PSYOP Tape of Vietnam." http://www.psywarrior.com/wanderingsoul.

Friesen, Bruce, and Jonathon Epstein. "Rock 'n' Roll Ain't Noise Pollution: Artistic Conventions and Tensions in the Major Subgenres of Heavy Metal Music." *Popular Music and Society* 18, no. 3 (1994): 1–18.

Geertz, Clifford. *Work and Lives: The Anthropologist as Author*. Stanford, Calif.: Stanford University Press, 1988.

Gilman, Lisa. "An American Soldier's iPod: Layers of Identity and Situated Listening in Iraq." Paper presented at the fifty-second annual meeting of the Society for Ethnomusicology, 25 October 2007, Columbus, Ohio.

Gittoes, George, director. *Soundtrack to War*. Melee Entertainment, 2006.

"Glenn Miller and His AEF Orchestra." BBC Propaganda Broadcasts. November 1994.

Goodwin, Andrew. *Dancing in the Distraction Factory: Music Television and Popular Culture*. Minneapolis: University of Minnesota Press, 1992.

Gorbman, Claudia. *Unheard Melodies*. Bloomington: Indiana University Press, 1987.

Gross, Robert L. "Heavy Metal Music: A New Subculture in American Society." *Journal of Popular Culture* 24, no. 1 (1990): 119–30.

Harbert, Benjamin. "Until Our Ears All Bleed: Poetics of the Grotesque in International

Extreme Metal." Paper presented at the fifty-second annual meeting of the Society for Ethnomusicology, 25 October 2007, Columbus, Ohio.

Harper, Jennifer. "'Army Strong' to be New Recruiting Slogan." *Washington Times*, 10 October 2006.

Harrell, Jack. "The Poetics of Destruction: Death Metal Rock." *Journal of Popular Music and Society* 18, no. 1 (1994): 91–103.

Hetfield, James. Interview by Terry Gross. *Fresh Air*. National Public Radio. 29 November 2004.

Hillman, Roger. "Narrative, Sound, and Film: Fassbinder's *The Marriage of Maria Braun*." In *Fields of Vision: Essays in Film Studies, Visual Anthropology, and Photography*, ed. Leslie Decereaux and Roger Hillman, 181–95. Berkeley: University of California Press, 1995.

Hintze, Wayne, and Jerry Lehnus. "Recognition of Military Advertising Slogans among American Youth." Paper presented at the International Military Testing Association (IMTA) Conference, 1996. http://www.ijoa.org/imta96/paper19.html. Accessed 2 June 2005.

Huron, David. "Music in Advertising: An Analytic Paradigm." *Musical Quarterly* 73, no. 4 (1989): 557–74.

Jameson, FredricFrederick. *Postmodernism, or, the Cultural Logic of Late Capitalism.* Durham, N.C.: Duke University Press, 1991.

Kaplan, Ann E. *Rocking around the Clock: Music Television, Postmodernism, and Consumer Culture.* New York: Methuen, 1987.

Keegan, John. *A History of Warfare.* New York: Vintage, 1993.

Keil, Charles. *Tiv Song: The Sociology of Art in a Classless Society.* Chicago: University of Chicago Press, 1979.

Kelley, Robin D. G. *Race Rebels: Culture, Politics, and the Black Working Class.* New York: Free Press, 1994.

Keyes, Cheryl. *Rap Music and Street Consciousness.* Urbana: University of Illinois Press, 2002.

Krims, Adam. *Rap Music and the Poetics of Identity.* New York: Cambridge University Press, 2000.

Latour, Bruno, and Steve Woolgar. *Laboratory Life: The Social Construction of Scientific Facts.* London: Sage, 1979.

Lifton, Robert J. "Existential Evil." In *Sanctions for Evil: Sources of Social Destruction*, ed. Nevitt Sanford and Craig Comstock. San Francisco: Jossey-Bass, 1971.

Lloyd, Mark. *The Art of Military Deception.* London: Leo Cooper, 1997.

Malcolm, C. A. *The Piper in Peace and War.* London: John Murray, 1927. Reprint, London: Hardwick Press, 1993.

Marple, Albert. "Wireless Music for Wounded Soldiers." *The Wireless Age* (April 1918): 590–93.

Marx, Karl, and Frederick Engels. *The German Ideology Part One, with Selections from Parts Two and Three, Together with Marx's "Introduction to a Critique of Political Economy."* New York: International Publishers, 2001.

McCoy, Alfred. *A Question of Torture: CIA Interrogation, from the Cold War to the War on Terror.* New York: Metropolitan Books, 2006.

McLaren, Carrie. "Salesnoise: The Convergence of Music and Advertising." http://www.stayfreemagazine.org/archives/15/salesnoise.html. Accessed 27 November 2006.

McNeil, Keith, and Rusty McNeil. *Colonial and Revolution Songbook.* Riverside, Calif.: Wem Records, 1996. http://www.mcneilmusic.com/rev.html. Accessed 3

November 2004.

Meyer, Leonard. *Emotion and Meaning in Music.* Chicago: University of Chicago Press, 1956.

Miller, David. *Conflict Iraq: Weapons and Tactics of the U.S. and Iraqi Forces.* St. Paul, Minn.: MBI Publishing Company, 2003.

Molino, Jean. "Fait musicale et sémiologie de la musique." *Musique en jeu* 17 (1975): 37–62.

Moore, Allan. *Rock: The Primary Text.* Burlington, Vt.: Ashgate, 2001.

National Research Council Committee on the Youth Population and Military Recruitment. *Evaluating Military Advertising and Recruiting: Theory and Methodology,* ed. Paul R. Sackett and Anne S. Maver. Washington, D.C.: National Academies Press, 2004.

Nattiez, Jean-Jacques. *Fondements d'une sémiologie de la musique.* Paris: Union Générale des Éditions, 1975.

———. *Music and Discourse: Towards a Semiology of Music.* Trans. Carolyn Abbate. Princeton, N.J.: Princeton University Press, 1990.

Nettl, Bruno. "The Institutionalisation of Musicology: Perspectives of a North American Musicologist." In *Rethinking Music,* ed. Nicholas Cook and Mark Everist, 287–310. New York: Oxford University Press, 1999.

Olds, Ian, and Garrett Scott, director. *Occupation: Dreamland.* Greenhouse Pictures, 2005.

Olson, Kenneth E. *Music and Musket: Bands and Bandsmen of the American Civil War.* Westport, Conn.: Greenwood Press, 1980.

Orbach, Israel. "Dissociation, Physical Pain, and Suicide: A Hypothesis." *Suicide and Life-Threatening Behavior* 24, no. 1 (1994): 68–79.

Page, Charles D. *History of the Fourteenth Regiment Connecticut Volunteer Infantry.* Meriden, Conn.: Horton Publishing, 1906.

Pettan, Svanibor. "Music and Music Research in the Context of Political Changes and War in Croatia during the 1990s." *Muzika* 5, no. 1 (2001): 20–40.

———. "Music, Politics, and War in Croatia in the 1990s: An Introduction." In *Music, Politics, and War: Views from Croatia,* ed. Svanibor Pettan, 9–27. Zagreb: Institute of Ethnology and Folklore Research, 1998.

Pielke, Robert. *You Say You Want a Revolution: Rock Music in American Culture.* Chicago: Nelson-Hall, 1986.

Pieslak, Jonathan. "Re-casting Metal: Rhythm and Meter in the Music of Meshuggah." *Music Theory Spectrum* 29, no. 2 (2007): 219–45.

———. "Sound Targets: Music and the War in Iraq." *Journal of Musicological Research* 26, nos. 2–3 (2007): 123–50.

———. "Text, Sound and Identity in Korn's 'Hey Daddy.'" *Popular Music* 27, no. 1 (2008): 35–52.

Piore, Adam. "Psyop: The Love's Not Mutual." *Newsweek,* 26 May 2003, p. 13.

Plenary Court Judgment of the European Court of Human Rights. Case of Ireland vs. The United Kingdom (Application no. 5310/71). Strasbourg, France. 18 January 1978.

Qureshi, Regula. "Islam and Music." In *Sacred Sound: Experiencing Music in the World Religions,* ed. Guy L. Beck, 89–113. Waterloo, Ont.: Winfrid Laurier University Press, 2006.

Randall, Annie J. "A Censorship of Forgetting: Origins and Origin Myths of 'Battle Hymn of the Republic.'" In *Music, Power, and Politics,* ed. Annie J. Randall, 5–24. New York: Routledge, 2005.

Rejai, Mostafa. "Ideology." In *Dictionary of the History of Ideas,* ed. P. P. Weiner, 553–59. New York: Scribner, 1973.

Rieber, Robert W., and Robert J. Kelly. "Substance and Shadow: Images of the Enemy." In *The Psychology of War and Peace: The Image of the Enemy,* ed. Robert W. Rieber, 3–38. New York: Plenum, 1991.

Roccor, Bettina. "Heavy Metal: Forces of Unification and Fragmentation within a Musical Subculture." *World of Music* 42, no. 1 (2000): 83–94.

Rose, Tricia. *Black Noise: Rap Music and Black Culture in Contemporary America.* Middletown, Conn.: Wesleyan University Press, 1994.

Run to Cadence: Special Forces Green Berets. Documentary Recordings, 460CD, 1996.

Sabis, Christopher. "Through the Soldiers' Ears: What Americans Fighting in Vietnam Heard and Its Effects." Undergraduate senior thesis, University of Rochester, 2000. http://www.geocities.com/afvn3/historymenu.html. Accessed 22 July 2007.

Sager, Michael. "Fact: Five Out of Five Kids Who Kill Love Slayer." *Esquire,* February 1992, 82–85.

Sajer, Guy. *The Forgotten Soldier.* Dulles, Va.: Brassey, 1990.

Sarkissian, Margaret. "'Religion Never Had It So Good': Contemporary *Nasyid* and the Growth of Islamic Popular Music in Malaysia." *Yearbook for Traditional Music* 37 (2005): 124–52.

Schachter, Daniel L. *Searching for Memory: The Brain, the Mind, and the Past.* New York: Basic Books, 1996.

Schneider, Edwin. *Suicide as Psychache: A Clinical Approach to Self-Destructive Behavior.* Northvale, N.J.: Jason Aronson, 1993.

Shelemay, Kay Kaufman. *Let Jasmine Rain Down: Song and Remembrance among Syrian Jews.* Chicago: University of Chicago Press, 1998.

Shiloah, Amnon. *Music in the World of Islam: A Socio-Cultural Study.* Detroit: Wayne State University Press, 1995.

Shoebat, Walid. *Why We Want to Kill You.* Newton, Pa.: Top Executive Media, 2007.

Smith, Stacy L., and Aaron R. Boyson. "Violence in Music Videos: Examining the Prevalence and Context of Physical Aggression." *Journal of Communication* 52, no. 1 (2002): 61–83.

"Soldiers in Iraq: Contaminated." *Economist.* 12 May 2007: 32.

Sun Tzu. *The Art of War.* Boston: Shambhala Publications, 1983.

Tapper, J., E. Thorson, and D. Black. "Variations in Music Videos as a Function of Their Musical Genre." *Journal of Broadcasting and Electronic Media* 38 (1994): 103–13.

Taylor, Philip. E-mail communication. 3 May 2006.

Totilo, Stephen. "EA Offers Up Snoop, Peas Tracks; Exec Talks Future of Video Game Music." http://www.mtv.com/games/video_games/news/story.jhtml?id=1553668. Accessed 1 March 2007.

Treaster, Joseph B. "G.I. View of Vietnam." *New York Times Magazine.* 30 October 1966. In "Songs of Americans in the Vietnam War." http://faculty.buffalostate.edu/fishlm/folksongs/americansongs.htm. Accessed 10 January 2005.

Tucker, Michael, director. *Gunner Palace.* Palm Pictures, 2004.

Today. BBC Radio 4. 20 May 2003. http://news.bbc.co.uk/1/hi/world/middle_east/3042907.stm.

Turino, Thomas. *Nationalists, Cosmopolitanists, and Popular Music in Zimbabwe.* Chicago: University of Chicago Press, 2000.

———. "Signs of Imagination, Identity, and Experience: A Peircian Semiotic Theory for

Music." *Ethnomusicology* 43, no. 2 (1999): 221–55.

U.S. Congress. Senate. Committee on Governmental Affairs, Subcommittee on Oversight of Government Management, Restructuring, and the District of Columbia. "Music Violence: How Does it Affect Our Children." Hearing before the Subcommittee on Oversight of Government Management, Restructuring, and the District of Columbia of the Committee on Governmental Affairs. 105th Cong., 1st sess., 6 November 1997, 105–395.

———. "The Convention against Torture and Other Cruel, Inhuman or Degrading Treatment or Punishment." 1990 Senate Resolution adopted by unanimous agreement of the United Nations General Assembly on 10 December 1984. http://www.unhcr.cr/html/menu3/b/h_cat39.htm.

———. General Accounting Office. U.S. *International Broadcasting: Challenges Facing the Broadcasting Board of Governors.* Testimony before the Subcommittee on International Operations and Terrorism, Committee on Foreign Relations, 29 April 2004. http://www.gao.gov/new.items/d04711t.pdf.

———. Record Labeling Hearing before the Committee on Commerce, Science, and Transportation. 99th Cong., 1st sess., 19 September 1985, 529.

U.S. Congressional Budget Office. "Recruiting, Retention, and Future Levels of Military Personnel." Washington, D.C.: Congressional Budget Office, October 2006.

Walser, Robert. "Rhythm, Rhyme, and Rhetoric in the Music of Public Enemy." *Ethnomusicology* 39/2 (1995): 193–217.

———. *Running with the Devil: Power, Gender, and Madness in Heavy Metal Music.* Hanover, N.H.: University Press of New England, 1993.

Washington, George. *The Writings of George Washington from the Original Manuscript Sources, 1745–1799,* vol. 8. Washington, D.C.: U.S. Government Printing Office, 1931.

Weinstein, Deena. *Heavy Metal:* A Cultural Sociology. New York: Macmillan, 1991.

West, Bing. *No True Glory: A Frontline Account of the Battle for Fallujah.* New York: Bantam, 2005.

West, Cornel. *Race Matters.* New York: Vintage Press, 1994.

Whiteley, Sheila. "Progressive Rock and Psychedelic Coding in the Work of Jimi Hendrix." In *Reading Pop: Approaches to Textual Analysis in Popular Music,* ed. Richard Middleton, 235–61. New York: Oxford University Press, 2000.

Wiley, Irvin Bell. *The Life of Billy Yank.* Indianapolis: Bobbs-Merrill, 1952.

INDEX

Page numbers in *italics* indicate photographs and illustrations.

The A-Team (television), 31–33
Abel, Ben, 82
Abu Ghraib prison, 96–97
AC/DC, 48, 85, 139
"Accelerate Your Life" campaign, 8, 27, 29–30, 37, 145
ACID Pro, 119
acoustic guitars, 110–111, *113*
Acrassicrauda, 168
Advanced Individual Training (AIT), 45
advertising. *See* recruitment
Aeolian/Dorian modes, 32, 35, 137, 204–205n8
Afasy, Meshary Rashid al-, 61
Afghanistan, 15, 43, 85, 97
African Americans, 146–47, 159, 174–75, 178–79. *See also* race issues
Agar, Michael H., 11
"Ahab Had a Camel," 45
Air National Guard, 1, *2*
Airborne Rangers, 45
Al-Agha, al-Moayad Bihokmillah, 67
Al-Aqsa mosque, 71, 72
Al-Aqsa television, 69
Al-Furqan Foundation, 62
Al-Jazeera television, 62
Al-Kut, Iraq, 118
Al-Qaeda, 58, 62
Al-Zawraa television, 76
The Alamo, 79
Ali, Abo (Abu), 58, 61, 64–65
Ali ('ud instructor), 118
"All I Really Miss is You," 119–21
"Allahu Akbar," 65–66, 74–75, 85, 166
Allied Expeditionary Forces (AEF), 47–48
Alpha Company, 52
ambushes, 56, 128, 153, 155–56
American Civil War, 47, 100
American Folklife Center, 106
American Music Therapy Association, 183
American Revolution, 15, 102, 105
"An American Soldier's iPod: Layers of Identity and Situated Listening in Iraq" (Gilman), 184

"an-Nuheim" (album), 64
. . . *And Justice for All* (Metallica), 40
"Angel of Death," 148–49, 150–52, *151*
Anthrax, 41, 140
anti-Americanism, 9, 57, 72–77, 165, 186
anti-gangsta rap, 174–81
anti-Israel movements, 9, 57, 72–77, 165, 186
Apocalypse Now (1979), 35, 85
Arabic language, 125, 199n32
Arafat, Yasir, 41
Araya, Tom, *2*, 41
"Are You Ready," 48
Arkansas National Guard, 52
Armed Forces Radio, 47
Armed Forces Vietnam Network (AFVN), 48, 160
Armstrong, Louis, 187
"Army of One" advertisement, 29, 55
Army Reserve, 27
"Army Strong" theme, *24*, 24–26
The Art of Military Deception (Lloyd), 80
The Art of War (Sun Tzu), 78
"Asad al-Fallujah" (Lions of Fallujah), 66–67
Askew, Kelly, 18
athletics, 185–86
Atkinson, Jennifer: on basic training, 44, 144; on combat preparation, 50, 147, 154; on gender issues, 158; on nostalgia, 181; on profanity, 187; on religious services, 111; on social ordering, 54
audio-vision, 19–20
Autoharp, 106
"Awake," 28, 30
"Axis Sally," 79–80

Bad Boy Records, 141
Baghdad, Iraq, 85
Baghdad Music Journal (Thompson), 125, *126*, 133
bagpipes, 79, 196n1
Bainbridge, David, 173
Bali, Indonesia, 164–65
"The Ballad of Ahmed Razooki," 121
"Ballad of the Green Berets," 106
"Ballad of the Hot Mic," 117
Bank Leumi bombing, 67
barracks humor, 123–25, 187–88

Basic Combat Training (BCT), 5, 44–45, 55, 144
Basserman, Albert, 89
battle. *See* combat
battle cries, 46, 65–66, 72, 74–75
"The Battle Cry of Freedom," 100
"Battle Hymn of the Republic," 100–102
BBC radio, 80, 89
"Be All That You Can Be" campaign, 27, 31
bebuten trancing, 164–65, 166
Becker, Judith, 164–65, 166–67
Behar, Ruth, 11
"Behind the Screens," 175
Bennett, William, 140
Berger, Harris, 11–12, 142, 157–58
"Beyond the Realms of Death," 139
Biggie Smalls (Notorious B.I.G.), 141
Biohazard, 140
Black Sabbath, 34
"Blame It On the ING," 121
"Blind," 39
"Block Rockin' Beats," 28
blogs, 6
"Blood On the Risers," 100–102
"Bloodline," 40, 41, 52, 162
The Blue Max (1966), 36
Blur, 39
"Bodies," 42–43, 52, 86, 148, 161, 170, 195–96n54
Body Count (Ice-T), 140
Bohlman, Philip V., 11
Bonham, Joe (film character), 40, 148
Boo-Ya Tribe, 140
Borchelt, Gretchen, 95
Botelho, Ronald: and indigenous Iraqi music, 5, 53; on interrogations, 98; on metal ideology, 141; and psychological operations, 81–82, 83–84; on radio propaganda, 174
Boym, Svetlana, 181
Boyson, Aaron R., 40
Brackett, David, 150
brass instrumentation, 25–26
"Brave Boys They Are," 100
Break Them Down: Systematic Use of Psychological Torture by US Forces (Borchelt et al.), 94–95
Briggs, Charles L., 11
"Bring the Noise," 140
"The British Grenadiers," 102
Brown, Bruce, 47, 106
Brown, Nick, 119–24, *120*
Buchholz, Horst, 90
"Burnin' in the Third Degree," 37–38
Bush, George H. W., 81–82
Bush, George W., 91, 155

Buzzell, Colby: on barracks humor, 187; on combat preparation, 50–51, 147, 150; on differences over music, 53–54, 171; on diversity, 4; on music in combat, 42–43; on "priming" function of music, 183; on race issues, 159; on social ordering, 55; on sound systems, 48–49; on sounds of combat, 56

Caddell, Allester, 46
Cage, John, 125
Cagney, James, 89–90
call-and-response melodies, 44–45
camaraderie, 55. *See also* social class and social ordering
Camp Taji, 111
Camp War Eagle, 127
Cannell, Stephen J., 32
care packages, 1
Carpenter, Pete, 32
Cash, Johnny, 29, 143
Castlevania: Symphony of the Night (video game), 39
casualties, 8, 14, 133, 146–47, 159, 179–80
Ceausescu, Nicolae, 199n33
censorship, 139–40, 140–41
Central Intelligence Agency (CIA), 86–87, 98
chanting, 166
Charlie's Angels (2000), 38–39, 145
Charlie's Angels (television), 34
The Chemical Brothers, 28
"Children of the Korn," 141
children's songs, 86, 88, 170–71, 182
Chion, Michel, 19–20, 73, 143
Chipmunks Christmas, 54, 171
Cisneros, Marc, 81
Civil War, 16
class issues, 157–59, 160
classical music, 76, 117–18
Clay, Henry Work, 100
Clay, Ronin, 127
Cleveland, Les, 100, 102, 123
Colonial and Revolutionary Songbook (American History Through Folksong) (McNeil and McNeil), 105
combat: and inspirational power of music, 46–54, 147; pre-combat music, 3, 5, 42–43, 50–51, 53, 54–57, 147–50, 153–54, 161–63, 173; and social ordering, 54–57; soldiers' accounts of, 49–54
commercialism, 177
commercials, 21, 144. *See also* recruitment
Como, Perry, 102
computers, 9, 119, 125–27, 133–34
Connor, Tommy, 102–104
conscription, 16–17

Continental Army, 16
Cook, Nicholas, 21
Coppola, Francis Ford, 85
Corkins, Bardley, 115, 128
Corrado, Mike, 117
Council of Europe, 92
Council of the Mujahideen, 63–64
Crawford, Rob, 1, *2*
"The Creed," 30–31, 36, 75, 145
critical phenomenology, 12
Croatia, 72
Crockett, James "Sonny," 33
Crotty, Joel, 136
cultural awareness, 53
Cunningham, Sally Jo, 173
Cusick, Suzanne, 86, 90–91, 172, 202n62
Cypress Hill, 140

D-Day, 47–48
"D-Day Dodgers," 102, 104–105
"Dagger X-Ray," 48, 106
Dallas Songwriters Association (DSA),
    115–16
*Dancing in the Distraction Factory: Music
    Television and Popular Culture* (Goodwin),
    40
"Danger Zone," 35, 36
*Dark Laughter: War in Song and Popular
    Culture* (Cleveland), 102, 123
Daughtry, J. Martin, 184
Davey, Monica, 115
Davis, Michael "Paperboi," 127
"The Day You Were Born," 133
death metal, 136
Death Row Records, 141
deep listening, 164–65, 166
DeGregory, Lane, 171, 172
"Deguello," 79
dehumanization, 162–65
Delorean, John, 17–18
demographics, 7–8, 142–43. *See also* class
    issues; gender issues; race issues
DeNora, Tia, 54, 55, 147, 182
"The Deployment," 128
detainees. *See* interrogations
Devereux, George, 11
The Devil's Rejects (2005), 39
diatonic modes, 118, *119*
"Die MF Die," 42, 43
digital technology, 3
dionysian themes, 137, 139, 156, 162
"Dirty," 128
diversity in the military, 4, 7–8, 159. *See also*
    gender issues; race issues
DMX, 147, 160
Documentary Recordings, 44–45

dog intimidation, 95, 97
Dole, Bob, 140
Doonesbury (Trudeau), 4, 160
Dope, 42, 43
Downie, J. Stephen, 173
Dr. Dre, 141
draft, 16–17
Dreyfus, Kay, 136
drill sergeants, 45
drive-by shootings, 155
Drowning Pool, 42–43, 52, 86, 148, 161, 170,
    195–96n54
Drummond, Javorn, 132
drums, 15, 46–47, 78
Durst, Fred, 141
Duvall, Robert, 85

EA Worldwide, 39
Eazy-E, 141
education, 68
Egypt, 173
Ehrenstein, David, 34–35
Eighth Amendment, 93
electronic music, 125–27
Eminem, 51, 85, 147, 156–57, 161
emotional power of music, 167. *See also*
    inspirational power of music
English Channel, 80
enlisted soldiers, 4, 160
"Enter Sandman," 86
Epstein, Jonathon, 136, 137
Escape from L.A. (1996), 39
ESPN, 185–86
ethnic diversity in the military, 4, 7–8, 159.
    See also race issues
ethnographic observance, 11
European Convention on Human Rights, 92
European Court for Human Rights (ECHR),
    87
*Evaluating Military Advertising and
    Recruiting: Theory and Methodology*
    (National Research Council), 73–74
Evangelical Christianity, 68, 186
Evans, Thomas W., 16
Ewing, Heidi, 68
executions, mock, 97
Experience Music Project (EMP), 184

Faith No More (band), 48, 140
Fallujah, Iraq, 51, 84–85, 153
fan mail, 1–3
Fast, Susan, 150
Fatah, 59, 67–70
Feld, Steven, 20, 147
female soldiers, 158–59
Field Manual 34–52 (FM 34–52), 94–95, 97

FIFA 98: Road to World Cup (video game), 39
fifes, 15, 46–47
Fifth Amendment, 93
"Fight the Power," 139
film, 34–39, 42, 89–90
Fischer, Becky, 68
Fish, Lydia, 102, 174
505th Parachute Infantry Regiment, 52
Flagg, James Montgomery, 16
"Follow Our Orders," 125
Follow the Leader (Korn), 141
food deprivation, 92, 95, 97
Foreign Correspondent (1940), 89
The Forgotten Soldier (Sajer), 47
Fort Benning, Georgia, 44
Fort Bragg, North Carolina, 82, 87
Fort Jackson, South Carolina, 44
Fort McNair, Washington, DC, 78
"The Four Horsemen," 51
Fourteenth Amendment, 93
Fourteenth Army (British), 80
Fourteenth Connecticut Volunteer Infantry, 47
Fourth Geneva Convention, 91–92
Fourth Infantry Division, 50
4th25 (rap group), 9, 10, 127–28, 132, 174–81
4th PSYOPS, 81
"Free America," 102
freestyle rap, 115–16, 132, 159
Friedman, Herbert A., 81
Friesen, Bruce, 136, 137
From Anxiety to Method in the Behavioral Sciences (Devereux), 11
Fruity Loops, 119
Furlong, Edward, 38
The Future of Nostalgia (Boym), 181

Gaddafi, Muammar al-, 41
gangsta rap: and combat preparation, 5, 52; and 4th 25, 10, 174–81; lyrical themes, 152–56; and rap ideology, 138, 142–43; and violent content, 206n46
GarageBand, 119
Gedrick, Jason, 37
Geertz, Clifford, 11
gender issues, 142–43, 145, 157–59, 184, 206–207n61
General Assembly Resolution 39/46, 93
Geneva Conventions of 1949, 91–92, 94, 95
genocide, 163–64
Gillars, Mildred, 80
Gilman, Lisa, 184
Gittoes, George, 52, 107, 115, 157, 162, 168
"Give Peace a Chance," 187

glam metal bands, 142
Glenn Miller's American Band, 47–48
"Go To Sleep," 51, 54, 147, 153–54, 162
Gobe, Herschel, 123
God Hates Us All (Slayer), 40
Godsmack, 8, 28, 30, 141, 145
Goldsmith, Jerry, 36–37
"The Good, the Bad, and the Ugly," 51
Goodwin, Andrew, 40
Gorbman, Claudia, 21, 25, 34, 36
Gordon Collection, 106
Grady, Rachel, 68
Great Britain, 87
The Greatest American Hero (television), 32–33
Green Zone, 6, 204n1
Gregory, Edward "Greg-O," 127
Grisham, C. J.: on class issues, 160; on combat preparation, 51, 56–57, 147, 153; on dehumanization, 162; on interrogations, 88, 94, 96, 97, 168; on personal music devices, 3; on "priming" function of music, 183; on psychological operations, 85; on recruitment, 43; on social ordering, 54, 55; on sound systems, 48
Gross, Robert L., 137
Grouchy Media, 42–43, 170, 195–96n54
group identity, 74–75
guerilla warfare, 155–56
guitars, 110–11, 137, 152
Gunner Palace (2004), 52, 115
Guns n' Roses, 38, 48, 85

Hadith, 59
Hadsell, Mark, 86
"Hail, Columbia," 100
Hamas, 59, 67–70, 73, 199n33
Hamilton, Linda, 37
Hammer, Jan, 33
Hanneman, Jeff, 148
Hardcastle and McCormick (television), 34
Hardson, Tre, 141
harmony, 137
Harrell, Jack, 137, 150
Hawaii Five-O (television), 34
Heavy Metal (Weinstein), 136
"Hell's Bells," 85
Helmet, 140
Hendrix, Jimi, 15
"Here We Go, Easy Run," 45
"Here Without You," 181
Hetfield, James, 40, 169, 171
Hezbollah, 59
Hezbollah Al-Manar television, 71
Highlanders, 181
Hillman, Roger, 18–19

Hispanic soldiers, 159
"Hit the Floor," 42
Hitchcock, Alfred, 89
Hitler, Adolf, 80
Hofer, Johannes, 181
Hoffman, Rick, 89
Hollings, Ernest, 139
Holocaust denial, 76–77
Holtan, Erik, 5, 7, 48, 110–111, 182
"Holy Wars," 40, 41
"Home of the Brave," 107–108, 110, 114, 132
"honorable duty" music: and ISI videos, 73,
    76; and recruitment, 8–9, 22, 26–27, 29–30,
    44, 195n50; and songwriting, 109
hooding, 92, 95, 97
House of Pain, 140
Howe, Julia Ward, 101
Humvees, 48, 51, 56, 64–66, 86
Hunter (television), 34
Huron, David, 21
Hussein, Saddam, 85, 129, 131
Hussein, Uday, 52
Hyland, Brian, 90

"I Don't Give a Fuck," 50, 54, 147, 154–55
"I Know a Song That Gets on Everybody's
    Nerves," 172
"I Love You," 86, 170–71, 172
"I Pledge Allegiance," 108–109, 110, 114
"I Ride," 175–76
"I Wanna Be a Dog," 172
"I Wore a Tunic," 102
Ice Cube, 140, 141
Ice-T, 140
"I'd Like to Teach the World to Sing (in
    Perfect Harmony)," 18
ideology of music styles, 135–36, 174–75,
    186, 208n101
Improvised Explosive Devices (IEDs): as
    background noise, 48; as inspiration for
    songs, 115, 128, 130; and Iraqi insurgency,
    155; and ISI videos, 62, 64–66, 73; and
    officers, 175
*In Country: Folksongs of Americans in the
    Vietnam War,* 106
"In My Merry Oldsmobile," 17
In the Hours of Darkness (2007), 111–14, *112,*
    133, 183
indigenous Iraqi music, 5, 53, 96, 173
individualism, 136, 208n101
indoctrination, 68, 69, 166, 186
inspirational power of music: and combat
    preparation, 46–54, 147–50, 153–54,
    161–63, 173; and metal/rap ideology,
    147–67; and social ordering, 54–57
insurgency, 155–56

intelligence gathering missions, 53
Intelligence Interrogation, 94
international law, 9
International Psychological Warfare Society,
    81
internet, 6, 59, 64, 119, 132
interrogations: and distortion in music, 169–
    70; and future research, 186; guidelines,
    202n62; music used in, 9, 10, 86–90; and
    security issues, 14; and timbre of music,
    167, 169–74; and torture, 90–99
interview process, 6–7
iPod, 3, 48, 185, 187
Iraq Unplugged (Brown and Schultz),
    119–24, *121,* 133
Iraqi National Guard (ING), 121, 124
Ireland, 92
Irish Republican Army (IRA), 87
Iron Eagle (1986), 37
Iron Eagle II (1988), 37
irritation/frustration operations, 83, 200n23
Islam, 59–62
Islamic Jihad Army, 76
Islamic State of Iraq (ISI), 58–59, 62–67,
    72–73
Israel, 59, 62
Israeli Defense Force (IDF), 56–57
Israelites, 15
"Itsy Bitsy Teeny Weeny Yellow Polka-Dot
    Bikini," 90, 172
iTunes, 185

Jabir, Tariq, 66–67
Jackson, Michael, 89, 168
Jagger, Aaron, 112–14
"Janel," 107–108, 132
Japan, 18, 80
Jericho, 79
Jesus Camp (2006), 68
jihad: and indoctrination, 166; and ISI
    videos, 76; and nasheeds, 61, 63–64, 66,
    68–70, 71–73; support for, 198n12
"John Brown's Body," 101–102
Johnny Got His Gun (1971), 40
Johnson, Mark, 20, 181
Johnson, Stephen, 5, 43
Jordan, 173
Judas Priest, 48
Judgment Night (1993), 140–41
"Just Before the Battle, Mother," 100

Keil, Charles, 20
Keith, Toby, 86
Kelley, Robin D. G., 156
Kelly, Robert J., 163
Keyes, Cheryl L., 156, 158, 162

Khattab, Umar Ibn al-, 198n12
"Kllna alqool qool" (The word is the word), 64–65, 66
Knoop, Jeff, 108–109, 110
Korean War, 16, 168
Korn, 39, 141, 194n30
"Kosher Blood," 68
Krall, Diana, 53
Krims, Adam, 136, 137–38, 149
Kuehl, Dan, 78–79, 82, 86, 171–74

Laboa, José Sebastian, 81, 82
"Lace Your Boots," 176
"LalaFallujah," 84–85
The Last Action Hero (1993), 39
Latour, Bruno, 11
Led Zeppelin, 34, 82
Lee, Stuart, 175
Leip, Hans, 102
Lennon, John, 187
"Liberation Army," 68
Library of Congress, 106
Lidov, David, 20
Lifton, Robert J., 163
lighting trucks, 84
L'il John, 50, 147, 154–55
"Lili Marlene," 102–104
Limp Bizkit, 141
Linkin Park, 42, 141
"Little GTO," 18
Live from Iraq (4th25), 9–10, 127–30, *129*, 132–33, 174–75, 179–81
"Live Wire," 38–39, 145
Living Colour, 140
Lloyd, Mark, 80, 83
Loggins, Kenny, 35
Lollapalooza III, 140–41
loudspeakers, 80–83, 98, 167
Lovett, Elliott, 115, 128
lyrical themes, 10, 137, 145, 152–56, 156–57

MacNoughton, Alexander, 46
Magnum PI (television), 33, 34
Major League Baseball, 39
Malcolm, C. A., 46
Malik, Abu Abdul, 61
marching cadences, 44–45
"Marching through Georgia," 100
The Marine (2005), 39
Marks, Johnny, 17
Martha Reeves and the Vandellas, 82
martyrdom, 70–72
Marx, Karl, 135
The Matrix (1999), 39
Maxwell, Bill, 33
McCain, John, 91

McLaren, Carrie, 17, 42
McNeil, Keith, 105
McNeil, Rusty, 105
"Me So Horny," 140
Megadeth, 40, 41, 48, 136
melody, 137
memory, 182–83
Mengele, Josef, 148
Merchants of the Myth (2006), 76–77
"Mercy Like the Rain," 61
Meshuggah, 194n30
metal music: and combat preparation, 5, 50, 52, 53; definitions of, 204–205n8; fan base of, 1–3, 75; ideology of, 10, 135, 136–43; inspirational power of, 147–67; and interrogations, 88; in Israel, 76–77; and lyrical themes, 174; and memory, 183; and psychological operations, 83–84; and recruitment, 8, 143–47; and social ordering, 54, 56; sub-genres, 136–37, 194n30; and timbre, 167–73
Metallica: and combat preparation, 48, 51, 56, 147–48; fan base of, 136; and interrogations, 86, 88–89; and metal ideology, 142; on sensory deprivation, 169; and violence themes, 40–41
Meyer, Leonard, 20
Miami Vice (television), 33–34
military occupational songs, 100
Military Occupational Specialty (MOS), 4, 5, 158, 184
Miller, Glenn, 47–48
Miner, Mark, 53, 150
misogyny, 145, 156, 158–59, 177
mode and harmony, 137
Molino, Jean, 20
Moore, Allan, 150
Moore, Robin, 106
morale, 82, 111
Morale, Welfare, and Recreation (MWR), 111
Morocco, 173
Moroder, Giorgio, 35
Morrison, Jim, 15
"Mortaritaville," 122–25, 187
Mötley Crüe, 7, 38–39, 142, 145
Mudvayne, 88–89, 147
Mujahideen Shura Council, 58
Mukasey, Michael, 91
"Music, War, and Reconciliation" (conference), 184
"Music as Torture, Music as Weapon," 90–91
Music in the World of Islam: A Socio-Cultural Study (Shiloah), 60
"The Music of War: An Interdisciplinary Conference," 184

Music Television (MTV), 18, 30–31, 39–44, 75
"Music Violence: How Does it Affect Our Children," 140
musical "code," 21, 26, 28, 34, 39, 42, 76
musical memory, 182
Mustaine, Dave, 41
"My Old Granny, She's 91," 45
"My Recruiter," 187

n-Track Studio, 119
nasheeds, 60–62, 64–67, 67–70, 79, 85, 198n12
Nashville, Tennessee, 1
Nasty As They Wanna Be, 140
National Defense University, 79
National Guard, 30, 52, 75, 124
National Hockey League, 39
National Research Council, 73–74
Native Americans, 106
Nattiez, Jean-Jacques, 20
Nazis, 89
Nettl, Bruno, 10
New Jersey National Guard, 30, 75
The New Seekers, 18
New York City Music Therapy Relief Project, 183
New York Times, 102, 115, 187
Ninth Symphony (Beethoven), 76
niveau neutre, 20
No Child Left Behind Act, 17, 193n5
"No One Comes Close," 28, 143
No True Glory: A Frontline Account of the Battle for Fallujah (West), 52, 84–85
Noriega, Manuel, 81–83
nostalgia, 181
nü metal, 28–30, 39, 76, 141, 145, 194n31
NWA, 140–41

obscenity, 140
Occupation: Dreamland (2005), 52, 54, 162
Office of Strategic Services (OSS), 86
officers, 160
Oldsmobile Motor Company, 17
Oliveros, Pauline, 164
"One," 40–41, 51, 56, 148
One, Two, Three (1961), 89–90, 171–72
Onyx, 140
Operation Desert Storm, 1–3, 48, 106
Operation Just Cause, 9, 81–82, 83, 87
original music compositions, 9, 105, 106
Osbourne, Ozzy, 139
"Over There," 100
Ozzfest, 150

Palestinian Authority television, 72

Palestinian Liberation Organization (PLO), 67
Palestinianian statehood, 59
Panama, 9, 81–82
Parents Music Resource Center (PMRC), 139, 140–41
parody songs, 102, 106–107, 122–25. *See also* text adaptation
party rap, 138, 142–43
Peirce, Charles, 20
Persian Gulf War, 1–3
personal computers, 9, 119, 125–27, 133–34
Pettan, Svanibor, 72, 86
Phelps, Michael, 185
Philips, J. J., 102–104
Phrygian/Locrian modes, 32, 46, 137, 152, 204–205n8
physical abuse, 97. *See also* torture
Physicians for Human Rights (PHR), 94–95
Pielke, Robert, 137
"Pilot Flying Low," 45
Piore, Adam, 86
The Piper in Peace and War (Malcolm), 46
Plato, 46
"Pledge of Allegiance," 109
poetry, urban, 174–75
Poison, 142
police profiling, 178–79
politics, 11–14
pop metal, 136
"porn rock," 139
portable audio devices, 3, 8, 48–49, 50
"Position Statement Against the Use of Music as Torture," 90
Post, Mike, 32
"Post Election News," 125
Post Exchange (PX) stores, 110
Post Traumatic Stress Disorder (PTSD), 183
power element in music: and class issues, 161; and combat preparation, 149; and distortion, 169, 194n30; and distortion, 204–205n8; and gangsta rap, 152–56, 178; and gender issues, 158; and music ideology, 137, 138–39, 146–47; and power chords, 152, 194n30; and power chords, 204–205n8; and recruitment, 143–44
"priming" function of music, 182–83
prisoners of war, 90–99. *See also* interrogations; torture
propaganda, 69, 73, 79–80, 83, 199n33
psychological operations (PSYOPS): described, 78–82; music used in, 7, 9, 83–90; on *The Simpsons*, 200n23; and timbre of music, 167–74; and torture, 90–99
Public Enemy, 139, 140
"Pussy," 179–80

"Qom" (Rise Up), 63–64, 66
Qur'an, 59

race issues. *See also* African Americans: diversity in the services, 7–8; and future research, 184; and gangsta rap, 157–60; and metal ideology, 142–43; and music preferences, 159; and rap ideology, 177, 178–79; and recruitment, 146–47
radio, 17, 47, 79–80, 89, 173–74
Radio Sawa, 173–74
Rage Against the Machine, 140–41
Ramadi, Iraq, 85
Rangda/Barong ritual, 164–65
rap music. *See also* gangsta rap: and combat preparation, 3, 5, 50, 53; and 4th 25, 174–81; and freestyle rap, 115–16, 132, 159; genres of, 136, 137–38; ideology of, 10, 135–36, 136–43; inspirational power of, 147–65, 167; and memory, 183; original compositions, 9–10; party rap, 138, 142–43; and psychological warfare, 83, 84; reality rap, 138; and recruitment, 145–47; and social ordering, 54, 56; and timbre, 168–70, 172–73
Rap Music and Street Consciousness (Keyes), 162
reality rap, 138, 175
Reconquista, 46
record companies, 177–78
The Recording Academy, 183
recording industry, 61
recording music, 119–34
recruitment: campaign themes, 24–28; counter-recruitment activism, 193n5; and film, 34–39; Hamas and Fatah, 67–69; history of, 16–18; and imagery, 18–21; and indoctrination, 186; and military advertising, 21–31; and MTV, 39–44; music styles in, 8, 143–47; and nasheeds, 64–67, 67–68, 72–77; overview of recruiting campaigns, 8; on *The Simpsons*, 195n50; and television, 31–34
"The Red, White, and Blue," 47
Reed, Bill, 34–35
Reign in Blood, 148
Rejai, Mostafa, 135–36
religion: Evangelical Christianity, 68, 186; and future research, 184; and indoctrination, 186; Islam, 59–62; and nationalism, 73; services, 111; themes in music, 23; and trancing, 166
"Remember Pearl Harbor," 100
Revak, Joshua, *113;* on combat preparation, 5, 52, 161; and freestyle rap, 159; and

songwriting, 111–15; on therapeutic use of music, 183
Revolutionary War, 46, 100
rhythm, 137
"Ride of the Valkyries," 47, 85
Rieber, Robert W., 163
Riminton, Hugh, 68
Robertson, Billy G., Jr., 117
Roccor, Bettina, 141
Rock on Film (Ehrenstein and Reed), 34–35
"Rocky," 51
Rolling Stones, 35
Romania, 186, 199n33
Root, George Frederick, 100
Rose, Tricia, 138
"The Rose of No Man's Land," 100
Rouse, Ed, 79, 80
Run-D.M.C., 140
"Run Me Some More . . . Hey," 45
running cadences, 44–45
Running with the Devil: Power, Gender and Madness in Heavy Metal Music (Walser), 35–36, 162
Rust in Peace (Megadeth), 40

Sagebiel, Jason, 7, 70, 117–18, 206–207n61
Sahir, Mustaqiim, 61
"Saigon Warrior II," 123
Sajer, Guy, 47
Saladin, Dann, 157–58
"Salvation," 117–18
"Sanakhudu Ma'arikana Ma'ahoum" (We will venture to battle with them), 66–67
Sandler, Barry, 106
"Sanitarium," 51
Santa Anna, Antonio López de, 79
Sarkissian, Margaret, 60
Sartre, Jean-Paul, 163–64
"Satisfaction," 35
Saudi Arabia, 58
Saunders, Neal: on combat preparation, 161–62; on individualism, 208n101; music composed by, 9–10; and music recordings, 127–32; on political issues, 13; and rap ideology, 174–81; on sounds of combat, 56
"Say Brothers Will You Meet Us," 101–102
Schachter, Daniel L., 10–11
Schnur, Steve, 39
Schultz, David, 52, 83, 119–24, *120,* 161, 187
Schultze, Norbert, 103
Schwarzenegger, Arnold, 37, 38
Scottish clansmen, 181, 196n1
sectarian violence, 69–70, 74
"Seek and Destroy," 51
Selective Service Act of 1948, 16–17
semiotics, 20–21

sensory deprivation, 83–84, 86–90, 92, 94–95, 169
September 11 terrorist attacks, 183, 195–96n54
75th Ranger Regiment, 81
sexual abuse/exploitation, 97, 156, 158
Shaam, 61
Sha'arawi, Hazim al-, 69
"shahid," 70, 72
"Shake, Rattle: Music, Conflict, and Change," 184
Shakur, Tupac, 140, 141
Shalev, Ziv, 56–57, 76, 148
sharing music, 5
"Sharpen My Bones," 67–68
Shelemay, Kay Kaufman, 11
"The Shell Hole Rag," 102
Shi'a militant movements, 69–70, 74
Shiloah, Amnon, 60
Shoebat, Walid, 67–68, 165–66
"Shoot to Thrill," 139
"Sick of Life," 28, 30
Simpson, Jessica, 182
The Simpsons, 195n50, 200n23
"A Singing Army is a Fighting Army," 100
The Six Million Dollar Man (television), 34
Skid Row, 48
Slayer: and censorship, 140; and combat preparation, 50, 52, 54, 148–49, 150, 162; fan base of, 1–3, 136; and metal ideology, 142; public perception of, 141; and sounds of combat, 56; and violence themes, 40, 41
sleep deprivation, 89, 92, 95
Slipknot, 88
slogans, 22–23, 194n29
Smith, Stacy L., 40
social class and social ordering, 54–57, 74–75, 142–43
Society for Ethnomusicology (SEM), 90, 184
"Soldier, Soldier Have You Heard," 45
soldier-created music, 100–107, 107–18, 119–34. See also 4th25 (rap group)
"Somebody, Anybody Start a War," 186
"The Song," 113–14
"Song 2," 39
Songs from the Soul of Service: A Collection of Songs Written by US Soldiers, Sailors, Airmen, and Marines, 117
songwriting, 107–18
Sonic Youth, 140
soul music, 160
sound systems in military vehicles, 48–49. See also loudspeakers
Soundtrack to War (2006), 52–53, 107, 115, 157, 162, 168
Spears, Britney, 88

sports, 185–86
St. Petersburg Times, 171
Staind, 141
"Stan," 156–57
Standard Operating Procedures, 95–96
Star of David, 76–77
"The Star-Spangled Banner," 47
Static-X, 160
Staves, Terrance, 127
Steel, William, 46
Steffe, William, 102
Stonehill College, 184
Straight Outta Compton, 140, 141
stress positions, 92
Strykers, 48
suicide bombers, 67–68, 165–66
"Suicide Solution," 139
Sunni militant movements, 62, 69–70, 74
Superman (film), 25–26, 26
"A Symphony of Bullets: Towards a Sonic Ethnography of Contemporary Baghdad," 184
Syrian Jews, 11

Tahnee Cain & Tryanglz, 37–38
"Taliban Bodies," 43
tanks, 48, 49–50
Taproot, 141
Taskforce 112, 127
technology: and music on the battlefield, 3; personal computers, 9, 119, 125–27, 133–34; and recording music, 119–34; and songwriting, 107
television. See also recruitment: Al-Aqsa television, 69; al-Jazeera television, 62; al-Zawraa television, 76; Hezbollah Al-Manar television, 71; Music Television (MTV), 18, 30–31, 39–44, 75; Palestinian Authority television, 72; and recruitment, 31–34
Terminator (1984), 37–38
Terminator 2: Judgment Day (1991), 38
Test Drive Unlimited, 39
Texas Revolution (1835–36), 79
text adaptation, 9, 100–105. See also parody songs
therapeutic use of music, 10, 183
"There's a Star-spangled Banner Waving Somewhere," 100
Third Geneva Convention, 91–92, 94, 97
Third Infantry Division, 44
Thirty Years War, 46
"This is Islam," 61
Thomas, Michael, 127
Thompson, William, 126; on class issues, 157, 160; on combat preparation, 52; formal music training, 125–27; on

interrogations, 95–97; music composed by, 7, 133; on nasheeds, 60, 165; on nonviolence, 167; on sectarian violence, 69–70, 74
thrash metal, 136
Three Doors Down, 181
300 (2007), 39
"thunder runs," 85
"Thunderstruck," 48
timbre, 10, 139, 149–52, 167–74, 176, 204–205n8
"Tokyo Rose," 79
Tomorrow's Pioneers, 69, 71
Top Gun (1986), 35, 36–37
torture, 9, 90–99, 186, 201n41
trance, 164–67
Transition Assistance Program (TAP), 124
Treaster, Joseph B., 102, 187
trench poetry, 175
Trice, Obie, 147
Trudeau, Gary, 4, 160
trumpets, 78–79
Tucker, C. Delores, 140
Tucker, Michael, 52, 115
Turino, Thomas, 20
"24 Hours," 128, 129–32
2 Live Crew, 140
2004 Summer Olympics, 185

'ud, 118
UN Resolution 242, 59
UN Resolution 3452, 92–93
Unheard Melodies (Gorbman), 21, 36
United Kingdom, 18, 92
United Nations Convention Against Torture and Other Cruel, Inhuman or Degrading Treatment or Punishment (UNCAT), 93–94, 97
United Service Organizations (USO), 1, 48, 184
Universal Declaration of Human Rights (UDHR), 92
urban poetry, 174–75
U.S. Air Force, 22, 28
U.S. Army: and the Abu Ghraib scandal, 96–97; official songbook, 100; and recruitment, 17, 22, 23–25, 27
U.S. Attorney General, 91
U.S. Coast Guard, 194n29
U.S. Congress, 48
U.S. Department of Defense, 8
U.S. Department of Homeland Security, 62
U.S. Department of Veterans Affairs, 124
U.S. Department of War, 47
U.S. General Accounting Office, 174
U.S. Marine Corps, 22–23, 29, 32

U.S. Navy, 22, 27
U.S. Navy SEALs, 33
U.S. PSYOPS Veterans Association, 89
U.S. Senate, 93, 139–40
US International Broadcasting, 174
Use Your Illusion II (Guns n' Roses), 38

video and computer games, 39, 144
videos, music, 18, 30–31, 39–44
Viet Cong, 80–81
Vietnam War: and barracks humor, 187–88; and dehumanization, 163; and the draft, 16; and interrogation techniques, 168; music of, 15, 174; and prisoner torture, 91; and psychological operations, 80–81, 85; and race issues, 146–47, 160; and radio broadcasts, 48; and songwriting, 106; and text adaptation, 102, 123
violent content in music: and censorship, 140; and gangsta rap, 176–77, 179, 206n46; and metal music, 40–42; and metal/rap ideology, 155–57; and "24 Hours," 129–32
visual perception, 18–20
vocal articulation, 137, 152, 204–205n8
volume of music, 136–37, 167

Wagner, Richard, 47, 85
wall-standing, 92
Walser, Robert: on dehumanization, 162; on gender issues, 158; on guitar solos, 35–36; on interrogation techniques, 168–69; on meaning in music, 20; on metal ideology, 136, 142
Walter Reed Medical Center, 183
wandering souls, 80–81
War is Heavy Metal (documentary), 52
"War Song," 106
Ward 57, 183
Warren, Joseph, 102
"Warrior Ethos," 30, 75
Washington, George, 46–47
water deprivation, 92, 95, 97
waterboarding, 91, 95, 97
Weinstein, Deena, 136, 137, 162
"Welcome to the Jungle," 85
"We're Airborne Rangers," 45
West, Bing, 52, 84
West, Cornel, 138–39
West Bank, 173
"What a Wonderful World," 187
"When Daddies Don't Come Home," 121
"When I Say Rhythm," 45
Whiteley, Sheila, 152, 169
Whitlock, Tom, 35
Williams, Dave, 170
Williams, John, 25

"Won't Back Down," 28–29, 143
Woodliff, Michael, 112
Woolgar, Steve, 11
World War I, 16, 40, 47, 100, 175
World War II: and barracks humor, 123; and interrogation techniques, 89, 168; music of, 15, 100; and propaganda, 174; and psychological operations, 79–80; and radio broadcasts, 47; and text adaptation, 102, 105

WWF/WWE professional wrestling, 39

X Games (television), 39

"Yankee Doodle," 47, 100
"You Could Be Mine," 38
YouTube, 61

Zemaryan, Jangli, 61–62
Zionism, 76–77

Jonathan Pieslak is Associate Professor at the City College of New York and Graduate Center, CUNY. His research interests include critical theory, rhythm in metal music, and music and war. He is also a composer and a recipient of a Goddard Lieberson Fellowship from the American Academy of Arts and Letters (2006). Jonathan's music can be heard at http://www.myspace.com/jpieslak.